The French
Family Feast

Mireille Johnston was born in Nice and educated in France, England and
America. She is the author of *The Cuisine of the Rose: Classical French Cooking
from Burgundy and Lyonnais*; *Cuisine of the Sun: Classical Recipes from Nice
and Provence*; *Central Park Country: A Tune Within Us*; and various articles
published in France and America. She is the translator of the films *The
Sorrow and the Pity* by Marcel Ophuls. stamped below. $10.99 The
Everyday Life

MIREILLE JOHNSTON

The French Family Feast

Traditional French Country Recipes

PENGUIN BOOKS

PENGUIN BOOKS

Published by the Penguin Group
Penguin Books Ltd, 27 Wrights Lane, London W8 5TZ, England
Viking Penguin, a division of Penguin Books USA Inc.
375 Hudson Street, New York, New York 10014, USA
Penguin Books Australia Ltd, Ringwood, Victoria, Australia
Penguin Books Canada Ltd, 2801 John Street, Markham, Ontario, Canada L3R 1B4
Penguin Books (NZ) Ltd, 182–190 Wairau Road, Auckland 10, New Zealand

Penguin Books Ltd, Registered Offices: Harmondsworth, Middlesex, England

First published in the USA by Simon & Schuster, Inc. 1988
First published in Great Britain by Penguin Books 1991
1 3 5 7 9 10 8 6 4 2

Printed in Great Britain by Clays Ltd, St Ives plc
Typeset in Linotron 10½/12½ Caledonia by Goodfellow & Egan, Cambridge

To Tom, Margaret-Brooke, Zabette, and all our friends who have shared so many heated conversations, gargantuan meals, and lazy siestas, I recall what Napoleon told his faithful Marshal MacMahon: 'Let us continue.'

ACKNOWLEDGEMENTS

I wish to thank my editor, Carole Lalli, wise, inspired and always full of cheer. It has been a joy to work with her in the making of this book. And to Charles Pierce my thanks for his helpful rigour.

Et que vive la fête! to M.F.K. Fisher who knows one when she sees one.

Contents

INTRODUCTION   1
    A Pretty Table   6
    This is No Time for Maybes   10
    Is That a Man I See in the Kitchen?   15
    Kitchen Equipment   19
    Measurements   20

HORS-D'OEUVRES   21
    Caviar d'Aubergines   23
    Crudités en Panier   24
    Gougère   28
    Gratin d'Aubergines   30
    Gratin Dauphinois   31
    Jambon Persillé   32
    Lentilles ou Pois Chiches en Salade   35
    Mouclade   36
    Olives Sautées, Olives Farcies   38
    Pissaladière   39
    Pissenlits aux Lardons   41
    Poireaux Tièdes Vinaigrette   43
    Ratatouille   44
    Soupe au Pistou   46
    Terrine aux Herbes   48

GREAT SUPERDISHES   51
    Agneau au Pistou   53
    Aioli Monstre   58
    Blanquette de Veau   66
    Boeuf à l'Orange Niçoise   72
    Boeuf Froid en Tranches   77
    Bouillabaisse Royale   81
    Brandade   87
    Canard Farci   91
    Cassoulet   97
    Chou Farci   104

Contents

Coq au Vin 110
Couscous 116
Daube de Boeuf en Gelée 124
Fondue Bourguignonne 130
Fondue Savoyarde 135
Gratin de Poulet au Fromage 139
Gratinée Lyonnaise 143
Hachis Parmentier 147
Jambon en Saupiquet 151
Marmite Dieppoise 156
Moussaka Provençale 160
Paella 165
Pietsch 170
Plat de Farcis 174
Porc aux Herbes 179
Pot-au-Feu 184
Potée 193
Poulet Fricassée Provençale 199
Poulet en Gelée 203
Poule Verte 207

DESSERTS 215
Cervelle de Canut 217
Compote de Poires 218
Crémets aux Fruits 219
Crêpes Normandes 220
Flan au Caramel 223
Grand Baba 224
Granité au Vin 228
Madeleines Tièdes aux Fruits 229
Mélange de Fruits 231
Mousse au Chocolat Glacée 232
Oeufs à la Neige et aux Fruits 234
Panier de Frivolités de Tante Yvette 236
Poires, Pruneaux, Oranges au Vin Rouge
    et aux Épices 238
Tarte au Citron et aux Amandes 239
Tarte Tatin aux Poires et aux Pommes 241

ACCOMPANIMENTS 245
Broccoli Purée 247
Cabbage Purée 247

Contents

Celeriac Purée   247
Fennel Purée   248
Green Salads   248
Rice   250

INDEX   251

INTRODUCTION

It has been proven that only around a good table do people reconcile and push away the clouds of indifference dissipated by the sun of good food.

GRIMOD DE LA REYNIÈRE

The true essentials of a Feast are only fun and food.

OLIVER WENDELL HOLMES

When one evokes the good life, there is nothing quite as heart-warming and reassuring as the thought of one's friends and relatives gathering round a full table. There is a communion of more than bodies when people share a meal. Indeed, if the destiny of nations depends on what and how they eat, the same is true of individuals.

What is potentially present in most people – love, humour, solidarity – can most of the time be exalted by a good meal shared with gusto. You address yourself to the sunny side of your friends and, trying to please eyes and palate, you may just reach the soul in the process. Inspiring food heightens inspired conversation and a heady blend of warmth and joy. It gives meaning and direction to the day, reality to the world.

We all have seen it again and again: as soon as a festive dish appears – an Easter ham, a soupe au pistou, a Christmas pudding, a cassoulet – suddenly everything falls into place round the table. One rediscovers the simple joys of impatience and curiosity with the first bite of food, and then delight, passionate discussions and soon a sense of well-being. The meal creates a bond, an exchange, an interaction of energies, a true connection. It is a truce when everybody round the table forgets hardships, evokes memories of golden times and moves towards new friendships. Among contented sighs, laughter, glowing eyes and the clinking of crystal and plates, the generosity and the concentration of energy take everyone round the table back to the simple joys of childhood.

The French did not invent Feasts, but over the centuries they have turned them into a national art. With love, care and intuition they have learnt to make each guest feel like the child of the house, pampered, secure and happy. Sunday meals in France are still very much a part of family ritual and are often a time one feels that food is the only thing agreed upon by impatient children, fragile grandparents, opinionated cousins, patronizing uncles, sophisticated gourmets and good-natured gourmands. There have always been many reasons in France to come together to celebrate, from religious and secular feasts to special days for tradesmen and artisans: Saint Thomas for the cobblers, Saint Joseph for the carpenters, Saint Catherine for the spinsters, Saint Barbara for the firemen, Saint Anthony for the absent-minded – not to mention all the births, weddings and anniversaries shared. And should this abundance of festive opportunities in a family ever seem insufficient, one could always recall how Alice in Wonderland discovered we each have 364 unbirthdays a year, and we are free to celebrate them as well.

Cuisine started at home, of course. Eating in restaurants is a modern notion that began after the French Revolution in 1789, when the aristocracy emigrated and their chefs decided to open their own establishments. It was, and still can be, strange, wonderful, exotic and exciting to eat out, but unfortunately one often visits a restaurant as if it were a museum, a library or a cathedral. Even if today, at long last, inventiveness at all costs and minimal art in food seem no longer the rage, most restaurant menus are still virtuoso exercises where pedantic skills prevail.

So good entertaining in France means home-cooking. Lusty 'real food', no-nonsense *cuisine de mère* has taste and soul and meaning, and remains a civilizing force, the cement of our social lives. This is why it is no thin compliment to be invited to share a family meal and all the ritual it implies.

Sometimes, forgetting that the best might be the enemy of the good, inspired and challenged by a famous chef's repertory, a humble citizen takes a deep breath, invites a group of friends and attempts single-handedly to prepare at home one of the chef's creations. The result is frequently a fussy, disheartening compromise because it is not realistic to think one can shop, trim, cut, cook and serve a major extravaganza while remaining the lovely, witty friend that people came to visit in the first place. Without the chef's professional staff, equipment and daily practice, this is an unequal battle that promises little real satisfaction for either the cook or the guests.

There are other ways to win the battle gracefully. In facing the challenges of cooking and entertaining at home today, most of us have come to understand that, just as in other realms as diverse as medicine, child-rearing and city planning, the past, intelligently examined, holds many of the answers to what are very modern problems. After endless bouts with fickle culinary fads, it seems that *cuisine bourgeoise, cuisine de ménage, cuisine de femme, cuisine de mère* and all their recipes sampled by so many generations remain the basis of serious, satisfying cooking. *Nouvelle*, Lean, *Haute* and other exotic exercises may come and go; refined home-cooking more than ever is the core of a successful family Feast.

We all know, of course, that nobody can expect every meal to be memorable. Most of the time one eats for sustenance and thinks no more of it. The road to the future may well be paved with fast-food eateries and convenience, industrialized products with fresh, frozen or vacuum-bagged take-away food, all swallowed on the run for efficiency and instant gratification. No doubt also that hamburgers and stuffed croissants may come in handy for everyday fare, but none of these trendy creations is either truly satisfying, efficient or economical. They cost two or three times the price of comparable home-made preparations, and often after one of those rather sleek meals gulped down in a jiffy, one remains strangely hungry.

When the time comes for a special occasion that breaks with the daily routine, when the time comes to say something that cannot be expressed otherwise, modern French and British men and women may choose home-cooking as their response to monotony and mechanization. The British man or woman who prepares a festive home-cooked meal today has much in common with his or her French counterpart. Neither has a professional entourage or an extraordinary amount of money to spend on food. Each has limited time for cooking and, as a result, most meals must be pulled together quickly and relatively effortlessly. There is no reason to turn our backs on the high-tech kitchen gadgets that save us real time and effort; there is nothing wrong with using frozen spinach to prepare stuffed Pietsch, or with grating cheese and slicing potatoes with a food processor for a Gratin Savoyard, or with whipping Brandade in a blender.

These men and women are willing to devote time and energy to a family Feast as long as they remain confident the results are going to be truly satisfying. This is why I feel the glorious 'one-dish meal' – *le plat unique* – the keystone to the French Feast, is the answer. It is a firm, decisive, totally reliable statement. Although often made with modest ingredients, since it is derived from peasant traditions, this ordinary food has been enhanced by centuries of editing into the most sophisticated of dishes. It represents the essence of a family tradition, the heritage of a region, and emerges from generations of shared experience.

Each of the thirty entrée recipes gathered in this book is an incantation to the memory of great simple, fresh, home-made meals shared by generations of congenial and convivial people. Curnonsky said that a great dish is the master achievement of many generations, and each in its way is just that – slow food as opposed to fast food. It is precisely this extra time and care, these real flavours mingled together naturally, that give each preparation its unique dimension.

These successful and exuberant dishes come principally from the French provinces, but a few foreign dishes such as Paella, Moussaka, and Couscous have been assimilated into French gastronomy in much the same way that painters such as Picasso, Chagall and Zao Wouki are shared by France with their native lands.

Our cuisine, like the rest of our heritage, is rooted in respect for the past but, as Goethe noted, true nostalgia should enhance, not limit, the quality of our experience. These traditional recipes must, therefore, fit the circumstances in which we enjoy them today. I offer you the fundamental classic recipes accompanied by the know-how, the *tour de main*, the *trucs*, the tips I have gathered along the way. We all enjoy hearty dishes, but they need not be 'Christian chokers', the name given by the French in the past to well-intentioned but heavy versions of these classic dishes. My Blanquette de Veau is thickened with shallots rather than flour, and I add a bit more lemon than my grandmother did when she prepared hers for us. My Brandade has less olive oil than hers, and it is often served with chicory or radishes rather than in a pastry shell. As you become familiar with these recipes, you, too, will want to alter them ever so slightly to suit your own preferences.

On the other hand, please remember that abundance – a touch of madness and excess – is essential in these meals. The platter of Jambon Persillé, the Gratin de Poulet au Fromage, the Potée and all the others must be spectacular in size as well as appearance. They should bedazzle and instantly communicate a feeling of uninhibited generosity. Don't fret over the left-overs. After each recipe I give advice on how to use them, and I promise you they will bring you tomorrows that sing.

This is where the sensible, practical, unsentimental approach to cooking by French mothers and grandmothers has been so helpful and reliable for us. These women are neither casual, chi-chi, sentimental nor vague. They have a knowing grasp of every problem, and they share all their serious, efficient knowledge with no frills as they transmit what they have gathered in their lives: cooking as a metaphor for the family life that nurtured them. Aside from personal interpretation, these dishes, little by little, will become a part of your life, for the taste for food comes from memory as well as imagination. As we contemplate the steaming tureen of spicy fish broth, our pleasure in anticipation of the rest of the Bouillabaisse mingles with reminiscences of Feasts past. How will it compare with the one we had last summer? Is the leek essential? Is lobster a distracting, ostentatious presence or should one simply relax and enjoy it? Is the colour of saffron more important than its taste? What ever did she do with that beautiful white silk blouse she stained that night?

I have selected thirty *plats uniques*, great dishes that are totally adaptable to the British kitchen and palate. To accompany them there are fifteen hors d'oeuvres that can be served with pre-dinner drinks or as a first course at the table, and fifteen desserts. Since the main dishes are generous, the beginning and the end of the meal should serve as light, relatively sober counterpoints to the heart of the matter – nothing elaborate, nothing heavy. Cooking, like music, is the art of mingling voices. The first course to awake the palate could be a vigorous tossed salad or a dish of crisp vegetables with a light sauce or a fragrant gratin, and the last course can be a satisfying cheese, a caramel custard, a light crêpe or a bowl of fruit.

Organizing a Feast is a serious business. It is a true demonstration of control where nothing of importance is left out. Preparing a meal is being able to face calmly a hundred little battles. Nothing happens by chance in such a party. Gratins, soups, stews are prepared in advance, reheated at the last moment and served in the container in which they were cooked or the next best pot.

On the day of the Feast, being in perfect command of the situation, you will go through the meal effortlessly, enjoying it as much as anyone else round the table, humming the old Charles Trenet refrain: 'Why wait to join the fun? Why wait to join the Feast?'

Sensibly organized, with all the cooking done in advance, this sort of preparation is a pleasurable experience for the host and for the guests. If there are friends, children or relatives at hand as you prepare your Feast, encourage them to shop, peel, chop, set the table and fold napkins. They will feel involved in the Feast and share its success, and they may save you a little time and energy.

Give a little thought to your guest list. Guests do contribute to the quality of a meal. Tell them about the menu in advance so they can anticipate the occasion and the food. They may want to bring wine, a special cheese, a cake or biscuits to enhance it. There must be time to eat, speak, listen and digest at a Feast. The luxury of having too much, the mindless abandon to idleness and small surprises leads to a *bonheur d'être*, a happiness of being that is truly contagious. For a few hours you join with your guests to create a suspended moment in which food is the most agreeable of pretexts.

Medieval banquets often ended with the guests swearing on a golden pheasant their willingness to depart for the Crusades. Your family and friends will sit at your table exalted and firmly convinced that while the cloudy future may be in the laps of the gods, the glorious present is happily in their plates. And they will leave reassured by the knowledge that the energy and grace, the carefree laughter and stimulating smells, the power of these great simple dishes – all of these miracles and more can be summoned up again at will.

A Pretty Table

French family cuisine is the very opposite of *cuisine de spectacle*, so the decoration of your table should not be ostentatious, grand or formal. There is no 'theme dinner', no central motif; at best, a wink toward the regional dish you place at the centre of the meal.

The setting should be consistently cheerful, warm, friendly and, above all, truly express your personal response to the occasion, the guests, the menu and the day.

With each dinner plan you will find a few suggestions for the table setting, but keep in mind at all times that it is the quality of the food and the quality of the friends sharing it, not a manicured, theatrical decor, that matters.

Your table should allow your guests to share the meal leisurely, to speak, to day-dream, to enjoy the occasion fully. An attractive table does not need to be an extraordinary one, but it must be comfortable. As long as your accessories are functional and as long as you do not try to express too many things or display too many themes at once, the setting will be right. There is no need for a sugar-spun temple, ice figures, baroque marzipan objects, antique silver – nothing contrived, cute, over-inspired or fussy. A confident superdish and a confident table setting will bring everyone together because the tone will be right and harmony will settle in the room.

A touch of insolence and insouciance, a rascal quality in the decoration as well as in the menu of your Feast will be welcome. Avoid anything pious, stiff or overdone in either. Guests are intimidated by overly fancy or overly exotic settings. The priority in a family-type Feast is making sure that a consistent tone, a discreet charm, a quiet confidence prevail. It should all feel cosy and familiar. However, there is no need to 'dress it down' either, in order to be reassuring.

Well done, a family Feast will bring intimations of a vegetable garden, a nearby fruit orchard, enjoying a long walk after the meal, gathering round a cosy fire later. There also may be memories of menus scribbled in purple, of lace-curtained windows, of jovial waiters in long white aprons, of all the pungent aromas, lusty stews and warm laughter you find in a no-nonsense, traditional bistro, because that is precisely the food style and atmosphere here.

After the guests have been invited and the menu has been chosen, you may even find a reason to celebrate something or someone – perhaps the first day of snow, the reconciliation of Aunt Elizabeth and Cousin George, the arrival of a foreign friend, the last strawberry, the first totally sunny day. Or you may depend on more serious events – our culture is never at a loss for ceremonies, rituals and anniversaries of all types. But it must be done tongue in cheek, and the thing never to lose sight of is the celebration of your family and friends gathered and sharing more than food round a pretty table.

Whatever the occasion, it will give you a good chance to display on your table lots of candles, flowers, wines, bright crockery and pretty fabrics. Generosity has to be your keyword throughout the preparation of the Feast, especially when tablecloths, cuts of meat or fish, eggs or vegetables – all the elements you use and work with in the following recipes – are reasonable in cost and easily available.

Use lighting to best effect. Carefully placed indirect lighting or spot lighting will transform the room. Place candles of different sizes round the table, but never too high and never scented, of course.

Use two glasses, for water and red wine or for white and red wines; this avoids getting up and it is thoughtful. Use heavy silverware if you have any, instead of brittle, amusing or exotic cutlery; comfortable silverware is a pleasure at a dinner table.

For your centre-piece try two round vases full of flowers around a tiny terracotta object you particularly like, or choose pretty bowls or containers made of copper, pewter, silver, ceramic, china; or use an old wooden bowl or a glass bowl, or arrange a cake-stand and several baskets. Fill your centre-piece with cut flowers or small branches of foliage, fruit and vegetables.

Mix nuts in their shells with tiny tangerines and kumquats, or mangoes with a few vines of ivy; mingle sweet peas and fresh fluffy roses in one or two birds' nests on each end of the table. Place a single flower in a bud vase in front of each guest, or scatter rose petals all over the table like the Romans used to do. You may like to fill a wide basket with tiny pots of fresh aromatic herbs, geraniums or ivy. You may float candles and multicoloured pansies in a wide, shallow crystal dish. Branches of tree shrubs, palmetto and flowers both in full blossom and in bud will also look lovely in a wide bowl.

If you have them nearby, pick some honeysuckle, wistaria, jasmine, ivy or any winding green vines you can find for your arrangement, intertwined or with their long stems stretching on the table 2–3 in/ 50–75 mm beyond the bottom of the container. Your centre-piece should have the casual grace of a country offering and feel as though it truly belongs there.

Ceramic, earthenware and terracotta from France, Portugal, Italy and Greece have a simplicity and charm that will cheer any table if you make sure the pattern is plain enough and the colours enhance one another. Avoid pristine white in favour of fresh blues, bold yellows, deep reds and muted greens.

Whether you prepare a *dîner fin* around Marmite Dieppoise or a dinner *à la bonne franquette* around Aioli Monstre, it is a fresh, unpretentious and easy feeling that must inspire your table so that everybody wants to belong to this spirited group, participate in its magic and merge into its energy. As you start to dress your table, think once more of a Renoir *Fête Champêtre*, a Bonnard table set in a garden, a country wedding in a cheerful inn or a crowded, good-natured bistro brimming with life.

The aim of your efforts is to give pleasure to your guests, not to show off. The meal, the decoration of the table and the feeling must mingle and harmonize so that everybody feels comfortable and elated. In a meal you have organized and orchestrated to the last detail there is still plenty of room for this gusto, this burst of happiness, this impromptu quality that transforms a fine meal into a genuine Fête.

Here are some things to have on hand for decorating your table for a Feast:

1. A few wide tea-towels or table-napkins to wrap casually round the soup pot, casserole or gratin dish when you take it from the oven or cooker to put on the table.

2. Many pretty baskets, some in natural wicker, some sprayed with a can of spray paint in pretty shades of dark red, ivory, white or bright blue, to serve breads (use at least three bread baskets when you have more than six guests), raw vegetables, boiled potatoes, biscuits or fruit, or to use for the centre-piece.

3. Two or three sets of solid-coloured, large, preferably cotton table-napkins to match your various tablecloths. Use dark red with different shades of brown in your napkins and accessories *or* dark red and various shades of greens for your autumn or winter Feasts. Use salmon, pale blue and ivory *or* all shades of yellow or pale green and pale pink in spring and summer. Avoid white – it may intimidate your guests as they

gingerly pass sauces and bowls round the table. There is nothing more pleasant and luxurious than wide, all-cotton napkins. Fold them and place them between the forks and knives at each place.

4. A few tablecloths. You can buy fabric by the metre for a very moderate price. Measure your table for an ample tablecloth that will reach the floor. If the fabric is not wide enough, seam two lengths together. Make a little hem all round the edges or simply cut the fabric with pinking shears. Choose coloured fabric to avoid the pretentious, stiff look of a white table. If you can avoid it, do not choose either a fragile fabric or 100 per cent polyester.

You may select a piece of quilted cotton for a Provençal effect and a pretty flowery or patterned cloth to make one, two or three tablecloths that will be inexpensive and interesting, and will last for years. If you don't want to sew at all, buy two printed king-size sheets; if you place one slightly overlapping the other, they will cover your table and reach to the floor. You may also look for a very large but simple pink-and-brown or green-and-blue patched Indian bedspread to cover the table generously. You may be tempted by a bright blue or dark red piece of vinyl-coated or American cloth; in solid colours, these wet-look cloths can be very dashing and also eminently practical. Over a tablecloth that touches the floor you may like a smaller square or round cloth in a contrasting colour. The main thing is to have plenty of fabric for a feeling of comfort and abundance.

5. A round wooden table-top larger than your table can be placed over it to increase your seating capacity, but within limits; certainly a round table for eight can become large enough for twelve.

6. Place a pad of felt, fabric or polyester foam under your tablecloth. It makes for a quiet and cosy table.

7. Coloured candles, beeswax candles and plain white votive candles in glass, wood, tin, brass, terracotta, silver or crockery holders. You may like to use a loaf of bread or a large cake (not too fresh, not too hard, just a bit stale), or vegetables or fruit as candleholders. Cauliflowers and artichokes seem to be the safest vegetables, and apples are perfect.

8. Pretty silver, wood, china or straw napkin-rings. Or you may want to wrap each napkin with a bright piece of ribbon or a long piece of grass and leaves, or tuck in a sprig of herbs. Napkin-rings are not necessary at a Feast, but they do give a feeling of homeliness. I often slip a place card in each napkin-ring.

9. Dry eucalyptus leaves or small white or coloured place cards, 1 x 2 in/

25 x 50 mm. If you use only the first name of your guest, it remains informal but is so very useful to plan your table arrangement in advance, to avoid last-minute decisions while the dish is on the table ready to be served and to prevent any awkward waiting. Just as you choose the menu and the decoration of your table, you must place your guests yourself so they enhance one another and are ready to participate in the easiest and most convivial of exchanges during the meal.

10. A collection of small and very large shells can be a very easy and effective centre-piece for certain meals, or try a collection of very small and large pebbles and stones in different shades if you can find them.

11. A wooden bucket, a copper bowl, a china tureen, an antique tin or earthenware utensil can be filled with flowers as a centre-piece.

12. As many pretty salt and pepper shakers and grinders in wood, terracotta, crockery or silver as possible.

13. Three or four wine decanters or wine jugs (for eight to ten guests you need at least three wine bottles in order to avoid getting up, passing too much and stretching across the table).

14. Water jugs.

15. Pots of delicate ferns, baby's breath, beige and red roses, geraniums and amaryllis to use as a centre-piece.

Keep your table in mind when you are in antique shops or at jumble sales. Some little object might add charm or amusement to it.

This is No Time for Maybes

A FEW WORDS ON STRATEGY

Most people don't have the time or the energy to cook a big meal very often, but when nothing else will do, when only a festive meal can give meaning and shape to a special day, that is the time to jump into the kitchen with confidence and gusto and prepare a Feast. Escoffier said that 'like music, the structure of gastronomy is built upon the harmony and sequence of its elements'. It is this graceful flow that the successful host masters; the point is to be decisive and efficient. To that end, the Feasts that follow are executed according to a strategy.

Success in cooking is basically the sum of a lot of small things done correctly. Two days before the Feast a cook must turn into a field marshal, making lists, checking all the details and doing the shopping. Most of the food is prepared a day in advance of the party. On the day, you will be able to deliver gracefully a perfectly synchronized meal and even be able to display the touch of abandon and spontaneity that spells happiness.

Although the truth is that a well-organized, calmly prepared festive meal is easy to cook, it is not the whole truth. In spite of organization and good sense, preparing an interesting meal is not a small pastime.

Cooking is no picnic, and one may just as well acknowledge it before one starts in order to avoid surprises later. When we entertain we must display a lot of energy and heart, a little imagination and a great amount of attentive care. All simple dishes rely on details; in good family food one does not hope for 'the sauce to cover up the fish'; things are not disguised here.

With processed food, frozen food and canned food we have become used to marching 'without fear and without hope' to the kitchen, as the troops of Napoleon did to Waterloo. Cooking has turned into a painless, disembodied activity. For a Feast we embark on a different path.

There are short-cuts to everything, yet the long way of preparing a rich family dish is not only the best and the surest, but also the easiest. Little, last-minute whipped-up creations are never totally foolproof, and they take more time than you can spare while your guests are waiting. It is far better to prepare calmly in advance and be confident throughout. And now to the strategy.

Well in advance, the guests are invited, the menu is chosen, all the silver, linen, glasses and chairs are checked. Make clear notes to yourself about wine, flowers, bread and accessories; be sure to have the right dishes and serving pieces for the menu in hand. Select serving baskets, tablecloths and napkins.

Keep in mind when you prepare your lists that although one does not actually *eat* one's guests, they are truly an essential part of a meal. So, as you invite your guests, avoid too many people who tend to talk shop and avoid too varied a group in age and professions. At the same time, people should be compatible on some ground and yet surprise and amuse one another. Generally, a good meal and a round table make for the most congenial dinner partners. Up to ten or even twelve at a round table is best for a general conversation, but eight is the most you should have at a rectangular one.

One or two days before your party carefully read the recipes you have chosen for your Feast. Take time to understand and even to visualize the different steps involved so that it is a clear process, not a mysterious exercise involving technical virtuosity.

Make a detailed shopping list with different sections for meat, vegetables and such things as candles and flowers; in this way you can shop quickly and you are less likely to forget anything.

Once you have gathered all that is needed, the actual preparation of the meal can begin. Peel and trim all the vegetables over a large piece of plastic or newspaper so the refuse can be discarded easily. For most of the Feasts that follow, the main dish, the sauces and the vegetables can be prepared and set aside a day ahead. You can even grate cheese and make breadcrumbs. You will not forget to sit down as often as you can during the process so you don't end up exhausted.

If you follow your schedule, by the end of the day most of your meal will be ready in the refrigerator and the silver, linen, glasses and tablecloths will be out and ready. Keep the flowers in large containers so you have only to arrange vases on the day. Have the wine ready to be opened or chilled. You should not have to purchase anything on the day of your party, and you should have a minimum of things to do, mostly reheat and serve.

On D-Day, lay the table and arrange the flowers, place cards and wine. The bread can be cut and wrapped in a napkin, then placed in a large plastic bag until the last minute, when it goes into its basket. As the time draws near, all the prepared or almost-prepared dishes are taken out of the refrigerator. Dessert plates and cheese tray are set out. Although it is not included in the Feast menus that follow, a cheese course may be added, if you like, after dessert or as a substitute.

Line a tray – the woven basket type, if possible – with fresh or dried leaves, vines, straw or a plain paper doily. Choose one large ripe Brie or one perfect big piece of Roquefort or two goat cheeses – a fresh one and a dry one – and a mellow Coulommiers, and arrange them, along with a bowl of walnuts, a few ripe pears and a bottle of old port if you have some. Cover the cheese with a glass bell or a napkin.

At formal affairs in France, host and hostess sit across from each other with their most important guests on their right. The other guests are then seated in order of dwindling importance. The *bouts de table* – the ends of table – are generally occupied by young, unclassified free spirits who lack authority and social credits but compensate with their wit. For family Feasts no stiff protocol needs to be followed, yet there should be no last-minute improvisation in the seating arrangement. Place cards – plain white – are best and save lots of time and confusion when the guests go to the table and your meal is piping hot, ready to be served. Seat your guests according to what you hope will be the best chemistry, the best *faire-valoir*, the most interesting counterpoints.

You must be dressed and totally ready an hour before your guests are expected, so that when the time comes to welcome them, you will be fresh and full of zest as well as attentive to the safe and steady progress of your meal. Whether the Potée is simmering or the Pietsch and Gougère are baking in the oven, all is under control.

Serve the hors d'oeuvres with the drinks if you possibly can; then when you sit down for the main dish you'll need only one change of plates for dessert. Make sure that all your guests have time to come to the table and find their places and are sitting before you bring the main dish. A good dish needs people waiting for its arrival, not the opposite. Select one or two friends to assist you with removing the plates. The next course will arrive gracefully and the meal will not be interrupted. A smooth, uninterrupted flow and your presence at the table are what you aim for.

Avoid running water, the clatter of dishes and the sound of the dishwasher operating from the kitchen. The process of changing plates should be simple, quiet and unobtrusive. A tea-trolley or serving cart is ideal. If you have one, pile the soiled dishes on it, cover them with a cloth and place the cutlery in a basket so it doesn't rattle or fall off.

After the main dish, especially if it is a very fragrant one such as a Fondue, Aioli Monstre, Bouillabaisse Royale or Paella, you might like to open the windows briefly to make the room fresh and light for the dessert.

Bring coffee and tea to the table with the cups and saucers. Don't waste time asking your guests in advance what they want to drink, just bring all the pots at once. Later, offer one or two brandies – a cognac, an Armagnac, an aged Calvados – some white fruit alcohol (eau-de-vie) such as Mirabelle (plum brandy) or Framboise (from raspberry). These are wonderful after such a meal. Eau-de-vie means water of life. They come from the fruits and are redolent with their tastes. And even if they do not aid the digestion as much as we like to think, they represent a delightfully superfluous touch that Voltaire, for one, thought so necessary to happiness.

Some time after the coffee, pass a tray of plain cold water, chilled fruit juices or mineral water with thin slices of lemon.

In the days following a Feast left-overs will be welcome in your house. Suggestions on how to use them best follow each recipe. Keep breadcrumbs (preferably home-made), fresh herbs, a good hard cheese, such as Gruyère or Parmesan and some wine in your kitchen, and your left-overs will easily turn into 'singing glorious tomorrows'.

We also have some suggestions for simple dishes when friends linger after a midday feast and seem never ready to part. Soupe au Pistou prepared the day before or Gratinée Lyonnaise reheated at the last moment and served with a bowl of fruit or a tray of cheese will save you from last-minute decisions and make the day longer. Keep almonds, olives, biscuits and fruit compote in your refrigerator; they may be helpful for this *après-fête*, this improvised second meal you never expected to serve. This is also a good scheme if you have weekend guests and the time of their departure is not quite clear.

Keep a book with the dates, the menus, the wines served, the names of the guests and the table setting used, and note your impressions of the evening. This will guide you throughout the years and prevent you from making the same mistake twice. It will also keep you from serving the same dish over and over to the same people and becoming a Johnny one-note, a Madame Blanquette to some, a Monsieur Daube to others.

Always remember Napoleon's advice to 'divide and conquer'. Clear strategy relies on a detailed list of the steps to be taken, which will help to complete each one separately without fuss or anxiety. Let's not speak of grace under pressure – who needs it? – but you can be assured that at the end of the day you will win the battle. And now, *que la fête commence* – on with the feast! Let it be glorious and contagious for all.

A WORD ABOUT WINES

Although rich, subtle, expensive wines are always an addition to a meal, they may not be the most appropriate choice with the regional family-type food served at festive gatherings. *Vins du pays*, light, fresh white wines, or simple robust red wines, reasonably priced, would be enjoyable. They are unpretentious and promote conviviality. Of course, this is to say nothing against the *crus classés*, the classified varieties, or *petits châteaux*. But with the dishes we offer, an honest, serious wine, one that you find appropriate, is really the only rule to follow. In any case, don't forget that if you have a superior wine, always offer it *after* the plainer one.

A robust, hearty wine can overpower a light and delicate dish, while a strong cheese or a highly spiced preparation needs a vigorous wine. Trust your taste, since classical rules and traditional combinations of wine and food are not always to be followed blindly.

Here are a few suggestions you will accept or discard according to your mood:

- Dry champagne is best served before the meal as an aperitif; sweeter varieties are perfect with dessert.
- Sweet wines generally are best with Flan au Caramel, Mousse au Chocolat Glacée, Panier de Frivolités and Tarte Tatin. Muscat wine,

a heady sweet wine, is perfect with most sweet dishes; it has appeared in all happy gatherings in France for centuries.

- Light, dry white wines such as Muscadet, Alsatian Riesling and Chablis are good with shellfish, fish, cold meats and omelettes. Or try Fumé blanc or Sauvignon blanc.
- Heavier dry white wines, such as Côtes du Rhône, Burgundy and Graves will do well with Gratin de Poulet au Fromage, Poulet Fricassée Provençale and Blanquette de Veau. The lighter reds can also be served with such dishes.
- Good rosés, such as the lovely Bandol wines of Tempier, are light, pleasant and unpretentious, and go with almost any dish.
- Simple, hearty, regional red wines go well with Bouillabaisse Royale, Daube de Boeuf en Gelée, Boeuf à l'Orange Niçoise and most rich strong cheese.

Is That a Man I See in the Kitchen?

Yes, Virginia, there *is* a man in your kitchen. See Harold. He is peeling and chopping vegetables *and* meticulously discarding the peels. *Oui,* Marie France, this is Jean Pierre officiating above the kitchen sink, scrubbing mussels *and* discarding the shells.

Let's take a closer look at this species. *Homo faber? Homo sensualis? Homo ludens? Homo sapiens?* As Nietzsche noted, the truly big events in our lives usually land in our midst with the lightness of a dove. No one can pin-point the beginning of this mutation, but men in the kitchen are a permanent part of the landscape today.

Once upon a time men contributed to the well-being of the family by hunting elephants and buffalo, building fires and roasting deer as a matter of course, while women gathered roots and berries. With civilization's advance, masculine participation took a different turn, and in the eighteenth century we find such individuals as the King of France cooking stews in his solid silver pans and brewing robust coffee every morning for his entourage.

But then a new Dark Age fell upon the home. Men forgot everything, including their way to the kitchen. Selecting, cooking, cleaning and serving became women's undisputed turf. Man went to war, raised skyscrapers and walked on the moon. Everyone seemed to agree that this was indeed a biology-is-destiny sort of certitude. Roles were clearly defined; one had only to play his or hers. Cuisine was woman's comforting response to man's frantic crusades and trivial pursuits. The

rich culinary heritage and precious tips from the past were now strictly
for her eyes only. Man did while woman . . . cooked.

Of course, men – at work, at play, travelling – liked to reminisce
about their mother's Pot-au-Feu, their wife's Mouclade, and when
eating out, they favoured bistros run by a husband-and-wife team that
felt just the way they thought home should feel. Men offered judicious
advice and measured praise, grading various culinary efforts of the
women in their lives, keeping up the good fight for high standards on
the dining table. Yet, left to their own devices, face-to-face with
hunger, they would walk to the kitchen reluctantly to survive mostly on
biscuits, crisps, beer and strong coffee, and occasionally gobble canned
soups or frozen dinners when inspired.

Their sense of not quite fitting in a kitchen was so clear they could not
even try. In films and novels men were described as perpetual
outsiders. Men identified with Dustin Hoffman's frustration preparing
breakfast for his child, Jack Lemmon straining his cooked spaghetti
through a tennis racket, and Bill Cosby's outrage: 'Why should I
prepare breakfast now? It's bad for the children's stomachs – they ate
just twelve hours ago!' Men were clumsy, nervous and out of place in a
kitchen. And when it was not considered off limits, since 'a man never
knew where anything was anyway', it was clear to all that he needed lots
of help, lots of helpers. Hence the almost military operation run by
great chefs in restaurants, the assumption that to be a cook a male needs
brigades of apprentices.

Once or twice a year, however, for a special occasion inspiration did
strike in some homes, and a thrust for challenge might send an
adventurous man into the kitchen. He would enter the arena with gusto
in a mood of 'anything she can do I can do better', and produce
elaborate, remarkable, bewildering creations. Such deeds were always
noted and highly praised before, during and after by all the friends and
relatives. Of course, peeling, chopping, trimming and cleaning were
never part of such exercises; men had other things in mind.

I remember my father's flamboyant *tours de force*. He would appear
in his double-breasted suit, cuff-links and all, tie flying to one side, a
hare or a lobster in hand – Lièvre à la Royale and Homard à
l'Armoricaine were his specialities. He walked in, we tiptoed out, but
did not go far and could reappear in a jiffy. Was the chef looking for
butter, salt, forks, chopped onions, an old cognac, a young Beaujolais?
In a minute we became disciplined apprentices, *petites mains*, trying to
help in this vertiginous creative process in which his demands seemed
so urgent, his aims so clearly defined, the elements in all the dishes so
noble. He did upgrade our daily fare. The hare and lobster dishes were

indeed fit for a king. Paul Bocuse could not have done any better.

The ritualistic importance of my father in the kitchen left strong memories in all of us. We were stunned, dazzled and a little exhausted. I remember the sink full of pots and pans, the blackened silver spoons used to stir his sauces ('silver is a noble metal; therefore . . .'). I remember feathers and vegetable peels, piles of tea-towels scattered here and there. Unused eggs would roll on the table, blocks of butter would melt by the cooker. I remember a Pollock-like ceiling once when, neglecting to place a lid on top, he used the blender for tomato sauce. Creators don't linger over such trivia.

A few years later my husband, full of nostalgia for his sweet Kentucky home, prepared ribs, fried chicken and corn pudding for a group of French friends. He came, selected his tools, inspected the assembled ingredients, created. My daughters and I stood aside and watched puzzled, awed, breathless. A thick smoke, the crackling of roasted pork – or was it the crackling of chicken crust? Our kitchen walls and ceiling would never be the same. But it was a perfectly wonderful meal. Prudhomme could not have matched it. We were stunned, dazzled and a little exhausted. Creators' manners did not seem to change very much from one generation to the next.

Then came the era of gadgets galore, a time of great splendour in gastronomical paraphernalia. Whenever men chose to enter the kitchen, they did it in full attire: large chef's hats, huge aprons decorated with humorous slogans and deep pockets, elbow-high oven mitts. They would beat the veal cutlets with shiny mallets, ponder and pontificate over the olive oil (Lord, may it be extra-virgin) for their Caesar salad, ignite chicken breasts, sweetbreads and shrimp with the finest Calvados and the oldest Armagnacs. Expectations were high and preparations were always conducted in the heroic mode; and whether the chef flew into a rage or kept his cool, the meal never appeared on the table before 11 p.m. The wives, children and friends would display loud admiration for the *grand artiste*, but faced with sleepy guests, a topsy-turvy kitchen and serving and cleaning still ahead of them, some of the female species present would secretly hope for the barbecue grill to melt, the lobster to escape and the food processor to crumble. The Thurber drawing in which an exasperated lady tells her dog, 'For heaven's sake, why don't you go outdoors and *track* something?' repeatedly came to mind at such moments.

But times have changed. The Amazon woman is tired, and so is Supermum. The flamboyant Rambos, the absent-minded husbands, are ready to go back to their huts. And a discreet mutant, a new breed of man appears on the scene and seems willing to save the day and carry the flame. He now tends the kitchen as if it were his own garden, sensitively and efficiently. Somehow anatomy and destiny are no longer at odds. He belongs.

'Elegance is the art of not astonishing,' said Cocteau, and today man's concerns in a kitchen are no longer to set criteria, to display panache, but rather to get into the game through legitimate means. No razzle-dazzle, no mad inventions. The new man is not transgressing, challenging, defying; he is following Margaret Mead's observations that a man's burden and glory lie in building a civilized home. And so he shops and chops and keeps the whole process under control. No longer an intruder, a fair-weather artist, an ineffectual virtuoso, he does not try to be stubbornly inventive. Lucid in front of exotic technology and rare ingredients, he respects the slow elaboration of plain ingredients into fine dishes.

And yet the mystery of man, his love for challenges, speed, sport and gambles, seems far from the gentle, patient art of women's cuisine. What draws him into the kitchen? Is cooking an escape, a solution, a means? If it is self-expression, what is he trying to express? Is it a need to control part of the universe? Does man finally discover the charm in small things? Is cooking a quest for authenticity or one more existential adventure in which he wants to measure his self and define his authentic values?

Can he cook by instinct as women are supposed to? Does he integrate the whole philosophy that comes with this type of traditional cooking? Is he anything other than a woman clone? Or is he cooking because no one else wants to be in the kitchen? Perhaps instead of asking questions such as these we should simply say, 'You've come a long way, my friend! Welcome to the kitchen.'

Virginia, Marie France and others like them who have gone through various degrees of suspicion, fear, amused tolerance, exhaustion, exasperation or 'forced liberal responses' to this new-man-in-the-kitchen situation have begun to sit back and enjoy the results. Male cooks no longer seem sweet and touching to their family; they are not fussed about, but are judged instead on the quality of their onion soup or stuffed cabbage. There is a weekly television programme in Paris called *Darling Man, What Are You Cooking Today?* and it is in those terms that man's odyssey in the kitchen will be measured from now on.

The old Manichean views seem silly and dated. We used to ask why a woman couldn't be more like a man and vice-versa, but now we see men and women becoming more alike in many ways that matter. *Cuisine de mères, cuisine de pères*, who cares? The gender of the Kitchen Vestal is irrelevant. Although men seem less sturdy in the kitchen than the epic women of the past, they bring good will and a special zest and freshness to their new turf.

The war of the sexes may not have ended, but there is at least a happy truce in the kitchen, a buffer zone across the butcher block. Some even go as far as to whisper that the couple that cooks together might stay together.

I look into the year 2000 and see my daughter leaning over her husband's heady Cassoulet and murmuring softly, 'Darling, this looks delicious, but when my daddy used to make it back in the eighties, he always added some fresh mint at the last minute. You might want to give that a try.' I see many such scenes in the future framed by a Dantesque arch declaring, 'Enter, brave souls, into this, the bravest of new worlds.' And next to it I see a small sign on which someone has scribbled, 'Relax and enjoy it.'

Kitchen Equipment

Here are a few labour-saving devices and a few tools worth having in your kitchen.

- Standard cook's measuring cups and spoons (*see* Measurements, p. 20).
- A large saucepan or soup pot for Bouillabaisse Royale, Marmite Dieppoise, Mouclade and other dishes.
- A large, heavy iron frying pan, still the best for sautéing.
- A 12-pt/7-l oval casserole, enamelled cast-iron or earthenware, with a tight lid, used to simmer. It can go in the oven and on the cooker.
- One 7-pt/4-l or two 5-pt/3-l (approximately) ovenproof dishes for gratins and for reheating food. They can go straight from the oven to the table.
- Two 7-in/175-mm crêpe pans.
- A pair of large kitchen scissors to cut fresh herbs, to get rid of gristle and cartilage, and for easy cutting of fruit tarts.
- A long-handled wooden spoon.
- Two wide, flexible, metal spatulas for sliding items on to plates.
- A big roasting pan and a rack for leg of lamb and other large joints.
- A wooden board the size of your terrine top so that as the ingredients cool under the board loaded with heavy cans, their texture becomes homogeneous. You will also use this wooden board when slicing. You may replace the board with a piece of cardboard wrapped with aluminium foil.

- A citrus zester, a small, flat type with tiny holes so precise it grates only the tasty, thin, coloured part of the rind.
- A multi-tiered steamer, which is wonderful to prepare Pot-au-Feu and vegetables. It also keeps food warm when your meal has to wait.
- A plate warmer. Plates for some dishes, such as Blanquette de Veau, Marmite Dieppoise, Brandade, and Coq au Vin, should arrive very warm on the table, so the sauce does not congeal.
- A 3-pt/1.8-l charlotte mould can be used for Moussaka, Poulet en Gelée and Daube de Boeuf en Gelée. You may also use a soufflé dish (but it has no handles) or a glass bowl 10 in/250 mm wide to make a dome.
- Ten individual porcelain soufflé dishes to be used for onion soup, Cassoulets, caramel custards and left-overs.
- A pretty, large glass bowl for Oeufs à la Neige, Granité au Vin, Cervelle de Canut and other dishes, and also as a centre-piece on the table, filled with floating candles and cut flowers.
- A tea-trolley or side table. This is so useful when you have a large gathering. Present the wonderful dish to your guests to admire, then settle it on the trolley or side table and serve each plate. Everyone can follow the process while the main table remains pretty and tidy. You can also keep a cheese tray, some dessert plates, a bowl of compote and a set of plates on a lower shelf. A good two- or three-level trolley is an absolute blessing.

Measurements

In this book many dry ingredients are measured by *volume*:

1. Spoons are standard cook's *level* measuring spoons, not just any household teaspoon or tablespoon;

2. A cup holds 8 fl oz/225 ml; this is not equivalent to a weight of 8 oz/225 g for all ingredients. Use cook's measuring cups for the best results.

Other quantities are given first in imperial and then in metric measurements. On any one recipe follow one set of measurements or the other; do not mix them.

HORS-D'OEUVRES

Caviar d'Aubergines

An aubergine purée seasoned with parsley, garlic, lemon juice and olive oil, and served with slivers of fennel, chicory, cucumbers, radishes and thin slices of warm bread.

This fresh, delicious purée can be passed round the table or served with drinks before the meal. It is accompanied by slivers of raw vegetables, large potato crisps, grissini breadsticks and thin slices of warm, oven-dried bread. It is presented in either scooped-out raw fennel bulbs or half-scooped-out raw aubergines, or it is piled as a dome in a wide, shallow dish decorated with very thin slices of lemon. The combination of cold Caviar with cool crisp vegetables and warm bread is irresistible. In France, where general conversation is the national pastime, this light and pungent hors-d'oeuvre with its rich offering of vegetables, is the best start to a warm and festive meal.

FOR 8 PEOPLE

PURÉE

> 4 large aubergines, unpeeled, with stems removed and cut in half
>   lengthways
> 5 cloves garlic, peeled and crushed
> Juice of 2 lemons
> 4 fl oz/100 ml olive oil
> Salt
> Freshly ground pepper
> 1 tbsp chopped onions or shallots
> 2 tbsp chopped flat parsley or basil
> 1 lemon, peeled or unpeeled, cut into very thin slices

VEGETABLES

> 1 bulb fennel, trimmed and cut lengthways into very thin slices, then
>   again in half if too wide
> 3 heads of chicory, trimmed, each leaf not wider than 1½ in/40 mm
> Handful of radishes, cleaned and trimmed, with a little stem left on
> 2 cucumbers, peeled and cut into sticks
> 1 celeriac, peeled and cut into very thin slices, then into 1-in/25-mm
>   slivers

BREAD

> 4 slices whole-wheat bread, toasted and cut in half
> 10 grissini breadsticks

Make a few slits on the flat part of the aubergines and rub a little oil on them. Preheat the oven to 400°F/200°C/Mark 6 and bake them, cut side up, for about 30–50 minutes, until soft.

Meanwhile, prepare the vegetables. Arrange on a serving dish, cover with cling film and refrigerate.

When the aubergines are soft, place them, skin and flesh, into a food processor or blender along with the garlic, lemon juice and olive oil; beat for a few seconds. When the purée is smooth, pour into a bowl, season with salt and pepper, and add the chopped onions. Cover with cling film and refrigerate. It should be served very cold.

A few minutes before you are ready to serve the Caviar, heat the slices of bread in a warm oven, then take the vegetables and Caviar out of the refrigerator. Stir the parsley or basil into the Caviar bowl, correct the seasoning with salt, pepper or more lemon juice and pour into a pretty bowl (or a scooped-out fennel or aubergine). Place very thin slices of lemon all over the surface of the dome and offer 2 baskets: 1 with warm crisp rounds or triangles of country bread and a few grissini breadsticks, and 1 with fennel, chicory, radishes, cucumbers and celeriac slivers, along with a bowl of large, good-quality potato crisps.

Crudités en Panier

A basket of trimmed raw vegetables served with five pungent sauces.

A wonderful way to begin a Feast and linger over aperitifs without a worry in the world, knowing you will be ready for the main course whenever you choose. This type of pretty, healthy, varied finger-food, with its assortment of lively sauces displayed on a side or coffee table, is a perfect introduction for a convivial dinner.

You may like to present your Crudités in an antique footed dish, in a long, shallow basket or a plump, round one, on a wooden platter, in tiny or big Chinese bamboo steamers, in an antique ice bucket, on a white china cake-stand, or in a bright ceramic bowl. If you choose to eat the Crudités seated at the table, they will be the most edible and engaging of still lifes.

Three sauces are generally enough, but the variety of vegetables has to be ample.

FOR 8 PEOPLE

VEGETABLES

> You may use a selection of:
> *tiny artichokes, trimmed*
> *small cos lettuce and chicory leaves*
> *sprigs of watercress*
> *cauliflower florets*
> *spring onions with green stems*
> *cucumbers, peeled and cut into thin sticks*
> *tiny mushrooms, cleaned and dried, with their stems*
> *carrot sticks or tiny carrots, peeled and washed, with their green*
>   *stems on*
> *tiny cherry tomatoes*
> *broccoli, washed and trimmed, in tiny branches*
> *fresh broad beans, shelled*
> *celery and fennel bundles, trimmed, cut vertically into very thin*
>   *slices with some ferny green left on*
> *courgettes, unpeeled and sliced, or peeled courgette sticks*
> *asparagus spears*
> *red peppers, cut into thin slivers*
> *radishes, trimmed, with a little green stem on*
> *bunch of breadsticks wrapped with thin strips of Parma ham*

Wash and trim all the vegetables in advance. Arrange them in their chosen container, sprinkle them with a little cold water and cover with cling film or foil as well as you can; chill until ready to use.

Puncture your elaborate pyramid of vegetables with shiny pea pods, thin spring onions, sprigs of flat parsley or some long stems of mint and basil twigs stuck between the Crudités for a rich and lively display.

For a more delicate offering, place a plate of thinly sliced turnips, cauliflower, mushrooms, green and red peppers and radishes in clumps in a glass bowl filled with crushed ice.

Prepare the sauces, cover with cling film and refrigerate.

SAUCES

THOIONNADE

> *1 egg yolk*
> *1 × 7-oz/200-g can tuna packed in olive oil; use the tuna and the oil*
> *2 cloves garlic, peeled and crushed*
> *Juice of 2 lemons*
> *1 tbsp Dijon mustard*
> *Freshly ground pepper*
> *Salt, if needed*
> *Tabasco to taste*

4 oz/100 g firm black or green olives, pitted and coarsely chopped
  (½ cup)
2 tbsp coarsely chopped capers

Put all the ingredients, except the olives and capers, in a blender or food processor; blend for a few seconds until you have a smooth paste. Chill and correct the seasoning with a little Tabasco. For added texture, add the chopped olives and capers just before serving. The sauce must be smooth but thick enough to stick to the vegetables as you dip them. Add a little oil if you find the sauce too thick; add a little crushed tuna if you find it too runny. Cover with cling film and refrigerate.

BAGNA CAUDA 1

4 cloves garlic, peeled, crushed and finely chopped
1 oz/25 g butter
1 tbsp olive oil
8 anchovy fillets, chopped and crushed, or 1 tbsp anchovy paste
8 fl oz/225 ml double cream
8 fl oz/225 ml soured cream
Freshly ground pepper

Sauté the garlic in the butter and oil until soft but not browned. Add the chopped anchovies, reduce the heat and stir for 1 minute. Add the double cream and soured cream, and sprinkle with pepper. Serve from a chafing dish. If you want to use it later, cover with cling film and refrigerate. Reheat over a low heat before serving.

BAGNA CAUDA 2

(A more pungent and spirited version)
20 anchovy fillets, crushed
2 slices of bread moistened in 2 tbsp water, then squeezed
2 cloves garlic, peeled and crushed
8 fl oz/225 ml olive oil
4 tbsp red wine vinegar
Freshly ground pepper
½ oz/15 g butter, softened

Place the anchovy fillets, bread and garlic in a blender or food processor. Add the olive oil to make a smooth mixture. Put the mixture on a very low heat, add the wine vinegar, pepper and softened butter, and when it is barely warm, pour into a crockery pot or chafing dish.

Note: The sauce must be only barely warm so as not to scorch the lips. If the sauce is not used immediately, cover, set aside and reheat gently over a very low heat.

PISTOU SAUCE

> 5 cloves garlic, peeled and crushed
> 1 tsp sea salt
> 2 cups basil leaves, washed, trimmed, and cut up with scissors a few
>   hours in advance so they lose their extra moisture
> 4 fl oz/100 ml olive oil
> ½ cup grated Parmesan, pecorino romano, or Gruyère cheese
> Freshly ground pepper to taste
> Salt to taste

Crush garlic and coarse salt in a mortar to make a paste, or use the back
of a fork and a small mixing bowl. Pour into a blender or food processor
with the basil leaves and olive oil and mix on a high speed. Cover and refrigerate. Just before serving, add the grated cheese, pepper and a little
salt if needed. If too thick, add a peeled, seeded and puréed tomato.

SAUSSOUN

> (A sauce I love but it might be an acquired taste, so try it first)
> 3 tbsp olive oil
> 1 cup chopped almonds
> 12 anchovy fillets, crushed
> 2 large bulbs fennel, coarsely chopped
> Drop of Tabasco
> 3 tbsp soured cream
> Salt, if needed
> 3 tbsp basil or fennel, cut with scissors

Put everything except the basil in a food processor or blender. It should
be smooth; if you feel it is too dry for a dip, add a little more olive oil.
Stir in the basil, pour into a bowl, cover with cling film and refrigerate
until ready to serve.

This sauce is also delicious served with warm or cold pasta.

TAPENADE

> (Which means 'capers' in Provençal)
> 1 cup black Nice olives or black Italian, Greek or Spanish oil-cured
>   olives, pitted
> 6 anchovy fillets, crushed
> 2 tbsp capers
> 1 clove garlic, peeled and crushed
> 1 tbsp Dijon mustard
> Juice of 1 lemon
> 4 tbsp (or more) olive oil
> Freshly ground pepper
> 1 tbsp cognac (optional)
> 2 tbsp chopped fresh basil

Place everything except the basil leaves in a blender or food processor. Mix at a high speed for 1 second, then pour into a bowl; correct the seasoning, adding more oil if the sauce is too thick. It should be smooth and soft. Sprinkle basil on top. Cover with cling film and refrigerate.

ANCHOYADE

> 20 *anchovy fillets, crushed*
> 5 *tbsp olive oil*
> 1 *tbsp wine vinegar*
> 2 *cloves garlic, peeled and crushed*

Place everything in a food processor; mix at a high speed for 1–2 seconds. Correct seasoning. Pour into a bowl, cover with cling film and refrigerate. Stir well before serving.

Note: Make a large quantity of this sauce – it is spectacular. The left-over sauce can be used as a spread on warm toast or, if there is enough, tossed on pasta.

Take everything out of the refrigerator just before your first guests arrive. Remove the cling film and foil and place the Crudités and sauces on the sitting-room table with the drinks. You may also offer a small basket of potato crisps with the Crudités, and add a bowl of sea salt, a bowl of Aioli Monstre or a bowl of Rouille to the tray on which you have displayed your sauce assortment.

Gougère

A cheese delight.

In most wine cellars of Burgundy, Gougère is served during the traditional tastings because it is the favourite counterpoint to a rich wine. It is a lovely hors-d'oeuvre to offer at home. It looks, smells and tastes delicious, and it wonderfully enhances drinks. Quickly and easily prepared, it is placed in the oven 1 hour before your guests are due.

Make sure you don't open the oven door for 45 minutes while Gougère is cooking, in spite of the tantalizing aroma. The following recipe makes for a very big Gougère, but, as you will see, 'less is more' does not apply to this dish.

Pass the plate of Gougère with the drinks. It is a time for shared memories, silly information heard as if it were essential, lively exchanges and gossip. The lovely cheese pastry and the fresh Kir drink make for a truly happy hour.

FOR 8 PEOPLE

INGREDIENTS

> *12 fl oz/350 ml milk*
> *4 oz/100 g butter*
> *1⅓ cups flour*
> *Salt*
> *Tabasco*
> *Freshly ground nutmeg*
> *6 eggs*
> *2 cups coarsely grated or finely diced Gruyère cheese (with additional cubes for garnish)*
> *1 tbsp Dijon mustard*

Preheat the oven to 400°F/200°C/Mark 6.

Pour the milk into a saucepan, bring it to a boil and add the butter. Remove from the heat and vigorously stir in the flour all at once. Use a wooden spoon or a whisk in a steady motion until the mixture comes away from the side of the pan and forms a ball. Add salt, Tabasco and nutmeg. Add the eggs one at a time, beating the mixture vigorously after the addition of each egg. Stir in the cheese and mustard. The mixture should be smooth, shiny and highly seasoned, so add a little extra Tabasco or salt if needed.

Butter a baking sheet and pile the dough on it by tablespoonfuls, forming a wide circle with a 2-in/50-mm hole in the centre. You may place a little round mould in the middle of the crown to form a perfect centre hole. Smooth the top with a little milk, using a brush or a piece of cheesecloth, then sprinkle a tablespoon of tiny cubes of cheese on top. Bake for 15 minutes, lower the temperature to 350°F/180°C/Mark 4 and bake 30 minutes more. *Do not* open the oven door, no matter how fierce your curiosity, no matter how seductive the smell.

After 45 minutes, open the oven and leave the door ajar for 5 minutes while you place a paper doily or clean napkin on your serving dish and prepare a stack of paper napkins.

Using 2 wide spatulas, place the Gougère on a serving dish. Take it to where the guests are so that everyone can marvel at the sight, then cut it into 2-in/50-mm slices. Pass round the plate. The Gougère can be eaten piping hot or lukewarm.

WINE

Kir, the aperitif made from white wine and blackcurrant liqueur, served chilled, or a good red wine, a dry white wine or a cool rosé is usually offered with Gougère, but you will discover that it is compatible with almost any drink, even mineral water with lemon.

Gratin d'Aubergines

A light and easy dish to prepare. You may serve it as a first course or as a garnish.

Make sure your aubergines are firm and shiny, and use a pretty ovenproof dish.

FOR 8 PEOPLE

INGREDIENTS

> 7 plump aubergines (about 4 lb/1.8 kg), unpeeled, stem removed, and
>   sliced lengthways
> Salt
> 4 tbsp (or more) olive oil
> About 2 lb/900 g tomatoes, peeled, seeded and sliced
> 6 cloves garlic, peeled and thinly sliced
> 2 tsp dried thyme
> 1 cup chopped flat parsley
> 1 tbsp freshly cracked peppercorns
> 1 cup freshly grated Parmesan, pecorino romano or Gruyère cheese
> 6 tbsp breadcrumbs (preferably home-made)
> 1 tsp olive oil

Sprinkle the aubergines with a little salt. (*Note*: Peel them *only* if they are not truly fresh and smooth.) Pile them on top of each other and place a heavy lid or board on top.

After 1 hour, dry the aubergine slices with a paper towel and cook them in hot olive oil until golden and tender on both sides. You will have to make several batches, so let the cooked aubergines drain on paper towels as you proceed. (Remember that although aubergines absorb oil, they exude it when they are cooked.) Add olive oil as you need it.

Add the tomatoes to the pan and cook for a few minutes, then stir in the garlic, thyme and parsley. Cook 2 minutes more, then turn off the heat.

Line a baking dish with a layer of cooked aubergine. Sprinkle with cracked peppercorns, salt and a little grated cheese, and then pour on some of the cooked tomatoes. Add another layer of aubergines, tomatoes, peppercorns, salt and cheese. Cover with cling film and refrigerate. An hour before the meal, take the gratin out of the refrigerator. Sprinkle with a little Parmesan and all of the breadcrumbs, and dot with olive oil.

Preheat the oven to 400°F/200°C/Mark 6 and bake for 10 minutes. Lower the temperature to 375°F/190°C/Mark 5 and bake 20 minutes more. Wrap a pretty tea-towel round the dish, place on a small tray and bring to the table. This may be served lukewarm or cold.

LEFT-OVERS

Add a little cooked rice, or 2 tbsp of moistened bread, and 1 egg. Fill halves of deseeded, parboiled courgettes or cucumbers. Sprinkle with breadcrumbs and bake until warm and golden.

Gratin Dauphinois

A gratin of potatoes, milk, onions and cheese.

This Gratin is a splendid start to a light meal or a succulent accompaniment to Agneau au Pistou, Daube de Boeuf en Gelée, Poulet en Gelée, Hachis Parmentier, Pietsch or Jambon en Saupiquet. It has defied all trends and remains its glorious lusty self no matter when or with what you serve it. It is one of those dishes that never go out of date and are never out of place.

If your guests are late or if you want to put the Gratin in the oven earlier, cover it with a piece of oiled foil and lower the temperature. Discard the foil during the last ten minutes for a crisp top.

FOR 8 PEOPLE

INGREDIENTS

> *4 shallots, peeled and minced*
> *3–4 lbs/1.25–1.8 kg potatoes, peeled, thinly sliced and well dried*
> *16 fl oz/450 ml milk or single cream or evaporated milk*
> *2 cloves garlic, peeled and crushed*
> *1 oz/25 g butter*
> *Salt*
> *Freshly ground white pepper*
> *Freshly ground nutmeg*
> *1½ cups grated cheese, half Gruyère and half Parmesan*
> *2 eggs, beaten*

You may prepare the shallots a few hours in advance and refrigerate them until you are ready to cook the Gratin.

An hour and a half before you are ready to serve the Gratin, preheat the oven to 350°F/180°C/Mark 4.

Peel the potatoes. Bring the milk to a boil. Slice and dry the potatoes. Rub a large or 2 small ovenproof dishes with the crushed garlic. Coat with butter and add the potatoes, salt, pepper, nutmeg and shallots. Mix with your hands to make sure all the slices are evenly seasoned. Add ½ cup of cheese and the beaten eggs, making sure they are distributed evenly throughout the dish. Pour the lukewarm milk over the potatoes. Sprinkle on the remaining cheese, dot with butter, cover with a piece of lightly oiled foil and bake for 1 hour. Remove the foil for the last 30 minutes. The Gratin should be creamy with a crisp top and utterly delicious.

Wrap a pretty tea-towel round the Gratin and bring it to the table with a long-handled serving spoon.

Jambon Persillé

A dome of fragrant ham aspic cooked in a tasty broth and seasoned with parsley, garlic and pepper.

A glistening dome of green and pink Jambon Persillé is a memorable sight. First created in Burgundy and served during Easter, it was often moulded in an old-fashioned washbowl for huge Feasts. For a lighter, more pungent hors-d'oeuvre, we have increased the quantity of herbs and seasoning and removed most of the fat from the ham.

You can offer this as a first course in an alfresco summer meal or as part of a buffet. You can serve it with toasted country bread, butter, fresh and tiny gherkins, or with a light herb Mayonnaise. But no matter where or how you offer it, its heady taste and mellow texture are always welcome at a festive table.

Jambon Persillé is best prepared at least one day in advance so that all the flavours mingle, and then you have only to take it out of the refrigerator and place it on the table at the last moment.

It is an uncomplicated dish, but, as always, choose the ingredients carefully and make the effort to secure the best. It will keep a week in the refrigerator, so make a generous bowl of Jambon Persillé and offer your guests a spectacular appetizer.

FOR 8 OR MORE PEOPLE

BROTH

> (to make approximately 24 fl oz/675 ml)
> *1 veal knuckle, trimmed and cracked (optional)*
> *1 lb/454 g veal bones, trimmed of fat (optional)*
> *1 stalk celery, cut into 2-in/50-mm pieces*
> *1 carrot, peeled and cut into large pieces*
> *2 bay leaves, crumpled*
> *10 peppercorns*
> *2 onions, quartered*
> *1 tbsp olive oil*

HAM

> *2 onions studded with 5 cloves each*
> *4 lb/1.8 kg ham, fully cooked*
> *10 peppercorns*
> *3 tbsp dried thyme*
> *2 tbsp tarragon or 1 tbsp chopped fresh tarragon*
> *3 bay leaves*
> *4 cloves garlic, peeled and crushed*
> *1 medium carrot, peeled and cut into 1-in/25-mm pieces*
> *1 piece orange rind, about 5 in/125 mm long*
> *24 fl oz/675 ml (or more) dry white wine*
> *About 1 tbsp unflavoured gelatin*
> *3 cups chopped flat parsley*
> *1 cup minced chives or spring onions, green part only*
> *3 cloves garlic, peeled and crushed*
> *3 tbsp minced fresh tarragon leaves (optional)*
> *2 tbsp red wine vinegar*
> *Salt and coarsely ground pepper*
> *Sprigs of parsley as garnish*

ACCOMPANIMENTS

> *Gherkins*
> *Toasted whole-wheat or country bread*
> *Unsalted butter*
> *8 fl oz/225 ml Mayonnaise with 2 tbsp double cream stirred into it and*
> *flavoured with 2 tbsp minced fresh herbs*

Prepare the broth. Combine all broth ingredients in a large stock-pot and cover with cold water. Bring to a boil, lower the heat and simmer for about 2 hours. Skim often. Allow the broth to cool and then remove the fat, which will have congealed on top.

Cut the onions studded with cloves in half and place them in a frying pan, cut side down. Brown over medium-high heat. These will give an amber quality to the broth.

Place 2 pt/1.1 l of broth, cooked ham, browned onion studded with cloves, peppercorns, thyme, tarragon, bay leaves, garlic, carrot and orange rind in a very large saucepan with enough wine to cover. Bring slowly to a boil. Skim. Simmer for about 2 hours, until the ham is tender enough to mash with a fork.

Remove the pot from the heat and let the ham cool to room temperature in the broth.

Remove the ham and set aside. Discard the rind, bones and veal bones. Reduce the cooking liquid to 2 pt/1.1 l. Discard the herbs, orange rind and vegetables. Strain the liquid through a sieve lined with a double layer of cheesecloth. Cool the liquid and then carefully remove the fat. Sprinkle the unflavoured gelatin over the liquid. Leave to dissolve for 5 minutes. Stir into the liquid to make aspic.

Coarsely shred the cooked ham with 2 forks into rather large chunks, about ½ x 1 in/12 x 25 mm or so, discarding fat and gristle. Stir in the parsley, chives, garlic, tarragon, vinegar, salt, pepper and the 2 pt/1.1 l of aspic.

Chill a 5-pt/3-l serving bowl in the refrigerator for a few minutes, then fill it with the ham, herbs and aspic. When full, cover with a plate, a piece of wood or foil-covered cardboard the size of the bowl top. Place a few cans on top to weigh it down for about 2 hours. Remove the cans and leave the bowl of Jambon Persillé in the refrigerator for 1 or more days. Unmould on to a large serving dish.

Just before serving, place a stem of parsley on top and surround the dome with tiny sprigs of parsley. Sprinkle a little red wine vinegar on the surface. Serve with warm toast, gherkins and unsalted butter. Cut in slices or scoop out. Pass round a bowl of Mayonnaise enriched with a little cream.

If you'd rather serve this dish unmoulded, sprinkle with vinegar and minced herbs on top and scoop out each serving with a long-handled spoon.

WINE

White Burgundy Aligoté or a dry white wine.

Lentilles ou Pois Chiches en Salade

A lukewarm lentil or chick-pea salad seasoned with fresh herbs, onions, oil and vinegar.

Whether served as an hors-d'oeuvre or as an accompaniment, this salad is always a treat. It is truly foolproof and can be served cold when needed. But the vegetables must be warm when the sauce is poured on them, so if you cook them in advance, reheat them gently before seasoning them.

Surround the lentils or chick-peas with lamb's lettuce leaves.

FOR 8 PEOPLE

VEGETABLES

> *4 cups dried lentils or chick-peas*
> *2 onions studded with 2 cloves each*
> *1 clove garlic, peeled and crushed*
> *3 bay leaves*
> *Twig of thyme*
> *Salt*
> *Freshly ground pepper*

DRESSING

> *9 tbsp olive oil*
> *Salt*
> *3 tbsp red wine vinegar*
> *Tabasco*
> *2 tsp chopped thyme*
> *1 tbsp coarsely crushed peppercorns*
> *3 shallots, peeled and chopped, or 2 onions, peeled and thinly sliced*
> *2–3 spring onions, trimmed and minced*

GARNISH

> *3 tbsp chopped parsley or chervil*
> *Handful of small lettuce leaves*

Soak the lentils or chick-peas in cold water, then drain into a pan and cover with cold water. Add the onions, garlic, bay leaves and thyme. Cook the lentils following the directions on the packet.

Meanwhile, prepare the dressing. Put the oil and salt in a bowl and beat with a fork or a whisk. Add the vinegar, Tabasco, thyme, peppercorns, shallots and spring onions. Beat until well blended.

When the lentils or chick-peas are tender, discard the onions, garlic and herbs, and pour into a large bowl. Season lightly, pour the dressing over and toss carefully. Pour into a clean bowl, sprinkle with fresh herbs (parsley or chervil) and tuck a few lettuce leaves all round before you bring it to the table.

If you have cooked the lentils or chick-peas in advance, reheat them gently so the vegetables are warm when you season them. Serve at room temperature. As long as it is seasoned with warm vegetables, this salad will be fragrant.

LEFT-OVERS

1. Soup: by adding a little broth, a crushed garlic clove and a twig of thyme, you will turn the left-overs into a lovely soup. Season it with a drop of raw olive oil and a little grated cheese just before serving.
2. Side dish: serve as part of Aioli Monstre or Couscous. Such a salad can also be served on a plate of cold hors-d'oeuvres or become the side dish for Fondue Bourguignonne, Pot-au-Feu or Poule Verte.

Mouclade

A spirited mussel stew prepared with cream and seasoned with curry.

The word mussel comes from the Latin word *musculus* (little muscle); hence the name of this mussel soup. Mussels have existed since prehistoric times and, as far as history records, have always been eaten by people. In Charente, where Mouclade was created, the culture of mussels started in the thirteenth century and has been prosperous ever since. Wild mussels are gathered in the rocks, or they are cultivated flat in parks or on wooden posts (*bouchots*) stuck in the sea or clinging in clusters on ropes. They are removed at low tide in flat boats.

This recipe comes from the Atlantic coast round La Rochelle, which, during the reign of Louis XIV, provided the King with this mussel soup every week. Given a chance, of course, most of the kingdom would have loved the same treat. Mouclade is truly a metaphor for all the good things the sea brings us. The traditional flavouring of curry powder goes back to the days when the spice trade was a seafaring endeavour and sailors unloaded their spices at the port of La Rochelle.

This is a glorious soup, easy to prepare and quite inexpensive.

Note: When you prepare mussels, remember they must always be closed. Open or broken ones should be discarded. The shell should be black or brownish black. Around Christmas time mussels have the most nutritional qualities, and Mouclade is a wonderful first course for a family Christmas dinner.

Mouclade is prepared in advance. You can serve it in a small amount as a first course or as a rich main course by leaving half of the shells in the plates and adding egg yolks to the sauce for a richer broth.

FOR 8 PEOPLE

INGREDIENTS

> *8 pt/4.5 l mussels*
> *1⅔ pt/900 ml white wine*
> *2 bay leaves*
> *1 large onion, chopped*
> *1½ oz/40 g butter, softened or kneaded with 6 tbsp flour*
> *3 cloves garlic, peeled and crushed*
> *6 shallots (approximately), peeled and chopped (½ cup)*
> *1 tsp curry powder*
> *8 fl oz/225 ml double cream*
> *Salt*
> *Freshly ground pepper*
> *Pinch of cayenne pepper*
> *Juice of 2 lemons*
> *3 egg yolks (optional)*
> *3 tbsp finely cut parsley*

Immerse the mussels in a sink filled with cold salted water for about 30 minutes. Scrub them and remove their beards.

Meanwhile, heat the wine, bay leaves and onion in a large saucepan. Add the mussels and shake the pan once or twice until they open. They should not cook through. Remove the mussels with a slotted spoon and shell them; you should have about 4 cups. Reserve 16 shells and discard the rest. Keep the broth hot and remove the onion. Place the shells with the mussels, cover with cling film and place in the refrigerator.

Pour the hot broth into a bowl through several layers of cheesecloth folded over a sieve. Stir the butter and flour in a saucepan for 2 minutes, then add the hot broth while stirring. Add the garlic, shallots and curry powder, and reduce for a few minutes over a high heat. You should have 1⅔ pt/900 ml of liquid. Add the cream to the broth. Simmer, stirring. Cool. Pour into a bowl, cover with cling film and place in the refrigerator.

Thirty minutes before the meal pour the broth into a saucepan and reheat slowly, without reaching boiling point, stirring once. After 20 minutes add the cooked mussels and the empty mussel shells. Add salt, pepper, cayenne and lemon juice. Check the seasoning. If this is your main course, stir 3 egg yolks with a little of the warm broth in a bowl, then quickly pour into the broth. Simmer and stir for a few minutes. Do not let the soup get near boiling point. Wrap a tea-towel round the cooking pot and bring it to the table piping hot, with warm soup plates and a bowl of chopped parsley.

Place a few mussels, a ladleful of broth and a few shells in each plate. Sprinkle with fresh parsley and pass to your guests.

WINE

A dry white wine.

Olives Sautées, Olives Farcies

A lively hors-d'oeuvre of stuffed olives and olives sprinkled with herbs and sautéd.

In the terraced olive groves of Provence, the dark, twisted olive trees with their dishevelled silvery foliage evoke an enduring civilization. All along the Mediterranean Sea a handful of olives and a slice of bread make the healthiest and best of meals. This peppery, fresh-spirited fruit is better than a 'poor man's truffle', as the saying goes. When you buy olives, make sure to choose carefully. You may choose from black and purple Greek olives, small black Nice olives, dark purple Gaeta Italian olives; all are very good. Never buy pitted or water-packed olives; they are soggy and tasteless.

Serve Olives Sautées and Olives Farcies together on a wide plate with thin slivers of oven-dried bread with a little unsalted butter, a few trimmed spring onions or trimmed radishes with a 2-in/50-mm stem, and a stack of paper napkins. If time is running short, you may want to serve only Olives Sautées, with or without warm almonds.

This is a pungent, unusual hors-d'oeuvre that is easy to serve with drinks before sitting down at the table for your *plat de résistance*.

FOR 8 PEOPLE

OLIVES SAUTÉES

> *1½ lb/675 g firm green, purple or black olives*
> *Thyme and savory*
> *3 bay leaves*
> *Pinch of coarsely ground black pepper*
> *2 tbsp (approximately) olive oil*

OLIVES FARCIES

> *12 oz/350 g large, firm green olives*
> *2 shallots, peeled and finely minced*
> *2 tbsp olive oil*
> *8 oz/225 g roughly chopped good country ham or cooked chicken*
> *2 tbsp chopped flat parsley*
> *1 tbsp grated Gruyère cheese*
> *1 egg*
> *Freshly ground pepper*
> *2 tbsp flour*
> *Dried thyme or savory*
> *Juice of 1 lemon*

To make Olives Sautées sprinkle the olives with the herbs and pepper. Sauté in warm olive oil, tossing them with a wooden spoon for about 5 minutes.

Note: The sautéd olives are nice accompanied by warm almonds. Bake some whole, shelled and skinned almonds at 300°F/150°C/Mark 2 for a few minutes until lightly coloured, then sprinkle with a little sea salt.

To make Olives Farcies, pit the olives. Sauté the shallots in the olive oil until soft. Add the ham, parsley, grated cheese, egg and pepper. Stir and remove from the heat. Pour into a food processor and process for a few seconds.

Stuff the olives with the mixture, then roll them in flour and the thyme or savory. Fry briefly on all sides, turning them with a wooden spoon. Sprinkle with lemon juice and serve warm.

Pissaladière

A crisp and mellow onion tart seasoned with herbs, anchovies and black olives.

This wonderful tart comes from Nice, where it is sold in the streets, in the markets and in bakeries; it is also prepared at home and is part of all the summer Feasts. Mediocre pizza-like tarts prepared with a few onions and some tomatoes are called Pissaladière, but the real article is unique and very distinctive. It has a crumbly, tasty dough and a thick filling of puréed sweet onions punctuated with spirited herbs, garlic, anchovies and olives. The result of this marriage of contraries offers an interesting counterpoint in texture and taste.

Light, crisp, sweet and highly seasoned, it is a perfect hors-d'oeuvre to serve with drinks before sitting down for the main dish at the dining-table.

It can be baked in a rectangular baking pan and cut into 2-in/50-mm squares or cooked in a round tart or flan tin and cut into wedges. Plan your decoration with anchovy fillets and olives according to the shape you choose.

You can make the Pissaladière in advance and reheat it for a few minutes just before your guests arrive.

FOR 8 PEOPLE

FILLING

> 3 tbsp olive oil
> About 4 lb/1.8 kg onions, peeled and sliced or coarsely chopped
> 2 cloves garlic
> 3 bay leaves
> 2 tsp thyme
> Salt
> Freshly ground pepper
> 8 anchovy fillets
> 1 tbsp dried thyme, oregano or marjoram
> Freshly ground pepper
> 20 (or more) tiny whole, unpitted Niçoise black olives or good
>   oil-cured olives from Italy or Greece, pitted and cut in half

CRUST

> 1/3 tsp dried yeast
> 2½ fl oz/65 ml lukewarm water
> 1⅓ cups flour
> 2 tbsp (approximately) cooking liquid from the onion purée
> 1 tbsp olive oil
> 1 tsp salt

Make the filling. Heat the olive oil in a large frying pan and cook the onions, garlic, bay leaves and thyme over a low heat stirring with a wooden spoon from time to time. Add salt and pepper to taste. Cover and simmer for about 2 hours over very low heat. The onions should turn a pale amber colour at the end of the 2 hours and never turn brown. You may want to make 2 batches for easier cooking if your frying pan is too small.

Remove the onions from the pan and pour all the cooking liquid into a bowl. You will use it for the crust. Set the onions aside while you prepare the dough.

To make the dough: dissolve the yeast in the lukewarm water and let it rest for a few minutes, according to the directions on the packet.

Preheat the oven to 225°/110°C/Mark ¼ for about 5 minutes, then turn it off.

Pour the yeast mixture into a large bowl. Add the flour, cooking juices, olive oil and salt, and knead for about 15 minutes with both hands. Your dough should become supple and very smooth. Add a little more oil if necessary and make a ball. Place in a clean, greased bowl, cover with a thick damp towel and allow to rest in the warmed oven for 1 hour.

Check after 1 hour. The dough should have doubled in bulk. Remove the dough from the bowl and punch it with your finger. Sprinkle a little olive oil on top, knead for a minute, replace in the bowl, cover with the damp towel and place it back in the oven for about 15 minutes.

Oil a large baking pan (about 11 x 17 in/280 x 430 mm) or 2 fluted round tart tins. Take the dough out of the oven and heat the oven to 375°F/190°C/Mark 5.

Pat down the dough and press it into the pan, spreading it one-quarter or one-third up the sides. Spoon the puréed onions on to the crust. Arrange the anchovy fillets in a lattice pattern on a rectangular pan or like the spokes of a wheel on a round one. Sprinkle with thyme, pepper and olive oil and bake for about 30 minutes. Add the olives and lower the temperature to 350°F/180°C/Mark 4. When the dough separates a bit from the sides, remove from the oven. Take care not to overcook Pissaladière, especially if you plan to reheat it before serving.

Reheat for about 10 minutes at 350°F/180°C/Mark 4. Cut in squares or wedges, sprinkle with a little cold olive oil and serve. You may wish to put a few twigs of basil leaves as garnish on your serving dish.

WINE

Spirited rosé or a light, strong red wine.

Pissenlits aux Lardons

A tossed salad of dandelion leaves or endive with crisp nuggets of bacon and a warm vinegar-and-oil dressing.

Gathering snails and dandelions is an exercise practised by the very young and the very old in France. As soon as the snow melts, dandelions show their pale, tender shoots and their tiny buds, and each spring they are picked by eager gourmets and docile children. Endive may be easier to find and can successfully replace dandelions in this recipe.

This robust, invigorating salad is prepared differently in each province. In Burgundy, herbs and verjuice are added; in Provence, garlicky *croûtons*; in Lyon, a soft-boiled egg is put on top of each plate. Sometimes a chopped hard-boiled egg is sprinkled on top of the salad, and sometimes a tablespoon of local brandy is stirred into the dressing.

FOR 8 PEOPLE

INGREDIENTS

> 2 cups (about 8 handfuls) dandelion leaves or endive, cut into
> 2-in/50-mm bits
> 2 tbsp olive oil
> 8 oz/225 g lean bacon or lean salt pork (about ⅔ cup when cut into
> ½-in/12-mm dice
> 4 tbsp red wine vinegar
> 1 tbsp Dijon mustard
> Freshly ground pepper
> Salt to taste
> 4 slices bread, each cut into 4 triangles and oven-dried (optional)
> 2 cloves garlic, peeled (optional)

Wash, trim and cut the salad greens. Keep them wrapped in a tea-towel and refrigerate until ready to use.

Pour the oil into a thick-bottomed frying pan and fry the pieces of bacon until crisp.

Meanwhile, fill a large salad bowl with warm water so it is thoroughly warm. Empty the bowl, dry it, fill it with the salad greens and pour the crisp bacon and warm cooking oil on top. Add the vinegar to the warm frying pan and bring to a boil. Stir in the mustard and then pour the whole mixture over the salad. Sprinkle with pepper and a little salt. Toss and serve.

You may also want to oven-dry the bread triangles, rub them with garlic, sprinkle them with a little oil and toss them in the salad just before serving.

Poireaux Tièdes Vinaigrette

Lukewarm leeks seasoned with a spirited vinaigrette.

Nicknamed the 'poor man's asparagus', it is only recently, with the *nouvelle* and lean cuisines, that leeks have acquired their *titres de noblesse*, but they always were a favourite in my home-cooking repertory.

A fresh and delicate dish, Poireaux Tièdes Vinaigrette is a traditional hors-d'oeuvre in family meals and on bistro menus. This is one of those dishes that at once gives the tone of a Feast and is wonderful when you plan a heavy main course.

FOR 8 PEOPLE

INGREDIENTS

> *24 thin to medium-size leeks (about 4 lb/1.8 kg)*
> *2 tsp Dijon mustard*
> *Salt*
> *Coarsely ground pepper*
> *2 tbsp red wine vinegar*
> *3 hard-boiled eggs, peeled and yolks separated from whites*
> *8 fl oz/225 ml olive oil*
> *3 tbsp coarsely chopped parsley*

Prepare the leeks. Trim off the roots, remove all withered or bruised leaves and cut off the dark green tops. Slice lengthways. All the leeks should be the same length, about 6 in/150 mm. Wash them thoroughly in cold water to remove all grit, spreading the leaves slightly apart. Tie them with string into 5 little bundles, as you would asparagus. Cook them in boiling water for about 10 minutes. They should not be too soft.

Meanwhile, prepare the dressing. Place the mustard, salt, pepper and vinegar together in a bowl. Mash and stir with a fork. Add the egg yolks, then stir in the oil until blended.

Drain the cooked leeks. Place them on a thick tea-towel or paper towel to absorb the excess moisture; remove and discard the strings, and place another thick towel on top. Slide the leeks on to a warm serving dish and pour the vinaigrette over them. Sprinkle with finely chopped egg whites and chopped parsley. Sprinkle a little oil on top. Serve with a spatula and a serving spoon. Pass round a basket of warm, toasted whole-wheat bread.

Note: If you have prepared your leeks in advance, cover the dish with a piece of foil and place it in the oven at 325°F/160°C/Mark 3 for a few minutes to take off the chill. Add the vinaigrette, egg whites, parsley and a little olive oil just before serving.

Ratatouille

A vegetable and herb stew.

The secret of this superstar summer dish is to simmer the vegetables separately and gently so they don't turn into a purée, and to cook them uncovered in a wide frying pan so they are not too watery. In other words, forget short-cuts; they never seem to work with this dish. Made carefully, this is a reliable dish that has never been touched by the dictatorship of the fickle, the inventive or the improved but remains truly popular. Expectations are always raised when one mentions Ratatouille, and fairly so. It can be served as an accompaniment with Agneau au Pistou, Canard Farci, Hachis Parmentier, Pietsch, Porc aux Herbes and Poulet en Gelée, or as an hors-d'oeuvre. Whether served warm, lukewarm, at room temperature or even cold, it is delicious and gets even better when prepared a day in advance.

FOR 8 PEOPLE

INGREDIENTS

> 3 large aubergines, peeled only if very large
> Sea or plain salt
> 8 courgettes, unpeeled, trimmed and cut into 1-in/25-mm slices
> 3 large, fleshy red or yellow peppers, seeded and cut into 1-in/25-mm strips
> 9 tomatoes
> 5 medium onions, peeled and sliced
> 6 cloves garlic, peeled and crushed
> 5 tbsp olive oil mixed with 5 tbsp peanut oil
> 3 bay leaves
> 2 large twigs thyme or 3 tsp dried thyme
> Freshly ground pepper or Tabasco
> Salt
> 6 fl oz/175 ml dry white wine
> 2 cups basil leaves or flat parsley, cut with scissors
> Juice of 1 large lemon (optional)

Trim stem end of aubergines and cut into 1-in/25-mm dice. Sprinkle with salt and leave to drain in a large colander while you prepare the rest of the vegetables.

Trim and cut the courgettes and peppers. Dip the tomatoes in boiling water for a few seconds and then remove their skins; cut them gently in half crossways and squeeze out the seeds. Prepare the onions and garlic.

Heat 1 tablespoon of oil in a large frying pan. Add the onions and sauté for a few minutes, stirring from time to time, until soft. Add the garlic, stir, then add the tomatoes, bay leaves and thyme. Simmer uncovered for about 10 minutes. Pour into a side dish and set aside.

Blot the aubergines and courgettes with paper towels and clean the frying pan with a paper towel. Add 3 tablespoons of oil to the pan and cook the aubergines for 5 minutes. Sprinkle with a little pepper and pour into the side dish. Clean the pan again with a paper towel, add 3 tablespoons of oil and cook the peppers for 5 minutes. Sprinkle with salt and pepper, and pour into the bowl with the rest of the cooked vegetables.

Clean the pan with a paper towel and heat 3 tablespoons of oil. Add the courgettes and cook uncovered for 5 minutes. Pour into a casserole or large thick-bottomed saucepan with the rest of the vegetables. Add the wine and basil, stir gently with a wooden spoon and simmer uncovered for 1 hour.

Cool, cover with cling film and refrigerate.

Thirty minutes before the meal, remove the herbs and pour off the top oil and excess juices. You should have a moist mixture but not a runny one. Correct the seasoning with salt, pepper and thyme. Pour into a pretty dish, sprinkle with basil and serve.

If you serve Ratatouille cold or at room temperature, sprinkle with the juice of 1 lemon and surround the edges of the dish with very thin lemon slices. If you reheat it gently to serve it warm, sprinkle a little basil or parsley on top and dribble with olive oil.

LEFT-OVERS

1. Soup: add a little broth or water, a twig of thyme and a crushed garlic clove. Bring to a boil and dribble a little olive oil on top just before serving.
2. Gratin: discard the excess juices, pour into a baking dish, sprinkle with grated cheese, chopped parsley, breadcrumbs and a little olive oil, and bake.
3. Omelette: prepare an omelette then pour the left-over lukewarm Ratatouille in the centre. Fold the omelette over and slide it on to a warm plate. Serve sprinkled with chopped basil and a little olive oil on top.

Soupe au Pistou

A vegetable soup seasoned with garlic, basil, cheese and olive oil.

Although it is a known fact that whoever pretends to please everybody and his father must be mad, I would venture to say that Soupe au Pistou can succeed where most other dishes might fail. I can testify that in my house it has pleased everyone and his father over and over.

The apotheosis of a vegetable extravaganza, this pungent and cleansing dish has been called *potage de santé*, health soup. When the heady mixture of basil and garlic is stirred into the warm broth, the wonderful scent rising from the tureen is so potent, so exquisite, so invigorating that it could give heart to the meekest – and to his father.

Soupe au Pistou is also the perfect answer when, after having shared one of your festive meals at lunch-time, no one seems in a hurry to go home. You have taken your guests for a long walk, they have played cards and now they are lingering and chatting and time seems suspended. Everybody is happy, no one is leaving and you know you must come up with a glorious solution.

A large pot of Soupe au Pistou prepared the previous day is exactly what you want. A light, fragrant, highly digestible dish, it is a meal in itself and will be the perfect ending to a perfect day.

It is better in the summer and autumn, of course, when there are plenty of fresh white beans, tiny carrots and good basil. But if you crave it off-season, keep a jar of frozen pistou and add fresh garlic, a handful of fresh flat parsley and a little raw olive oil at the last moment. Prepare your soup with the best fresh vegetables available. Soupe au Pistou may be served warm, lukewarm or cold.

FOR 8 PEOPLE

VEGETABLES

> *1 lb/450 g green beans, trimmed and cut into 1-in/25-mm pieces*
> *6 large or 8 small carrots, peeled and diced*
> *6 onions, peeled and sliced*
> *3 turnips, peeled and diced*
> *6 courgettes, unpeeled and diced*
> *6 potatoes, peeled and diced*
> *1 head celery, trimmed and diced*
> *2 leeks, white part only, trimmed and diced*
> *1½ lb/675 g white beans, preferably fresh in summer or dried, precooked*
> *8 oz/225 g fresh or frozen small broad beans*

Olive oil
½ cup (about 3 oz/75 g) diced lean ham or bacon
3 bay leaves
Twig of thyme
Pinch of sage
Salt
Freshly ground pepper

PISTOU

4 cups shredded fresh basil leaves
8 cloves garlic, peeled
1 cup grated Parmesan or Gruyère cheese
6 fl oz/175 ml olive oil (approximately)
Salt
Freshly ground pepper

GARNISH

Bowl of grated Parmesan or pecorino or Gruyère cheese
Basket of sliced oven-dried bread
Basket of sliced fresh bread

Wash, trim and cut all the vegetables. Shell and blanch the white beans and broad beans.

Heat 3 tablespoons of olive oil in a large frying pan. Sauté the sliced onions until golden. Add the ham or bacon and cook for a few minutes. Slide the contents of the pan into a large bowl with the beans.

Add a little oil to the frying pan, then sauté the rest of the vegetables in batches for a few minutes.

Note: If you are in a hurry, the vegetables need not be sautéd before being added to the soup.

Bring a large saucepan of water to a boil. Add the bay leaves, thyme, sage, all the vegetables, salt and pepper. Simmer uncovered for 30 minutes. Add to the bowl of meat and beans. Correct the seasoning. Cool, cover the bowl with cling film and place in the refrigerator.

Meanwhile, prepare the Pistou sauce. Place the basil leaves, garlic and cheese in a food processor and blend for a few seconds. Add a little olive oil, stir with a spoon, process again for a minute and add more oil. You should have a smooth mixture. Correct the seasoning with salt and pepper, and pour into a bowl. Cover with cling film and place in the refrigerator until ready to use.

Thirty minutes before the meal, grate some cheese and put it into 2 pretty bowls. Reheat the soup on a low heat and pour into a large tureen.

Bring the soup and the bowl of Pistou to the table. Stir the Pistou into the soup tureen when all your guests are seated – the stunning aroma is intoxicating. Serve and pass the plates round the table along with the bowls of cheese and the baskets of oven-dried and fresh bread.

Terrine aux Herbes

A country pâté of veal, ham, chicken livers, herbs, garlic and wine.

This is a creation made with beautifully interrelated ingredients: meat, herbs, spices and wine. All you need when you prepare it are love, confidence and, of course, quality ingredients.

Technically, a pâté is a mixture of meats enclosed in pastry (*en croûte*). When it is not *en croûte* but simply cooked in crockery, it is a terrine. A good terrine must have a variety of meats and a diversity of textures and flavours. This terrine is a bright, reliable, rich star in the firmament of terrines. It will keep – and improve – for about a week and be prettier if you serve it with a spatula out of its own porcelain or earthenware cooking dish, rather than sliced on a plate. Serve with a crisp, bitter dandelion or endive salad, butter, gherkins and toasted whole-wheat bread.

FOR ABOUT 10 PEOPLE

INGREDIENTS

> *8 oz/225 g chicken livers, clean and as lightly coloured as you can find*
> *Flour*
> *½ oz/15 g butter*
> *2 tbsp vegetable oil*
> *1½ lb/675 g lean veal, lean pork and boiled ham, coarsely chopped separately by hand (about 4 cups altogether)*
> *1 tbsp dried thyme or savory*
> *4 cloves garlic, peeled and crushed*
> *2 onions, peeled and chopped by hand*
> *1 tbsp red, green and black peppercorns*
> *3 eggs*
> *1 tbsp juniper berries*
> *8 fl oz/225 ml dry white wine*
> *2 tbsp port*
> *½ cup chopped parsley*
> *A few strips of back fat or streaky bacon about ⅛ in/3 mm, enough to line your mould*

2 × ½-in/12-mm thick slices of cured ham, each cut into 4 strips
4 bay leaves

GARNISH

> *Gherkins*
> *Bitter tossed salad*
> *Whole-wheat bread, toasted and sliced*
> *French bread*
> *Unsalted butter*

Trim the chicken livers; rinse and pat them dry. Dredge with 1 tablespoon of flour. Heat the butter and oil in the frying pan and sauté the chicken livers on all sides for 2 minutes. Remove from the heat and set aside.

Mix the coarsely chopped veal, pork and ham with a wooden spoon. Add the herbs, garlic, onions, peppercorns, eggs and juniper berries. Stir in the wine, port and parsley and cook for a few minutes.

Note: Don't use a food processor to chop and combine the ingredients or the terrine will turn pasty and dry. You should have a smooth, grainy texture, not a baby food purée.

Preheat the oven to 350°F/180°C/Mark 4.

Line the bottom and sides of the terrine with half the slices of back fat or bacon. Put one-third of the stuffing, including chicken livers, in the bottom of the terrine. Cover with the strips of cured ham and pat down gently with the palms of your hands. Spread half of the remaining stuffing, the remaining strips of cured ham, then the rest of the stuffing. Place 4 bay leaves on top and cover with the remaining slices of back fat.

Place a piece of foil on top of the fat, put on the lid and set in a roasting pan half-filled with hot water. Set in the preheated oven and bake for 2 hours. Remove the foil and lid, and bake 15 minutes more, uncovered, to allow the top to brown.

The terrine should shrink from the sides and the juices should run yellow. Take the terrine out of the oven and cover it with a wooden board or piece of cardboard (the shape and size of the inside of the top) wrapped in a piece of foil. It should fit as snugly as possible. Place 2 or 3 cans on top to weigh down the terrine as it cools. When cool, refrigerate the terrine, still weighted down, and keep it 1 or 2 days before serving. In this way all the flavours will blend and the terrine will have a nice, firm texture.

When you are ready to serve the terrine, remove the weighted top. Slice the terrine lengthways with a long, sharp knife (so each slice is then easier to cut and take out), then place a knife and a narrow spatula in the mould and let each guest cut his slices directly. It will be pinkish, moist and homogeneous.

Pass the terrine from guest to guest with a bowl of gherkins, a bitter tossed salad and a basket of toasted whole-wheat bread as well as a basket of sliced French bread.

WINE

A dry white wine, a rosé or a light red wine, such as Beaujolais or a domestic wine.

GREAT SUPERDISHES

Agneau au Pistou

Marinated roasted leg of lamb served with a warm puréed garlic sauce and a cold Pistou sauce

SUGGESTED MENU

Caviar d'Aubergines
Crudités en Panier

Agneau au Pistou
Gratin Dauphinois
Easter Salad

Granité au Vin
Panier de Frivolités

Beaujolais

This is the traditional spring meal to celebrate Easter. In Latin countries this festivity is more important than Christmas. It is a time of rejoicing with family and friends, a challenge, a revenge on long, lonely winter. After such a meal, in which lamb, ham and eggs all speak of resurrection, the bleak, cold days are forgotten and everyone leaves the table confident in the renewal powers of spring.

Genuine spring lamb, *agneau pascal*, is on sale in April, but a leg of such a lamb weighs only about 4 lb/1.8 kg. In winter it is twice the size, and although the taste is not as delicate, it is still called lamb until it is 1 year old. Always choose lamb with dark pink meat (not red), tight flesh, light, thin bones and very white – never yellow – fat. If you are on very good terms with your butcher, have him detach the bone. Place some sliced garlic cloves in the cavity, and then slide the bone back while it cooks. Remove the bone only when the meat is cooked and you are ready to slice it. For eight people, choose a 7 lb/3 kg leg of lamb, which means the lamb should be a little under 1 year old and will absorb the marinade without losing its fresh quality.

This could be served with Gratin Dauphinois, a warm Ratatouille, a dish of white haricot beans, fresh green beans or diced celeriac blanched for 20 minutes and then sautéd with butter, lemon juice and parsley.

Prepare the Caviar and start marinating the lamb the day before your Feast (see Strategy, page 57). Make sure an accompaniment such as Ratatouille is prepared in advance and reheated when you roast the lamb, so both arrive together piping hot at the table.

FOR 8 PEOPLE

MARINADE

> *8 bulbs of garlic (about 48 cloves)*
> *3 tsp dried thyme or a few twigs fresh thyme*
> *2 onions, peeled and thinly sliced*

2 *bay leaves, crushed*
Salt
Freshly ground pepper
24 fl oz/675 ml dry white wine such as Muscadet or white Burgundy
2 *tbsp olive oil*
4 fl oz/100 ml Dijon mustard
A bowl of chopped fresh herbs: basil, parsley, thyme, coriander

LAMB

7 *lb/3 kg leg of lamb, with bone in but separated, if possible (see above), and trimmed of excess fat*
2 *tbsp red dried rosemary or thyme or savory*
Olive oil

COLD SAUCE

Pistou or *Aioli Sauce*

ACCOMPANIMENTS

Choose from:
Gratin Dauphinois
Ratatouille
Blanched white beans with butter
Boiled green beans
Easter salad: watercress or chicory with Vinaigrette and 2 hard-boiled eggs

Prepare the marinade the day before the dinner. Set aside 8 cloves of raw garlic to insert in the meat. Blanch the rest of the garlic cloves in salted water for 10 minutes. Drain. Mix together the remaining marinade ingredients and add the blanched garlic cloves.

Note: Such an enormous quantity of garlic will not be overwhelming once it is blanched. The strong taste when raw will be replaced by a sweet, delicate and nutty flavour.

Put the lamb in a large dish. Add the marinade, cover and leave overnight on the lower shelf of the refrigerator, turning the lamb a few times.

Prepare the Ratatouille if this is your chosen accompaniment. Cover and keep it refrigerated.

Cool, peel and pass the hard-boiled eggs through a sieve into a small bowl. Cover with cling film and refrigerate.

On the morning of the dinner, peel and chop the shallots and garlic for the Gratin, and keep them tightly wrapped in a piece of foil.

Two hours before the dinner, take the lamb out of the refrigerator, dry it with a paper towel, then add dried rosemary or thyme or savory herbs. Cut the remaining 8 cloves of garlic into slivers. If you have the bone detached, insert the slivers into the cavity, then replace the bone. If you have not had the bone detached, make slits in the flesh and insert the slivers.

Preheat the oven to 400°F/200°C/Mark 6.

Rub the lamb with a little olive oil. Pour a little marinade in the bottom of the roasting pan, put the rack in place and set the leg of lamb on it. Set aside the rest of the marinade.

Don't use any marinade on the meat while the lamb is cooking. A very hot oven is necessary initially to dry the lamb, which is still a little moist from its marinade no matter how carefully it has been patted. A strong, dry heat will lock in the juices and produce a crisp skin. After 10 minutes of cooking, baste the surface of the lamb with a little olive oil, then lower the heat to 375°F/190°C/Mark 5. Turn the lamb on the other side and roast for 1 hour more, turning it once again. As your lamb cooks, baste it with a brush dipped in olive oil – not with the marinade, which would make the lamb soggy. When the skin is crisp enough, stop adding fat (it would turn brown or black).

Meanwhile, peel the potatoes, slice them, heat the milk and prepare the Gratin. Bake the Gratin for 1 hour. Reheat the Ratatouille or prepare the other accompanying dish you have chosen.

Prepare the tossed green salad. Pour the dressing into the bottom of a large bowl, cross a serving spoon and fork over the top, then place the green leaves and minced hard-boiled eggs on top, ready to be tossed later for a perfect Easter salad.

The lamb should cook, uncovered, for about 9 minutes per 1 lb/450 g.

When it is done, remove it from the oven and let it rest for 15 minutes before you slice it.

Skim off the fat from the roasting pan. Discard the herbs from the marinade. Crush the cooked garlic cloves with a fork and return them to the warm juices in the roasting pan. Boil briskly on top of the cooker for 5–10 minutes, scraping the coagulated juices with a fork. Transfer all the juices into a small saucepan and reheat on a low heat.

Bring the warm plates, salad, gratin or other side dish to the table. Also bring a bowl of chopped fresh herbs – basil, parsley – warm sauce, cold sauce and the leg of lamb on a serving dish with the carving knife and fork.

Make sure everybody has a chance to see the whole display. Remove the bone and start carving the lamb in thin slices, cutting parallel to the bone so the juices won't run out. Give each guest some gratin, other accompaniment and 2 small slices of lamb. Pour a little warm sauce, sprinkle fresh herbs over the meat and pass each plate.

When you have served everyone, place the bowls of warm sauce and cold sauce on a little tray and pass them round for each person to help himself. Place the bowl of salad on the table and let your guests help themselves.

WINE

A rather strong red wine, such as a Bordeaux Graves, a Beaujolais, a Bourgogne Beaune; or a dry white wine, such as Muscadet, Pouilly sur Loire, Bordeaux Graves or Bourgogne Meursault.

WHAT TO SERVE BEFORE AND AFTER AGNEAU AU PISTOU

HORS-D'OEUVRES TO BE SERVED WITH THE DRINKS

1. Caviar d'Aubergines with Crudités en Panier
2. Olives Sautées with warm almonds
3. Gougère
4. Jambon Persillé, for a traditional Burgundian Easter meal

DESSERTS

1. Granité au Vin
2. Panier de Frivolités with a fruit salad
3. Tarte Tatin aux Poires et aux Pommes
4. Oeufs à la Neige et aux Fruits

TABLE DECORATION

This is a joyful time and the inspiration here is spring, so you may want to choose an ivory, white or pale yellow tablecloth because these colours evoke Easter and induce joy.

Place one or two cake-stands on the table and pile on fresh, exotic, rustic or antique eggs. Arrange daffodils, lilies, daisies – all the white and yellow flowers you can find – in a white enamelled basket, a white porcelain tureen or a glass bowl, and place them in the centre of the table surrounded by white or yellow candles.

It should be a cheerful, festive, beautiful table but not an overly elegant, glitzy one. Be careful not to go wild with accessories or be excessive.

In France it is believed that the bells of cathedrals, chapels and the churches of the land fly to Rome to be blessed and that on Easter morning they come back full of goodies, which they pour on lawns, round trees and on dining tables wherever the fancy hits them.

For dessert, plates of chocolate – bitter, milk and white – in the shape of tiny chickens, bells, fish, rabbits and eggs are passed round to the guests.

STRATEGY FOR THE SUGGESTED MENU

- Guests invited for 7.30 p.m.
- Meal served at 8.30 p.m.

- One day before the Feast: marinate the lamb; prepare the Caviar, the sauces for the Crudités and the lamb, the Ratatouille or other side dish, the hard-boiled eggs and the Granité au Vin.

- On the morning of the Feast: peel and chop the shallots and garlic and wrap them in foil. Wash the greens for the salad or prepare the vegetables for the Crudités and refrigerate. Prepare the salad dressing.
  7.00 Preheat the oven and oven-dry the bread for 30 minutes. Take the lamb, shallots, salad greens and Crudités out of the refrigerator. Peel and slice the potatoes and heat the milk.
  7.25 Bake the Gratin in the oven. Bake the lamb in the oven. They take about the same time. Reheat the Ratatouille or other side dish.
  7.30 Your first guests arrive. Bring the Caviar, Crudités and warm bread to the living room.
  8.15 Remove the lamb from the oven and finish the sauce according to the recipe. Take the cold sauce out of the refrigerator.
  8.30 Light the candles. Ask your guests to the table. Bring the warm plates, Gratin, lamb, sauces, side dishes and salad to the table.
  9.00 Serve the Granité au Vin with a plate of biscuits or a basket of Frivolités and, of course, a plate of tiny chocolate eggs, fish, chicken, bells and rabbits.

LEFT-OVERS

1. A fresh spring mixture: dice lamb and sauté in olive oil with diced turnips, carrots and potatoes. Sprinkle with chopped parsley or basil.
2. Moussaka Provençale, page 160.
3. Curried lamb: sauté onions; add tomatoes, curry powder and diced left-over lamb. Cook for a few minutes. Correct the seasoning. Serve with rice.
4. Hachis Parmentier, page 147, replacing the beef with left-over lamb.

Aioli Monstre

Aioli – ai *for garlic*, oli *for oil* – *is the heady sauce that is the soul of one of the most loved and celebrated superdishes of Provence.*

SUGGESTED MENU

Roasted Hazelnuts and Almonds

Aioli Monstre

*Granité au Vin
Panier de Frivolités*

Full-bodied Dry Rosé

Garlic was introduced to France from the Middle East after the Crusades and adopted at once in the south of France as a sacred herb. It was, and still is, rubbed on babies' lips, given to athletes and soldiers, used against evil spirits, rheumatism, plague, diabetes and dull temperaments. 'It is not an exaggeration to say that peace and happiness begin geographically when garlic is used in cooking,' said a famous French gourmet. And Aioli, the marriage of garlic and olive oil, is more of a philosophy than a dish. As Proust's Madeleine vividly evoked with full intensity the charm of long-lost afternoons, a mere dot of Aioli evokes all the bright, fragrant world of Provence. Mistral, the Provençal poet, wrote: 'Aioli intoxicates gently, it fills the body with warmth and the soul with enthusiasm. In its essence it concentrates the strength, the gaiety of the Provençal sunshine.' This fabled dish requires a true passion for garlic, and timid individuals fulfilled with the elusive whiff of that vegetable should either fasten their seat-belt and enjoy it, or abstain.

In Provence Aioli is traditionally served with dried salt cod on Fridays, which were once Catholic fast days and from that habit continue often to be meatless days in Latin countries. The dish also appears on Ash Wednesday and for Christmas Eve supper, along with snails, before midnight mass. But Aioli is in full attire as *Aioli Monstre* throughout Provence every summer, when it concludes the 3-day festivals that celebrate each village's patron saint.

Seated side by side at long tables set out in village squares, tourists, farmers, children, local dignitaries, shopkeepers and cousins gather to share the huge plates of fish, vegetables and meats. Through a long afternoon they visit, gossip, joke and digress, and the bowl of Aioli passes from hand to hand, spreading a good-natured communion among all. Aioli fills the soul and pleases all the senses with its fiery, satiny sauce; with its blissful embarrassment of offerings as rich and diverse as a Provençal market, it makes for a memorable Feast.

It is difficult to describe fairly a Feast organized round Aioli. Some claim it is not unlike a trip to paradise: to understand it fully, you must have been there. Others – myself among them – claim that although Provence is the cradle of Aioli, Aioli cannot stay eternally in its cradle and, unlike local wines, travels well.

This is not a dish for timid souls; it is not the sort of dish one can eat or prepare, so to speak, on tiptoe. Aioli is exhilarating and overwhelming, and one must prepare properly for it the day before the Feast.

Aioli needs very little in the way of additional accompaniments. The wonderful display of dishes on the table is spectacular in colours, flavours and textures, and its diversity enables every guest to choose according to his taste and appetite. Each one creates his own meal – a bit of this, a touch of that. The heady sauce enhances the bland vegetables and meats, and challenges the spirited salt cod and the firm squid. Fortified against evil spirits and diseases of all kinds, your guests will leave the table contented, drowsy and in a blissful state of well-being, ready for a little siesta or a peaceful chat. And that's the way it's meant to be.

Since there is no general agreement on what an Aioli Monstre should include, I give here the exhaustive list of possibilities. Even the most extravagant Aioli Monstre would not include all of this, so choose according to the season and what your market offers, the size of your party and your purse. Essential ingredients are dried salt cod, hard-boiled eggs and a wide variety of vegetables, including boiled potatoes. Snails, squid, octopus and, certainly, lobster are optional.

For each guest plan on two or three raw, and two or three cooked vegetables, one hard-boiled egg, some canned tuna fish, some fresh fish, some salt cod and a slice of meat. Always choose the smallest, freshest vegetables. Aioli Monstre, with its staggering variety of ingredients, is wonderful for an out-of-doors meal, but you can serve Aioli, the sauce itself, in any way and in any season you like. Even simply spread on a warm slice of country bread, it is a delightful treat.

Generally, Aioli sauce is served from the mortar in which it traditionally is made, but, of course, it can also be served in bowls. There are many truly 'authentic' recipes, and I am giving you the version I find most delectable – and the most overwhelming!

FOR 8 PEOPLE

FISH

Choose 1 or more of the following fish:
2-3 lb/900 g-1.25 kg dried salt cod
4 bay leaves

3 lb/1.25 kg squid, cleaned, trimmed and sliced into ½-in/12-mm
    strips
2 lb/900 g octopus, trimmed and sliced into ½-in/12-mm strips
Salt
Freshly ground pepper
1¾ pt/1 l mussels, thoroughly cleaned, in their shells
Wine for broth
2 lb/900 g snails or periwinkles
1 × 7 oz/200 g can of tuna
1 uncooked lobster (or 2 if you feel extravagant)
3 lb/1.25 kg fillets of lean fresh fish such as cod, striped bass, halibut,
    whiting, swordfish

MEATS

Choose 1 of the following:
4 lb/1.8 kg rump joint of beef, sliced
4–5 lb/1.8–2.25 kg chicken, cut into 6 or 8 pieces
4 lb/1.8 kg boned leg of lamb

RAW VEGETABLES

Choose 2 or 3 of the following:
4 heads of chicory, trimmed and halved lengthways
4 tomatoes, cut in half, or 8 whole if small
1 cauliflower, cut into florets
4 very small artichokes, cut in half lengthways
1 lb/450 g broad beans, shelled
1 head celery, trimmed and cut into sticks
2 lb/900 g very thin green asparagus, trimmed

SAUCE

14–16 cloves garlic
Pinch of salt
8 fl oz/225 ml vegetable oil
2 egg yolks
1 tsp Dijon mustard
8 fl oz/225 ml olive oil
Juice of 2 lemons
2 tsp lukewarm water
Pinch of freshly ground white pepper
Pinch of crushed saffron

COOKED VEGETABLES

Choose 3 or 4 of the following:
1 lb/450 g dried or canned chick-peas, well rinsed

8 thin carrots, whole and peeled
8 beets
4 turnips
8 bulbs fennel, trimmed, or 4 halved if they are large
1 cauliflower, trimmed
8 small artichokes, trimmed
8 potatoes, unpeeled if they are new
2 lb/900 g runner beans, trimmed
2 lb/900 g purple-tipped asparagus, trimmed
8 courgettes, whole if small, otherwise cut lengthways
4 sweet potatoes, peeled

GARNISH

4 hard-boiled eggs, peeled and halved
A little watercress
2 lemons, sliced
Bunch of parsley, washed and trimmed
A few lettuce leaves

Two days before the Feast, place the pieces of salt cod, skin upwards, on a plate or in a colander in a deep bowl. Cover with cold water and soak for at least 24 hours, changing the water 5 or 6 times.

The day before the Feast place the cod in a saucepan and cover with fresh cold water. Add a bay leaf and bring the water to a boil. Turn off the heat and let the fish cool in the water. Drain. Keep covered in the refrigerator.

Wash and trim the squid and octopus, and slice into ½-in/12-mm strips. Place in a pan of water with 2 bay leaves, salt and pepper, heat and simmer for 30 minutes. Drain and keep in the refrigerator until ready to use.

Cook the cleaned mussels in a little wine for a few minutes, until the shells open. Keep in the refrigerator until ready to use. Do not remove the mussels from their shells.

Cook the snails in a pan of salted water for 10 minutes, drain and keep in the refrigerator until ready to use. Serve in their shells.

If using dried chick-peas, cook according to the directions on the packet and drain.

If using canned chick-peas, rinse them under cold water. Pour the chick-peas into a bowl and keep until ready to use.

Roast or boil the piece of beef or chicken, or roast the lamb. Let the meat cool to room temperature, then slice it, wrap it in foil and keep it in the refrigerator. Add a few twigs of watercress to the centre of the dish before serving.

On the day of the party, trim, wash and cut the raw vegetables. Place them in a pretty basket or dish, sprinkle with a little cold water, cover with cling film and leave in the refrigerator until ready to use. Trim the vegetables and fish, which will be cooked at the last moment.

For the garnish, slice the lemons and wash the parsley, and cover with cling film until ready to use. Everything is thus prepared in advance.

Some hints before preparing the sauce: boiled garlic cloves instead of raw garlic will make a highly digestible but milder Aioli. A boiled potato can be added to the raw garlic cloves for a smoother, lighter Aioli. A slice of toasted bread soaked in vinegar may be added to the garlic and egg-yolk base.

To prepare the sauce using a mortar and pestle have all the sauce ingredients at room temperature, away from draughts, as you make it. Peel the garlic cloves and remove the green germ in the centre, if any, to make it more digestible. Place the garlic in a large mortar. Add a pinch of salt and 1 tablespoon of vegetable oil and crush with the pestle. Continue to pound the mixture until it is a paste. Add the egg yolks and mustard and mix in thoroughly.

Combine the rest of the vegetable oil with the olive oil and then dribble in *very slowly*, stirring all the while, until the sauce thickens to a custard-like texture. Aioli, like mayonnaise, is an emulsion that can occur only if the oil is incorporated into the yolks very slowly, especially at the beginning. The experienced Aioli-maker merely holds a finger over the opening of the oil bottle to control the flow, estimating the quantities by eye and feel.

Beat in the lemon juice and the water. Check the seasoning and add salt and pepper to taste. Your sauce should be satiny and gold. Place half of the Aioli in a bowl and cover with cling film. Add a pinch of crushed saffron to the other half and stir well. Place in another bowl, and cover with cling film. Place both bowls on a low shelf of the refrigerator until ready to use.

To prepare the sauce using a food processor force the garlic through a press to make it into a paste. Put the garlic paste into the processor bowl with the egg yolks and mustard, and whirl together for a few seconds to combine. Add the oil as described above, *very slowly*, through the feed tube while the machine is running. When the sauce is firm, add the lemon, water, salt and pepper. Whirl again briefly to combine. Complete as in the method using a mortar and pestle.

Note: If your Aioli sauce separates, add 1 teaspoon of hot wine vinegar and stir until it becomes firm again, or start with a fresh egg yolk in a clean bowl and beat in the sauce slowly until firm and smooth.

On the day of the Feast, 1 hour before the guests are due to arrive, take all the raw vegetables, squid, octopus, mussels, salt cod, snails, sliced meats and chick-peas out of the refrigerator. Arrange them on serving dishes and decorate with lemon slices and lettuce leaves, watercress and parsley. Open the can of tuna fish, drain it and place the tuna on a plate with a few lettuce leaves tucked around it. Place the serving dishes on the dining-table.

Boil or grill your fresh fish according to its size and quality, for about 30 minutes. Place it on a serving dish, garnish with a small bunch of parsley and a few lemon slices, cover it with a piece of foil to keep it lukewarm and place it on the table with the rest of the dishes.

If you are including lobster, boil it in a large pot of salted water for about 12 minutes per 1 lb/450 g. Drain, break it in large hunks and place it on a plate.

If you have a multi-tiered steamer, fill the bottom part with hot water. If possible, put the eggs in here to hard-boil; otherwise cook them in a small saucepan. In the first compartment place your choices among carrots, beets, turnips, fennel, cauliflower and small artichokes, cover and cook for 10 minutes. Then add the second compartment on top and fill it with potatoes, runner beans, asparagus, courgettes and sweet potatoes, cover and cook 10 minutes more. Turn off the heat. The vegetables will still be lukewarm when they are served with the Aioli.

A few minutes before serving the meal, place the cooked fresh fish on a piece of foil on top of the vegetables in the steamer.

If you don't own a steamer, cook your choices among carrots, beets, turnips, fennel, cauliflower and artichokes in a large pan of boiling salted water for about 30 minutes, or until they are just cooked. Remove vegetables as they finish. In another pan of salted water cook the eggs and your choices among potatoes, runner beans, asparagus, courgettes and sweet potatoes for 15 to 20 minutes.

Peel the eggs, cut them in half and serve them around the lukewarm fish. Place the lukewarm vegetables on a large plate. The selection of meats, raw vegetables, snails, mussels, squid, tuna and chick-peas are already on the table. Check to see that every bowl and dish is decorated with lemon slices, watercress or parsley. Take the Aioli bowls out of the refrigerator. If you have a pretty marble or wood mortar, serve one of the Aioli sauces in it. It is traditional, and if the mortar is marble, it will help to keep the sauce pretty and cool.

Have your guests pass the serving dishes and bowls round to one another and then leave everything on the table because it is beautiful, and because everyone will have second and third helpings. You should not have to get up until dessert.

WINE

There are no special rules on the wine you should serve with Aioli. Some people think only cool water is appropriate, some think you should serve a strong red wine, some a very dry white or rosé wine. I suggest two jugs of water and a dry, full-bodied red, white, or rosé wine.

WHAT TO SERVE BEFORE AND AFTER AIOLI MONSTRE

This is an abundant dish, so the hors-d'oeuvres and dessert should be mere counterpoints.

HORS-D'OEUVRES TO BE SERVED WITH THE DRINKS

You may start the meal with a glass of dry white wine with a drop of blackcurrant or raspberry liqueur for a light Kir aperitif, or a glass of sweet vermouth or anise-flavoured *pastis*, and offer:

1. Roasted almonds and hazelnuts warmed for a few minutes in the oven for extra crunchiness
2. Olives Sautées
3. Pissaladière
4. A thin slice of Terrine with gherkins and thinly sliced country bread

DESSERTS

1. Cold Mélange de Fruits
2. Granité au Vin
3. Panier de Frivolités
4. Poires, Pruneaux, Oranges au Vin Rouge
5. Tarte au Citron

TABLE DECORATION

A printed tablecloth in warm tones of blue, peach, yellow and all the shades of ochre is perfect for a Mediterranean feeling.

Use as many straw or lacquered baskets as you can find and pretty crockery serving dishes. Wide cotton napkins are essential, and finger-bowls, wet paper towels or paper napkins as well are a good idea.

Place a bowl filled with flowers and fruit, perhaps dotted with a few shiny pea pods or asparagus spears, in the centre of your table. This is a very crowded table with all the plates of raw and cooked vegetables, fish and meat and bowls of sauce, so food is truly the heart of the matter here – and your centre-piece must be attractive but small.

STRATEGY FOR THE SUGGESTED MENU

- Guests invited for 7.30 p.m.
- Meal served at 8.30 p.m.

- One day before the Feast: prepare the Frivolités, Granité, Aioli sauce, meats, fish and chick-peas. Refrigerate.

- On the day of the Feast:
  6.30 Arrange serving dishes of raw vegetables, prepared snails, squid, octopus, mussels, salt cod, meat and tuna fish and place them on the table. Cook the fresh fish and other vegetables.
  7.30 Guests begin to arrive. Serve hazelnuts and almonds with drinks.
  8.30 Place the Aioli and plates of cooked vegetables and fish on the dining table. Give a final check to the table. Light the candles. Call the guests to the table.
  9.30 Change plates. Serve the Frivolités. Unmould and serve the Granité au Vin.

  Later After the meal offer strong coffee and a very pungent herb tea, such as Mint or Anise Tisane. And *to help refresh the breath* offer mints or parsley, a few coffee beans, or a piece of lemon peel or bitter chocolate to nibble, or glasses of cold water with lemon juice.

LEFT-OVERS

In a family Feast nothing is lost, all is transformed and this alchemy of glorified left-overs shows the genuine French gift of leaving nothing to waste and doing wonders in the process. All the ingredients of an Aioli Monstre always provide singing tomorrows, with delicious dishes such as those listed below.

1. A light lunch, a true bistro dish. Hard-boil some eggs. Remove the shells and cut in half lengthways. Add an additional pinch of saffron and a little lemon juice to the left-over Aioli sauce and spread it on the hard-boiled eggs. Serve the eggs on a bed of watercress or cos lettuce.
2. Sprinkle some chopped fresh basil into your left-over Aioli sauce and serve it as a dip. Place it in the centre of a flat basket surrounded by chicory leaves, slivers of young courgettes, celery sticks, and very thin breadsticks.
3. Prepare a big bowl of steamed mussels. Strain, shell and let cool. Add diced celery. Stir the juice of 1 lemon into the Aioli sauce and then stir it into the celery and mussels. Check the seasoning, sprinkle with chopped parsley and serve as a lunch dish or as a first course.

4. For a tureen of Bourride soup serving 8 people, stir 8 tablespoons of Aioli sauce into 2 egg yolks, then add about 3 pt/1.7 l of warm fish broth, stirring all the while. Check and correct the taste, adding salt, pepper or more Aioli. Place over a low heat while continuing to stir for a few minutes. The soup will thicken, but don't let it come to a boil or the eggs will curdle.

Pour the creamy soup into a tureen and serve with crisp slices of toasted French bread. This is usually a first course followed by the fish used in making the broth and served with a bowl of Aioli. Genuine Bourride is prepared with white-fleshed fish, but you may use any light fish soup with your left-over Aioli sauce.

5. Cut the left-over vegetables into slivers or dice and pour warm vinaigrette (2½ fl oz/65 ml wine vinegar, 5 fl oz/150 ml olive oil, salt and pepper) over them. Serve as a first course sprinkled with fresh herbs.

6. With left-over fish: peel and slice 2 onions and sauté them in ½ oz/ 15 g butter and 1 tablespoon oil until golden. Add the fresh fish, salt cod and squid, and lower the heat, stirring once. Sprinkle on 3 tablespoons of wine vinegar, freshly ground pepper and chopped basil or chives. Serve warm as a lunch course with either toast points or warm boiled potatoes, thickly sliced.

Blanquette de Veau

A veal stew with onions, mushrooms and capers in a lemony sauce.

This is a real jewel of the family repertory. However, like all living things, it has changed and evolved a little over the decades. For instance, there tends to be less flour, more vegetables and more lemon in my version than in my grandmother's.

This delicate and elegant dish can be prepared entirely a day in advance, and it

SUGGESTED MENU

Gougère

Blanquette de Veau
Rice
Mange-touts

Poires, Pruneaux,
Oranges au vin Rouge et
aux Épices

Fumé blanc

is not difficult to execute but, as always, organization is essential. The sensible strategy given here will have you fresh and ready to enjoy your guests on D-Day and share with them a memorable meal. Whether you honour a friend's arrival, commemorate an anniversary or celebrate your favourite cousin's plan for a summer in Patagonia, Blanquette de Veau will turn your meal into a coherent and exciting Feast.

Always choose a very white, mother-of-pearl-coloured veal, and try to select different cuts. You should have lean meat for the most part, but also some bones and cartilages for texture, body and flavour. Choose firm, creamy-coloured mushrooms and small pearl onions; cook them separately and add them to the Blanquette at the last moment so they retain texture and flavour. By adding leeks and celery to the broth, and lemon peel, lemon juice, capers and nutmeg to the sauce, Blanquette de Veau becomes a truly festive dish.

Choose a large earthenware, enamelled ironware or stainless-steel casserole, pretty enough to bring to the table. Avoid a black iron pot, which would turn the veal grey.

In spring Blanquette de Veau served with boiled new potatoes and asparagus is a wonderful treat. But you may serve the Blanquette with a dish of plain rice cooked with bay leaves, a dish of buttered pasta or boiled artichoke hearts, as it is often served in Brittany. You may also offer tiny broad beans, mange-touts, braised sliced chicory or blanched celery as a second accompaniment. Both accompaniments should be brought to the table with the warm plates and the Blanquette.

FOR 8 PEOPLE

INGREDIENTS

2 lb/900 g mushrooms, cleaned and trimmed into roughly the same
*   size*
1 tsp lemon juice
24 small pearl or pickling onions, peeled
2 large carrots, peeled and sliced
2 leeks, washed and sliced lengthways
2 stalks celery, chopped
5 cloves garlic, peeled
4 tbsp freshly chopped chervil or flat parsley
4 lb/1.8 kg veal breast, shoulder or knuckle, cut into 2-in/50-mm
*   pieces; at least 30 pieces of firm, lean meat with all the fat trimmed off*
1 (or more) cracked veal bones (optional)
1²/₃ pt/900 ml water (approximately)
1²/₃ pt/900 ml dry white wine
2 onions, peeled and studded with 2 cloves each
Handful of parsley, washed
2 bay leaves
A few thyme twigs or tsp dried thyme
2 × 1¹/₂-in/35-mm pieces lemon rind (no pith)
Salt
Freshly ground pepper

3 oz/75 g butter
Juice of 1 large lemon, or more to taste
5 tbsp flour
4 egg yolks
8 fl oz/225 ml double cream
Zest of 1 lemon, grated
Pinch of freshly grated nutmeg
4 tbsp capers
Salt to taste
Pepper to taste

ACCOMPANIMENTS

Rice
2 lb/900 g mange-touts

The day before the Feast, wash and trim the mushrooms, and sprinkle with 1 teaspoon lemon juice to prevent discoloration. Submerge the pearl onions in boiling water for 1 minute so they are easier to peel. With the tip of a knife, pierce a cross in the root end of each onion. Prepare the carrots, leeks, celery, garlic and chervil. Set the chervil aside for garnish.

Place the meat and bones in a very large saucepan and cover with cold water. Bring slowly to the boil. As it simmers, a greyish-white scum rises to the surface. Remove it with a large slotted spoon and discard. Stir once or twice with a long-handled spoon and skim the top carefully. After 30 minutes all the scum should be removed.

Add the white wine, onions with cloves, parsley, bay leaves, thyme, lemon rind, carrots, leeks, celery and garlic. Sprinkle with salt and pepper, cover partly and simmer for 1½ hours. Pierce a piece of veal with a fork; it should be tender but not overcooked.

Remove the meat and bones from the saucepan. Pour the broth into a colander placed over a large pan. Discard the bay leaves and thyme, and use the back of a spoon to press the rest of the vegetables through the colander into the pan.

Place the cleaned mushrooms in a large saucepan. Add 1 oz/25 g butter, the juice of 1 lemon, and 6 fl oz/175 ml of the meat broth. Cover and cook over medium heat, stirring occasionally. Remove the mushrooms with a slotted spoon, and keep in a bowl to cool. Add the pearl onions to the liquid in the pan, cover and bring to a boil. Simmer for about 25 minutes, until tender. Pour into the bowl of mushrooms and cool completely. Cover with cling film and place in the refrigerator for later use.

Bring the large pan of meat broth to a boil and allow it to reduce until you have about 2 pt/1.1 l of broth left.

Meanwhile, prepare the meat. Discard the bones and, with a pair of kitchen scissors, carefully remove all the gristle and gelatinous parts from the meat and discard. Cover the meat with a piece of foil and set aside.

If you choose rice as an accompaniment (you may prefer plain noodles), cook it in accordance with the directions given in the recipe on page 250.

For the vegetable accompaniment, cook the mange-touts for a minute or so, cool them, then cover with cling film and keep in the refrigerator.

Melt 2 oz/50 g of butter in a large, heavy-bottomed saucepan. Add the flour, stirring until it foams. Beat in the hot broth, little by little, stirring vigorously with a whisk. As it reaches boiling point, lower the heat and simmer, stirring, for about 10 minutes. Remove from the heat and let it cool. Add the meat, cover with cling film, and set in the refrigerator along with the mange-touts and rice.

The day of the Feast, 1 hour before dinner, preheat the oven to 350°F/180°C/Mark 4. Take the rice, mange-touts and Blanquette out of the refrigerator. Prepare and bake the Gougère. Place the rice in a gratin dish and stir it with a fork. Sprinkle a few dots of butter and a bit of water on top. Bake for about 30 minutes, stirring delicately with a fork once. Turn off the oven and leave the rice inside; it will keep warm and firm. Meanwhile, reheat the mange-touts with a little butter in a covered saucepan on a very low heat.

With a spoon, carefully remove and discard the congealed layer of fat that has accumulated on the top of the Blanquette. Reheat the Blanquette slowly for about 30 minutes, stirring once with a long-handled wooden spoon. Add the mushrooms and onions after 15 minutes, cover and cook 5–10 minutes more.

Meanwhile, beat the egg yolks and double cream with a whisk. Gradually stir in a ladle of the hot broth, then pour the mixture into the Blanquette. The sauce should thicken a little while the meat and vegetables blend with the sauce, but never simmer.

Check to see that everything is thoroughly heated. Add additional lemon juice, if desired, grated lemon zest, nutmeg and capers. Stir gently. Add salt and freshly ground pepper, if needed. The sauce should be very flavourful.

Remove the rice from the oven, stir it with a fork and remove the bay leaves. Place the dish, wrapped in a pretty tea-towel, on a tea-trolley, side table or dinner table. Pour the warm mange-touts into a bowl and place it on the table with a bowl of chopped chervil and the warm plates. Bring the Blanquette casserole wrapped in a large tea-towel.

Serve 2 pieces of meat, a few onions, some mushrooms and capers in the centre of each plate. Spoon the velvety sauce over this and add rice and mange-touts round it. Sprinkle the whole plate with chopped chervil. When passing a plate to each guest, suggest that he or she start at once. This delicate dish is at its best when eaten piping hot.

WINE

Generally, a white wine is advised, but many people prefer a good red wine or even a chilled rosé with Blanquette, so forget the rules and follow your whim.

WHAT TO SERVE BEFORE AND AFTER BLANQUETTE DE VEAU

HORS-D'OEUVRES TO BE SERVED WITH THE DRINKS

1. Gougère
2. Crudités à la Tapenade, au Saussoun, à l'Anchoyade

WHILE SEATED AT THE TABLE BEFORE SERVING THE BLANQUETTE:

1. Jambon Persillé
2. Terrine aux Herbes
3. Pissenlits aux Lardons or a plain tossed salad

DESSERTS

1. Poires, Pruneaux, Oranges au Vin Rouge et aux Epices
2. Grand Baba, with Compote de Poires
3. Granité au Vin
4. Mousse au Chocolat Glacée
5. Tarte au Citron et aux Amandes

TABLE DECORATION

The meal is a metaphor for all rich, cosy family treats one longs for in efficient, sleek, insipid times. It is a Sunday-best type of meal, and since it is not messy to serve, you may use a rich printed piqué or solid quilted fabric on your table. Make sure you have a lot of warm colours because Blanquette is all white. You may like to scatter tiny bowls of cut flowers across the table or weave a delicate narrow wreath of cut flowers or leaves between the glasses.

Display your most precious salt and pepper shakers, butter pots, tiny plates filled with nuts, decanters and all the napkin rings you own. Your table will be the setting for a rich and festive performance, filled with delicious food and lively participants. Make sure sparkling glasses, graceful flowers and a bold use of colours give the table your glorious Blanquette Feast deserves.

STRATEGY FOR THE SUGGESTED MENU

- Guests invited for 7.30 p.m.
- Meal served at 8.30 p.m.

- The day before the Feast: prepare the Blanquette, mange-touts, rice and Poires, Pruneaux, Oranges au Vin Rouge et aux Epices.

- On the day of the Feast:
  6.45 Prepare and bake the Gougère.
  7.30 Your first guests arrive.
  7.45 Bring the Gougère with drinks to the sitting-room. Place the rice in the oven. Reheat the Blanquette on a low heat. Reheat the mange-touts. Prepare the tossed salad and dressing.
  8.15 Add onions and mushrooms to the Blanquette. Light the candles. Bring the chilled wine and cold water to the table.
  8.30 Ask your guests to the table. Add cream, egg yolks and lemon to the Blanquette. Bring warm plates, rice, mange-touts and tossed salad to the table. Bring in the Blanquette.
  8.50 Bring the Poires, Pruneaux and Oranges dish and a plate of thin biscuits to the table.

LEFT-OVERS

1. Soup: chop the pieces of left-over meat and place in a saucepan. Add the Blanquette sauce, and the rice. Pour in some good chicken or beef broth or milk and gently bring to a boil, stirring. Correct the seasoning with more salt, pepper and nutmeg before you serve this luscious soup.
2. Crêpes: fill salty crêpes with the chopped left-over meat and vegetables. Roll them, place them in an ovenproof dish, and spoon Blanquette sauce, thinned with a little milk, on top. Dot with butter, and heat.

Boeuf à l'Orange Niçoise

A marinated beef simmered with veg-etables in red wine, herbs, garlic and orange rinds.

This is a traditional beef stew revisited by the good fairies of Nice and Provence. They brought fresh orange rind, herbs and garlic for a sharp and distinctive accent. They simmered the wine mari-nade for a more mellow and more fragrant taste. They cooked the whole dish very slowly and evenly to let the flavours mingle and enhance one another. They skimmed the fat for a moist, lean and lively stew, and thanks to them we now have a perfectly accented dish, truly worthy of a Provençal *festin*.

A few points to remember in case the fairies are not looking over your shoulder during the entire operation: the meat must be of good quality, trimmed and well cut. It must be thoroughly sautéed and then simmered in a tasty marinade to absorb slowly all the spices, herbs and wine flavours. A gentle, even cooking is essential, and carefully removing the fat from the sauce after a night in the refrigerator will make for a light and delicious dish. Start this two days in advance for a perfect blending, but note that it is very easy to prepare; nothing can go wrong with this dish. Remember, cooking is not as holy (or as grave) as a mass; it is a Feast, so relax and enjoy it.

Boeuf à l'Orange is traditionally served with boiled noodles seasoned with a little olive oil or with new jacket potatoes. Nice's little black olives or good firm green or purple olives are ideal; never use the soft, watery, canned olives.

FOR 8 PEOPLE

MARINADE

> 4 tbsp olive or vegetable oil
> 4 onions, peeled and sliced
> 1 carrot, peeled and sliced
> 2 stalks celery, peeled and chopped
> Salt
> 3-in/75-mm piece dried orange peel (if you do not have dried peel, place a fresh piece in a low oven for 15 minutes)

SUGGESTED MENU

Pissaladière

Boeuf á l'Orange Niçoise
Boiled New Potatoes
Green Salad

Oeufs à la Neige et aux Fruits

Pinot Noir

24 fl oz/675 ml hearty red wine
2 cloves garlic, peeled and crushed
3 bay leaves
Twig of thyme

BOEUF À L'ORANGE

5 lb/2.25 kg boneless beef (rump sirloin tip or top round), trimmed of
*   all fat and gristle and cut into 1½-in/35-mm cubes*
3 tsp thyme or marjoram
3 tbsp vegetable oil
16 fresh baby onions or small white onions
8 oz/225 g lean salt pork or bacon, with no rind and cut into
*   ½-in/12-mm dice*
1 tbsp flour
3 tbsp cognac or grappa
16 fl oz/450 ml beef broth or red wine
3 cloves garlic, peeled and sliced
Salt
Freshly ground pepper
8 carrots, peeled, cut in half lengthways, and then sliced on the bias
Rind of 1 large orange (no pith), finely grated
3 tomatoes, plunged into hot water and peeled, seeds removed, and
*   then diced*
1 cup small Nice black olives, unpitted, or firm large green or purple
*   olives (optional)*

ACCOMPANIMENTS

New potatoes boiled in their jackets or boiled noodles
A salad of chicory or endive and watercress or rocket and Batavian
*   endive, with a vinaigrette dressing*

GARNISH

3 tbsp chopped parsley
1 cup grated Parmesan cheese

Make the marinade two days before the Feast. Heat 4 tablespoons of oil in a cast-iron frying pan. Add the onions, carrot and celery. Sprinkle with salt and sauté for a few minutes. Add the orange peel, wine, garlic, bay leaves and thyme, and cook for 15 minutes. Remove from the heat and cool to room temperature.

Place the pieces of beef in a large bowl and pour the cooled marinade over them. Cover and keep in the refrigerator overnight.

Remove the pieces of meat from the marinade and dry with paper towels. Sprinkle the meat with a little thyme. Heat 2 tablespoons of the oil in a cast-iron frying pan and sauté the meat, a few pieces at a time.

They should brown on all sides for about 10 minutes. Turn them carefully using tongs. Meanwhile, heat the remaining tablespoon of oil in a large enamelled cast-iron casserole. As the pieces of beef are browned, transfer them to it. You will have to make several batches.

When all the meat is browned, add the onions to the frying pan, sauté on all sides until golden and then pour into the casserole. Sauté the salt pork over a moderate heat for a few minutes, then add to the casserole. Sprinkle the flour over the casserole and stir carefully.

Pour the brandy into the frying pan, scrape the bottom and transfer the contents to the casserole. Pour the marinade and the beef broth into the frying pan, heat for 1 minute and transfer to the casserole. Add the garlic, salt and pepper to the casserole and bring to a simmer on top of the cooker, uncovered. Cover and simmer for 2½ hours. Add the carrots and cook 20 minutes more. The dish is cooked if a fork can pierce the meat easily, but the carrots should not be mushy. Remove from the heat. You should have about 1½ pt/800 ml of sauce, and it should coat a spoon lightly. If you seem to have too much sauce, pour it into the frying pan and reduce it over a medium heat for a few minutes. Pour the sauce into the casserole. Cool, cover and refrigerate.

On the day of the Feast, wash and dry the ingredients for your salad. Wrap and keep them in the lower part of the refrigerator.

One hour before serving the meal, remove all the items from the refrigerator. Discard the bay leaves, thyme and orange rind from the beef stew in the casserole. The fat that has accumulated on the surface, which should have a waxy texture, is easy to remove with a spoon. Discard as much as you can. Stir 1 tablespoon of water into the sauce and bring it to a simmer. Cover and cook slowly, basting twice with a wooden spoon.

Bring a large saucepan of salted water to a boil and cook the accompaniment (potatoes or noodles).

Check and correct the seasoning of your stew, if necessary, and just before you are ready to serve, stir in the grated orange rind, diced tomatoes and olives. Turn off the heat at once.

Drain the potatoes and transfer them to a basket or dish (or drain the noodles, sprinkle them with a little olive oil or butter and transfer them to a dish).

Place the dressing, spoon, fork and then the salad in a bowl.

Wrap the casserole in a tea-towel and take it, covered, to the table with the warm plates, potatoes and bowls of salad, chopped parsley and Parmesan cheese.

Place a few pieces of beef, a few dice of bacon, 2 onions, a few carrot slices, a few tomato dice and a few olives on each plate. Spoon some sauce over this and sprinkle a little parsley on top. Add some potatoes (or noodles) and hand the plates to your guests. Pass the bowl of Parmesan and the bowl of salad round the table. Leave the covered casserole, as well as the basket of potatoes (or noodles) and the bowl of salad, for your guests to help themselves to seconds.

WINE

Any red wine – Bordeaux, Bourgogne, Côtes du Rhône, Pinot Noir – will be welcome as long as it is generous and potent. If you can, use the same wine for cooking as you serve with the meal.

WHAT TO SERVE BEFORE AND AFTER BOEUF À L'ORANGE NIÇOISE

HORS-D'OEUVRES TO BE SERVED WITH THE DRINKS

1. Pissaladière
2. Poireaux Tièdes Vinaigrette
3. Jambon Persillé
4. Crudités en Panier
5. Pissenlits aux Lardons

DESSERTS

1. Oeufs à la Neige et aux Fruits
2. Grand Baba
3. Crêpes Normandes
4. Raspberries or strawberries surrounded with sliced lemons, sprinkled with lemon juice and sugar, and served with Crémets
5. Sliced peaches or raspberries sprinkled with orange and lemon juice and a few mint leaves

TABLE DECORATION

Display carrots, fresh parsley, white onions and shiny black olives appetizingly. One is overcome by the sight and tantalizing smell of Boeuf à l'Orange Niçoise. Therefore the setting will be whatever inspires you as long as it is unfussy, inviting and cheerful: a sharp tablecloth, perhaps a simple Indian fabric, so Provençal in feeling, or a beautifully printed king-size sheet; lively napkins; a bowl filled with lots of fluffy cut flowers, with a few long, sinuous twigs of ivy or honeysuckle stuck among them and wandering towards the guests; deeply coloured candles in simple earthenware, wood, white china or crockery holders;

two pretty bowls filled with grated cheese; pretty baskets filled with fresh and oven-dried breads; two or three decanters of wine; and perhaps wooden or earthenware salt and pepper shakers.

STRATEGY FOR THE SUGGESTED MENU

- Guests invited for 7.30 p.m.
- Meal served at 8.30 p.m.

- Prepare the marinade two days in advance and the Boeuf and the Oeufs à la Neige a day in advance.

- On the day of the Feast:
  Prepare the Pissaladière and salad greens.
  7.00 Preheat the oven. Take the Boeuf out of the refrigerator. Place the Pissaladière in the oven to warm.
  7.30 Your first guests arrive. Serve Pissaladière with drinks in the sitting-room.
  8.00 Cook potatoes. Arrange the salad bowl. Reheat the Boeuf on a medium heat.
  8.30 Light the candles. Ask your guests to the table. Bring warm plates, a basket of warm potatoes, the Boeuf and bowls of chopped parsley and Parmesan cheese to the table.
  9.00 Remove Oeufs à la Neige from the refrigerator. Heat the caramel and dribble it over the egg whites. Bring to the table.

LEFT-OVERS

1. Stew: add sliced carrots, quartered turnips, fresh onions and quartered potatoes to your left-over stew. Reheat it slowly, adding a little broth if needed. Sprinkle with parsley and serve.
2. Ravioli: mince the left-over beef and salt pork or bacon (a small cup). Add 5 oz/140 g of cooked spinach, 1 egg, a little cheese and stir well. Use this mixture to fill your ravioli according to your favourite recipe. You should have about 40 ravioli. Cook in a pot of boiling water, drain and serve with the beef sauce and grated Parmesan.
3. Boiled green croquettes: cook 1 cup of spinach and ½ cup of rice. Drain well, then add 1 cup of finely chopped left-over beef. Stir in 1 egg, salt, pepper and 3 tbsp of grated Parmesan or Gruyère cheese. Make small round balls. Sprinkle a tray with flour and roll them in it. Drop the balls in a large pot of boiling water for 10 minutes. They rise to the surface as soon as they are cooked. Drain, sprinkle with olive oil and Parmesan cheese, and serve at once.

Boeuf Froid en Tranches

Slices of marinated beef cooked to pink and then served cold in their juices with a raw tomato and tarragon sauce.

SUGGESTED MENU

Poireaux Tièdes Vinaigrette

Boeuf Froid en Tranches
Gratin Dauphinois
Watercress Salad

Crêpes Normandes

A Full-bodied Red Wine

Whether your guests are 'meat and potato' people or normally shun spicy preparations for other reasons, this will be a winning combination: seasoned cold beef with a fragrant sauce, peppery watercress salad and luscious Gratin Dauphinois. This menu is a gourmet's delight but is still simple and healthy. For a lighter meal, Gratin d'Aubergines or a warm Ratatouille can replace the Gratin Dauphinois. Cold beef can be the best or the most mediocre of dishes. When it is rolled in cracked pepper, carefully cooked, thinly sliced, basted in its deglazed roasting juices and served with a fresh sauce of raw tomatoes and tarragon, it is a delicious dish and the perfect counterpoint to a mellow Gratin Dauphinois.

Boeuf en Tranches is prepared entirely the day before your party and needs no last-minute touch to ensure its success. It's a wonderful addition to an all-cold summer meal for a buffet, a picnic or a late supper.

FOR 8 PEOPLE

BEEF

> *3 lb/1.25 kg beef fillet, 4 in/100 mm in diameter, trimmed of all fat, or 3–4 lb/1.25–1.8 kg beef tenderloin, the central section preferably, about 3 in/75 mm in diameter, trimmed of all fat*
> *Olive oil*
> *Coarsely ground peppercorns*
> *4 tbsp red vermouth or sherry, approximately*
> *Salt*
> *Freshly ground pepper*

SAUCE

> *3 tomatoes, peeled, deseeded and diced*
> *3 tbsp fresh tarragon, chervil or flat parsley leaves*
> *1 tbsp coarsely ground coriander*
> *Salt to taste*
> *6 fl oz/175 ml virgin olive oil*

WATERCRESS SALAD

> *2 or 3 bunches watercress*
> *1 tbsp minced chervil*
> *10 tbsp olive oil*
> *3 tbsp red wine vinegar*
> *Salt*
> *Freshly ground pepper*

The day before the Feast remove the meat from the refrigerator at least 3 hours before you are ready to cook it. Dry the surface with a paper towel. Rub with the olive oil and peppercorns, pressing them firmly into the meat with the palms of your hands. Cover with greaseproof paper or foil, and leave for a few hours at room temperature.

Preheat the oven to 425°F/220°C/Mark 7.

Remove the foil or paper, place the meat in a large roasting pan and slide it into the hot oven for 10 minutes, turning once so all sides are seared. Discard the fat from the pan, lower the heat to 325°F/160°C/Mark 3 and cook for 20 minutes more.

Remove the roast from the oven and cool to room temperature. Meanwhile, add the vermouth to the roasting pan and scrape the coagulated juices in the bottom of the pan with a fork. Pour the juices into a large bowl with the roast, cover carefully with foil and refrigerate.

On the day of the Feast, remove the meat and juices from the refrigerator a few hours before you are ready to serve the dinner. Discard any fat from the juices. Place the meat on a board. Cut the beef crossways into slices about ¼ ins/6 mm thick. Pour any juices into the bowl of cooking juices. Carefully spoon some juice on to each slice of meat. Replace the slices tightly against each other, wrap them in foil and place them on the serving dish. Leave them so they will be at room temperature when you serve them; the meat will soak up some of the juices.

Meanwhile, prepare the cold tomato and herb sauce. Plunge the tomatoes in a bowl of boiling water for a second before peeling off their skin, then open and deseed each tomato. Cut each one into ½-in/12-mm dice and place them in a bowl. Pluck the tarragon leaves from the stem and place them in the bowl. Add crushed coriander, salt and olive oil. Stir and check to correct the seasoning. Cover and leave for later in or out of the refrigerator.

To prepare the salad, remove the tough ends of the watercress, wash and drain. Add the chervil. Combine the oil, vinegar, salt and pepper to make the dressing.

One and a half hours before serving the meal, prepare the Gratin Dauphinois. Put the Gratin in the oven.

When you are ready to serve, bring the towel-wrapped Gratin to the table with the watercress salad, the plate of sliced meat and the bowl of sauce. Sprinkle a little salt and pepper on the meat and spoon a little of its juices on top. Serve each guest 2 slices of beef and a portion of Gratin. Spoon a little cooking juice and then some of the tomato and herb sauce on top of the meat. Pass the bowl of sauce round the table.

WINE

Any good red wine you like.

WHAT TO SERVE BEFORE AND AFTER BOEUF EN TRANCHES

HORS-D'OEUVRES TO BE SERVED WITH THE DRINKS

1. Crudités en Panier, with a variety of sauces
2. Poireaux Tièdes Vinaigrette
3. Jambon Persillé

DESSERTS

1. Grand Baba
2. Crêpes Normandes
3. Tarte Tatin aux Poires et aux Pommes

TABLE DECORATION

This is the most workable of menus and the easiest to serve. You may have as elaborate and busy a table as you choose since this is an unfussy menu. You may like a pretty blue and honey-coloured scheme: a fresh, flowered, chintz cloth, and blue and ochre candles in glass candlesticks. You may like to put a huge hollowed pumpkin in the centre of the table filled with an assortment of blue cornflowers, bluebells, peonies, marigolds and tea roses – all carefully arranged in a glass container and then placed in the pumpkin. You could tie each blue napkin with an ochre or yellow ribbon and slide a name card in it.

You may like to wrap a blue or white napkin round the neck of each bottle and arrange two linen-lined baskets of bread, a few tiny bowls of mustard and a few small pots of whipped butter on the table.

STRATEGY FOR THE SUGGESTED MENU

- Guests invited for 7.30 p.m.
- Dinner served at 8.30 p.m.

- The day before the Feast: prepare and cook the meat. Cool, cover and refrigerate overnight.
- Prepare Gratin Dauphinois, Poireaux Tièdes or Jambon Persillé and a basket of Crudité vegetables. Prepare the Crêpes Normandes. Cover with foil and refrigerate.

- On the day of the Feast:
  6.00 Slice the meat. Dip each slice into the juices. Cover and set aside at room temperature.
  Prepare the Vinaigrette. Reheat the Poireaux.
  7.00 Bake the Gratin. Prepare the watercress and dressing but don't toss.
  7.30 Place the dish of Poireaux or Jambon bowl and Crudités with the drinks as your guests arrive.
  8.30 Bring the warm Gratin, sliced beef, bowl of sauce and watercress salad to the dining-room. Put the Crêpes in the oven and reheat. Start the meal.
  9.00 Add a little redcurrant sauce on top of the Crêpes. Change plates and bring the warm Crêpes to the table with dessert plates.

LEFT-OVERS

1. Hachis Parmentier, page 144.
2. Brown and cook some sliced onions. Cut the beef into slivers and add to the onions. Cook for a few minutes, season, then serve with chopped parsley, a few drops of red wine vinegar and boiled potatoes.
3. An omelette: sauté 1 sliced onion in a little warm oil. Cut the left-over meat in small pieces and sauté for a minute. Pour a few beaten eggs on top and stir until the omelette is set.
4. Cold salad: mix diced boiled potatoes, diced left-over beef and quartered hard-boiled eggs. Season with a hearty vinaigrette and sprinkle with fresh herbs.
5. Pasta: sauté 1 sliced onion. Add the finely chopped left-over beef and pour in a good tomato sauce. Serve with *al dente* spaghetti and a bowl of grated Parmesan cheese.

Bouillabaisse Royale

A spectacular fish and vegetable soup – or is it a stew? – heady with saffron and herbs, and served with a red pepper and garlic sauce.

SUGGESTED MENU

Olives Sautées

Bouillabaisse Royale

Panier de Frivolités

White Bordeaux

This high-spirited fish stew, this glorious mythical dish is truly a Feast by itself. Nothing timid, nothing cautious about it. Bouillabaisse embodies the excess, the joy, the fire of Provence; it speaks of 'Pétanque' ball players under silvery plane trees, of cypresses and olive groves, of the purple sea and the rocky jagged coast. With its delicate combination of fish, herbs, vegetables and olive oil cooked on a high heat, this potent broth is the magical golden soup that Venus invented to please and distract her husband, Vulcan, while she attended to questionable matters with a young shepherd.

Labelled Marseille's very own speciality, it is such a great combination that every fisherman, every restaurant's chef, every housewife along the French Mediterranean coast is proud to claim his or her very own 'authentic' version.

Originally, of course, a fisherman's Bouillabaisse depended solely on what the nets brought that day, though everybody seems to agree there should never be mussels or clams in a serious Bouillabaisse. But should there be potatoes? Garlicky rounds of toasted bread? Pastis? Which Rouille is acceptable? Fierce arguments, endless quarrels persist.

There are fifty ways to make the 'right, the only' Bouillabaisse. The 'royale' version may include bass and lobster; the 'fisherman' version insists on four different kinds of fish; others are made with dried salt cod, sardines, sorrel, spinach, Swiss chard and squid. There is even a 'one-eyed bouillabaisse', made with poached eggs and no fish at all! Fresh firm fish and a light, pungent broth emulsified for a few minutes with a good olive oil ('bouillabaisse' means brought to a quick boil and cooked quickly) and served with a fiery sauce are the sensible basics of success.

Choose from monkfish, flounder, scorpion fish, porgy, red whiting, John Dory, red snapper, perch, sole, conger eel, haddock, sea bass, cod, mullet and soft-shell crabs for a spectacular Bouillabaisse. Be sure to avoid mackerel and sardine, both when you prepare the broth and as a fish.

'Rouille', the glossy, peppery, garlicky sauce, comes in many versions. Sometimes it is made with a variety of small fish caught in the rocks; they are coarsely cut up and then crushed, cooked with herbs, blended with a boiled potato and seasoned with saffron, cayenne and olive oil. Most of the time it is simply a saffron and garlic mayonnaise or a red pepper and garlic sauce, which must be very hot and have a smooth consistency in order to enhance and challenge the strong flavour of the Bouillabaisse. In the eighteenth century this fiery, intense sauce, because of its antiseptic and antibiotic qualities, was even used to fight plague.

The broth and the fish are presented as two separate courses in restaurants. The broth is served and the Rouille is spread on fried or oven-dried bread rounds and floated on the soup. One must wait for a second before biting. Plates are changed; the platter with a combination of fish is presented, head and all; then each fish is filleted and served with the potatoes on a large plate along with a bowl of Rouille.

At home matters are conducted differently. This is, after all, a fisherman's dish, and the ritual does not have to be so elaborate. Broth, fish and shellfish, served together with potatoes, make for a crammed but splendid plate, and a simpler process allows less opportunity for the fish to be overcooked. Although mussels and lobsters are not traditionally used in Provence, you may like to add them. For practical reasons lobster must be served in a separate plate, which is some trouble when you serve 8 or 10 people on your own.

The rich, dark, intense broth, the sweet shellfish, the tasty fish and the saffrony potatoes are a glamorous combination. Miracles occur when this 'golden broth' appears on the table. The pungent aroma and the bright colours exalt life and radiate joy and energy. It is a spectacular, exciting sight, a truly euphoric process. Nibbling, sipping, smelling, mopping up the last drops of sauce, marvelling with unrestrained abandon make the sharing of this dish a total, vital experience.

In the galaxy of glorious superdishes Bouillabaisse stands high, extracting with gusto the essence of the sea and converting all the guests around a table into grateful disciples. Nothing could be more conducive to conviviality and animated conversations than Bouillabaisse.

FOR 8 PEOPLE

FISH

> 8 lb/3.5 kg fish, cut into 2 × 4-in/50 × 100-mm chunks or thick slices;
> flavourful fish: striped bass, cod, sea bass, halibut, eel, haddock,
> hake, porgy; delicate fish: whiting, sole, flounder, red snapper
> 2 tbsp olive oil
> 2 tbsp dried thyme
> Salt
> 2 tsp saffron powder, according to taste and depending on the quality
> you use
> 2 tbsp fennel seeds
> 1 lb/450 g shellfish: 8 soft-shell or small crabs; 8 large shrimp,
> unpeeled if possible, peeled if your guests are finicky

BROTH

> 4 tbsp raw olive oil (approximately)
> 6 onions, peeled and chopped
> 2 large leeks, white part only (optional)
> 5 tomatoes, chopped
> 6 cloves garlic, peeled and crushed
> A few sprigs parsley and stems
> 2 lb/900 g fish bones, fish heads and trimmings; the fishmonger will
> give them to you after he has filleted sole, cod or any other lean fish
> Bouquet garni (1 sprig parsley and stems, 1 sprig thyme and 1 bay
> leaf)
> Few twigs dried wild fennel or fennel seeds or extract anise
> 3-in/75-mm orange rind (dried in the oven for 15 minutes)
> 8 thyme twigs or powder
> Salt to taste
> 1⅔ pt/900 ml (approximately) dry white wine
> 3¼ pt/1.8 l water
> Freshly ground pepper
> 1 tbsp Pernod or 2 tbsp anise extract

SAUCES

ROUILLE 1

> 8 cloves garlic, peeled and crushed
> 6 red chilli peppers, peeled and crushed or Tabasco to taste
> 1 slice bread, crust removed, moistened with water and squeezed
> 5 tbsp olive oil
> Salt
> 3 tbsp broth

ROUILLE 2 (THE EASIEST)

> *16 fl oz/450 ml Aioli sauce*
> *Tabasco to taste*
> *1 tsp saffron (optional)*
> *1 tbsp broth*

VEGETABLES

> *8 potatoes*

GARNISH

> *20 very thin slices of French bread, approximately; oven-dried to*
>   *crisp*
> *2 cloves garlic*
> *Grated Gruyère cheese*

On the day before the Feast, trim and cut the fish into big chunks. Pat them dry with a paper towel. Make the marinade with the olive oil, thyme, salt, saffron and fennel. Rub each piece evenly with the marinade and leave in the bowl, covered, for a few hours.

Prepare the broth. Heat a little oil in a large saucepan or stock pot. Add the chopped onions and cook for a few minutes until golden. Add the leeks after a few minutes, then the tomatoes, the garlic and the parsley. Add the fish bones, fish heads, a bouquet garni, the twigs of fennel (or some seeds), the orange rind, thyme, salt, white wine and water. Bring to a boil. Lower the heat and simmer, covered, for 1 hour.

Meanwhile prepare the Rouille; you should make 12–16 fl oz/350–450 ml for 8 people.

If you choose Rouille 1, put the garlic and peppers (or Tabasco) in a mortar and pound them until crushed and blended. Add the bread and stir until you have a smooth paste. Work in the oil slowly. Add a dash of salt to taste. Stir in the fish broth. Your sauce should have the consistency of a light custard. (You may use a food processor for this.)

If you choose Rouille 2, prepare an Aioli sauce and add Tabasco and saffron to taste. It should be a fiery sauce. Add the broth. Pour the entire mixture into a bowl, cover with cling film and refrigerate.

Pass the broth through a food mill or thick sieve, pressing with a spoon against the mesh to extract as much as you can from the mixture. Discard the herbs and bones. Taste and add freshly ground pepper and more salt if needed. Cool, cover with cling film and refrigerate.

On the day of the Feast, 1 hour before the meal, remove the broth and the marinated chunks of fish from the refrigerator. Remove the fish chunks from the marinade.

Peel the potatoes and cut them into 1-in/25-mm thick slices. Dry well and place in a saucepan. Pour enough fish broth to cover the potatoes and bring to a boil; lower the heat and cook.

Meanwhile, heat the soup plates and rub the slices of oven-dried bread with a clove of garlic.

Remove the Rouille from the refrigerator. Put the Rouille and the grated cheese in pretty bowls. Put the garlicky, crisp bread in a basket and bring to the table.

Bring the rest of the broth in the stock pot to a boil, uncovered. Add the flavourful fish first, along with the shrimps and crabs. Five minutes later add the delicate fish and about 3 tablespoons of olive oil. Add the Pernod or anise extract at the last moment.

Check if the potatoes and fish are ready. Lift out the fish, but not the shrimps or crabs, with a wide skimming spoon and place in a shallow dish. Do the same with the potatoes and pour a ladle of broth over each. Bring the dishes of fish and potatoes to the table along with the pot of broth, crabs and shrimps, and, of course, the warm soup plates.

Make sure everybody has seen and smelled the grand Technicolor display of your dramatic production, then start serving. Pass the Rouille bowl round.

Place 2 pieces of fish, 1 shrimp, 1 crab and 1 slice of potato in each dish and pour some hot broth on top. Ask each guest to pass the Rouille bowl, the crisp, garlicky bread and the garlicky cheese.

Put the left-over fish, potatoes and shellfish into the pot, cover and keep for second helpings. Meanwhile, pass some warm broth to pour over the guests' plates as they are enjoying their first helping.

WINE

A semi-dry or a mellow white wine is good. A rosé is often served in Provence. Bordeaux, Anjou, Monbazillac and Jurançon white wines are also recommended.

WHAT TO SERVE BEFORE AND AFTER BOUILLABAISSE ROYALE

A Bouillabaisse, whether sophisticated or simple, is truly a *plat unique* except, perhaps, for a tossed salad and a light dessert, but you may choose the following:

HORS D'OEUVRES TO BE SERVED WITH THE DRINKS

1. Bowl of Olives Sautées
2. Bowl of warm almonds
3. Pissaladière

DESSERTS

1. Mélange de Fruits
2. Cervelle de Canut
3. Panier de Frivolités
4. Granité au Vin

TABLE DECORATION

This extravagant, brilliant dish dazzles and scatters its bright colours and aromas generously all round; in other words, it is a beautiful but quite messy dish. Your table could be covered with a bright blue American or vinyl-coated cloth for a safe and pretty meal, and you could place a pile of large shells filled with green leaves in the centre. Or you may wish to use a Provençal, heavy, quilted fabric and set a white tureen filled with fruit in the centre. Blue, ochre or bright yellow could make a pretty backdrop. You should place baskets all round the table for discarded shells, and use an assortment of pretty bowls to serve the Rouille, grated cheese and oven-dried bread. If you can, don't forget to have finger-bowls or a stack of paper napkins, and, of course, nice, wide, all-cotton napkins.

STRATEGY FOR THE SUGGESTED MENU

- Guests invited for 7.30 p.m.
- Meal served at 8.30 p.m.

- One day before the Feast: marinate the fish for a few hours, then prepare the Bouillabaisse, the Rouille and the Frivolités.

- On the day of the Feast:
  7.25 Remove the Bouillabaisse from the refrigerator and reheat it over a low heat. Peel and cook the potatoes. Prepare Olives Sautées.
  7.30 Your first guests arrive.
  7.40 Bring Olives Sautées with the drinks.
  8.00 Oven-dry the bread, take the Rouille out of the refrigerator and add the fish to the hot broth. Rub garlic on the crisp, oven-dried rounds of bread.
  8.25 Add shellfish and final ingredients to the hot broth. Light the candles. Place the Rouille bowl, grated cheese bowl and bread basket on the table. Ask your guests to the table.
  8.30 Bring to the table the potatoes, the fish moistened with warm broth in two shallow dishes, and the large pot of broth and shellfish.
  9.00 Bring the basket of Frivolités to the table.

LEFT-OVERS

1. An interesting and unusual way to serve Bouillabaisse is in a cold jelly of its own broth on a bed of bitter greens, such as endives.
2. You can reheat the left-over Bouillabaisse and add a few potato slices and a little white wine.

Brandade

A fluffy, dried salt cod, potato and milk mousse seasoned with nutmeg and raw olive oil.

Cod is a voracious creature that lives in deep waters, loves cold climates and feeds on other fish and shellfish. Because Norwegian sailors dried it in the wind and sun and brought it to the coasts of Provence as an exchange for olive oil, fruit and vegetables, it has become a staple in Mediterranean cuisine. Its flesh is rich in protein and mineral salts. It is peppered with tomatoes, spinach, carrots, leeks, onions, potatoes, peppers or anchovies in an endless variety of dishes.

SUGGESTED MENU

Soupe au Pistou

Brandade
Tossed Green Salad

Fruit Compote

Meursault

Brandade, an unctuous purée of shredded dried salt cod, lukewarm milk and oil, is a ritual food in Provence. Stirring the warm mixture with a wooden spoon for hours in a slow, steady movement tests your patience and teaches you that one should work hard at one's pleasures. And the metamorphosis of grey cod into this smooth, ivory mousse is one of the mysteries we depend on to be happy.

Whether the original idea came from Venice, Béziers or Nîmes is of little importance. The traditional Provençal recipe is now made with shredded cod, twice as much olive oil as cream, and truffles or parsley. Garlic, potatoes and even a drop of orange juice are added according to taste and custom.

Brandade is served lukewarm or cold, either in a crisp pastry shell or piled in a white dome. It is eaten throughout Provence on Fridays, on Christmas night, or on New Year's Eve.

There is no need to possess special keys; there is no secret to unlock as you prepare the Brandade. The cardinal fact about this dish is your

ability to unsalt the cod and your patience to check and correct texture
and flavour as you go.

Instead of pounding the cod in a mortar with oil and milk, we use a
food processor or a blender for a fluffier texture. We also use more
potatoes, less oil and more spices in our Brandade so that we can serve
it as the core of a Feast.

Always taste cod with the tip of your tongue before boiling it to make
sure it has soaked enough and is not too salty. The flesh should be
white-brown on one side, grey-blue on the other.

FOR 8 PEOPLE

BRANDADE

> *3 lb/1.25 kg dried salt cod*
> *3 large potatoes*
> *Salt*
> *2 bay leaves*
> *1 onion, studded with a clove*
> *8 fl oz/225 ml olive oil*
> *8 fl oz/225 ml warm milk*
> *3 cloves garlic, peeled and crushed*
> *Pinch of nutmeg*
> *Pinch of freshly ground white pepper*
> *2 tbsp lukewarm cream or milk*
> *Lemon juice to taste*

ACCOMPANIMENTS

> *3 slices of bread cut into toast points or 9 slices of French bread,*
> *   oven-dried*
> *1 tbsp olive oil*
> *1 tbsp chopped parsley*
> *2 tbsp firm Niçoise or Greek black olives, pitted*
> *Bowl of rocket or chicory or endive tossed with a vinaigrette dressing*

Two days before the Feast, place the salt cod in a large saucepan or
basin and cover with cold water. Soak for at least 24 hours, changing the
water 5 or 6 times. Drain.

The day before the Feast, boil the potatoes in their skins in a large
pot of slightly salted water until soft.

Place the cod in an enamelled or stainless-steel saucepan and cover
with cold water. Add the bay leaves and onion, and bring slowly to a
boil. Lower the heat and simmer for 3 minutes, then let the fish cool in

the water. Drain. Remove skin and bones and shred. You should have about 4 cups of shredded cod.

Heat the olive oil and milk in separate saucepans. They should be warm, not hot. Peel the potatoes. Place 1 potato and a few pieces of cod in a food processor and whip briefly. Add the crushed garlic, more flaked cod, another potato and continue processing, alternately pouring in milk and oil. Finally, add the nutmeg, pepper and even salt, if needed. You should have a smooth white purée. Spoon and scrape into a bowl. Cover with cling film and place in the refrigerator.

On the day of the Feast, 30 minutes before serving, stir in the 2 tablespoons of warm cream and reheat at medium heat, stirring. Add pepper, salt and lemon juice to taste.

Meanwhile, prepare the bread. Preheat the oven to 350°F/180°C/Mark 4. Place the slices (rounds of bread or triangles) on a baking sheet. Sprinkle a little olive oil on top and bake until brown. Turn them on the other side after 2 minutes and turn off the heat after about 3 minutes.

Pour the Brandade purée into a warm dish, add a few drops of cold olive oil on top and stir. Dip a tip of the triangular or round croûtons in Brandade, then into chopped parsley and place round the edge of the serving dish. You may like to place a handful of pitted black olives in the centre of the dome of Brandade.

Serve with a large bowl of tossed green salad seasoned with vinaigrette dressing.

WINE

Because of the milk or cream in the Brandade, you should serve a mellow white wine, Bordeaux, for instance, or Barsac, Anjou or Monbazillac; but because of the garlic you should choose a dry white wine such as a Pouilly-Fuissé, Cassis, Bellet or Meursault, so choose according to your taste and to the amount of garlic used.

WHAT TO SERVE BEFORE AND AFTER BRANDADE

HORS D'OEUVRES TO BE SERVED WITH THE DRINKS

1. Soupe au Pistou
2. Gratin d'Aubergines
3. Jambon Persillé
4. Terrine aux Herbes

DESSERTS

1. Panier de Frivolités served with either Granité au Vin or Mélange de Fruits
2. Poires, Pruneaux, Oranges au Vin Rouge et aux Épices
3. Grand Baba served with apple compote

TABLE DECORATION

This delicious dish is not very colourful in spite of the parsley croûtons and the black olives. Therefore, it would be best to choose a cheerful tablecloth and a bright centre-piece, perhaps a bunch of short fluffy roses or bright geraniums gathered in a shallow basket. You may also like to spread tiny glass containers of multicoloured cut flowers round the table. Along with the salt and pepper shakers, put tiny bottles of olive oil so each guest can add a few drops of cold oil to his warm Brandade.

STRATEGY FOR THE SUGGESTED MENU

- Guests invited for 7.30 p.m.
- Meal served at 8.30 p.m.

- One day before the Feast: prepare the Soupe au Pistou, Brandade, the salad greens, Frivolités and cooked fruit.

- On the day of the Feast:
  7.30 Your first guests arrive.
  8.00 Reheat the soup on a low heat. Reheat the Brandade on a low heat. Oven-dry the bread triangles, sprinkling a little oil on top. Prepare the salad.
  8.30 Light the candles. Ask your guests to the table. Bring the linen-wrapped soup and bowl of Pistou.
  8.50 Bring a basket of Frivolités and a bowl of cooked fruits to the table.

LEFT-OVERS

1. Crêpes: fill crêpes with left-over Brandade, cover with a light cream sauce and bake.
2. Omelette: stuff an egg omelette with the left-over Brandade. Add a little milk if it is too dry, and sprinkle with chopped black olives and a drop of olive oil just before serving.

3. Croquettes: add 2 eggs to the left-over Brandade and stir. Make into small round patties, dip in breadcrumbs and fry in oil. You may want to fry a few twigs of parsley and serve them with the Croquettes.

4. *Oeufs Benedict*: poach eggs and serve on top of a tablespoon of left-over Brandade. Cover with a well-seasoned Hollandaise sauce in individual dishes.

5. Flan de Brandade: add a little milk and 2 beaten eggs to the left-over Brandade. Pour into a baking dish, sprinkle with a small amount of breadcrumbs, and bake for 1 hour at 350°F/180°C/Mark 4. Serve with cooked spinach or sautéd mushrooms.

Canard Farci

Crisp pieces of duck served with a stuffing of apples, liver, prunes, ham and herbs, with a light, crisp garnish of chestnut, lemon and spring onions.

SUGGESTED MENU

Pissenlits aux Lardons

Canard Farci
Puréed Cabbage

Grand Baba

Alsatian White Wine

In the eighteenth century women of quality were always given three orations for their funeral. One was delivered by a philosopher (a must in the century of enlightenment when philosophers were what the stock exchange raiders or the *haute couture* wizards are to us now). The other two orations were given by regular guests at her table. It was not a case of social disease, such as 'dining out as an alternative to living', but rather dining out as an intensification of life, a fulfilling of all senses, an effort at making civilized contact, a desire to give soul and heart to daily life. Serve this Canard Farci and you may rest assured that when the time comes and you have to leave this valley of tears or joys, your orations will all be of the very best quality. Canard Farci may well be your *passeport gourmet* to immortality.

But back to the nitty-gritty. You need a whole duck for every 2 people, so for 8 people buy 4 ducks. If you can find duck thighs only, buy 9 thighs and cut each in half at the joint; these will be easier and neater to cook and serve than whole ducks.

Note: Duck has a very high fat content. Long roasting allows the excess fat to be removed. You will be happy and grateful to have it later to pour on sautéd potatoes, chestnuts and vegetables of all kinds.

Four cooked stuffed ducks on a serving dish in a dining room are a lovely sight, but they spell trouble for the hostess. They are a problem to carve, to scoop out the stuffing and then to serve, during which most of the meal gets cold and guests become impatient.

The following preparation overcomes the problems that make Canard Farci difficult to deal with when one has no help and insists on serving this dish piping hot, crisp and moist.

The cut-up duck is cooked slowly and pricked frequently to rid it of all excess fat and to produce a crisp skin. The stuffing is baked separately until the very end when the crisp duck is added for a few minutes. Meanwhile, the chestnuts and spring onions brown in duck fat.

This is a precise process tested over and over by generations of generous women eager to provide unforgettable Feasts for their families, with the result being a preparation with no last-minute surprise or virtuoso tricks and a harmonious dinner that flows gracefully round a sumptuous platter.

Everything in a successful Feast is based on planning, planning and planning, and that is why we are so elated when the Canard Farci is set on the table. There is nothing left to plan or worry about. We can enjoy it and flow along with the happiness running through the room. You may feel pedestrian and disciplined during this rather long preparation in the solitude of your kitchen, but as the Canard Farci appears, it will seem as if it had been created by no less than a brigade of gourmet guardian angels.

FOR 8 PEOPLE

MEAT

> *4 ducks, thawed if frozen*
> *Freshly ground black pepper to taste*
> *2 tsp dried thyme or 3 sprigs fresh thyme*
> *Juice of 1 lemon*
> *2–3 tbsp sea salt*

BROTH

> *2 onions, studded with cloves*
> *2 carrots*
> *1 stalk celery*
> *Salt to taste*

STUFFING (about 9 cups are needed)

> *2 × 10-oz/295 g cans whole chestnuts in water*
> *1½ cups prunes, pitted*
> *3 oz/75 g unsalted butter*

*1½ lb/675 g tart apples (Granny Smiths), peeled, cored and thinly
    sliced to make 3 cups*
Salt
Freshly ground pepper
¾–1 cup duck or chicken livers, cut in half
3 large onions, peeled and thinly sliced
Vegetable oil
6 oz/175 g cooked ham, trimmed of fat and cut into ¼-in/6-mm cubes
1½ cups chopped parsley
8 fl oz/225 ml red vermouth or port
3 eggs, lightly beaten

ACCOMPANIMENTS

3 tbsp duck fat (approximately)
40 whole chestnuts (part of the 2 cans bought for the stuffing)
1 lemon rind, finely grated
*5–10 spring onions, trimmed, with 2-in/50-mm of green stem on, and
    halved lengthways*
Cabbage or Fennel Purée or Ratatouille

SAUCE

8 fl oz/225 ml dry white wine (approximately)
2 tbsp brandy
8 fl oz/225 ml duck broth
1–1½ oz/25–40 g unsalted butter, softened

GARNISH

Parsley or watercress

If using frozen duck, be sure to thaw according to the directions on the
wrapping. The day before the Feast pull away the excess fat from the
tail end of cavity. Cut away excess neck skin. Remove the wishbone,
wing tips, backbone, breastbone, and neck; you will use them along
with the gizzard to prepare a fragrant broth. Separate the legs from the
body and cut each leg in 2 parts across the joint. Cut down the length of
the breastbone on either side of the ridge and lift each breast out in one
piece. Trim all pieces of any fat, keeping the skin intact. Rub them with
pepper, thyme, lemon juice and salt.

   Place in a roasting pan large enough to hold all the pieces flat in one
layer. Use 2 pans if necessary. Cover and refrigerate for 4 hours or until
ready to use.

   To prepare the duck broth, place the gizzards, wings and necks in a
saucepan of water with the onions, carrots, celery and salt. Bring to a
boil and then simmer, covered, for 1 hour. Drain. Cool. Remove top
fat, then cover with cling film.

Prepare the stuffing. Open the cans of chestnuts and set aside about 40 whole ones for the garnish. Add the broken pieces to the stuffing. Soak the prunes in enough lukewarm water to cover, for 30 minutes. Melt 1 oz/25 g of the butter in a large frying pan. Add the apples. Cook quickly over moderately high heat, stirring often, until soft and lightly coloured, about 10 minutes. Season with salt and pepper. Transfer to a large bowl.

Add 1 oz/25 g of butter to the frying pan. Add the livers and cook for about 1 minute on each side. Add to the bowl of apples. Melt the remaining butter and cook the onions for 5–10 minutes, or until soft. Transfer to the bowl of apples. Melt a little vegetable oil and quickly sauté the diced ham. Add to the bowl. Combine the apples, livers, onions and ham, the broken chestnut pieces, parsley and pepper to taste. Drain the prunes and add them. Add the vermouth. Mix well, cover and refrigerate for 2–4 hours, or until ready to cook.

Prepare the Cabbage or Fennel Purée or the Ratatouille. Cover and refrigerate.

On the day of the party, 3 hours before the guests are due to arrive, preheat the oven to 350°F/180°C/Mark 4. Prick the duck breasts and leg pieces and place on a rack in a pan. Cook uncovered for 30 minutes, then pour off the fat into a bowl and reserve. One hour later pour off more accumulated fat into the bowl. Continue cooking about 1½ hours more. Prick the duck with a fork to see if the juices run clear, indicating that the duck is done. Remove from the oven. Slice the breasts on the diagonal about ¼-in/6-mm thick. Arrange the slices to overlap one another in a big ovenproof dish, then place the thighs and legs alongside. Cover with a large piece of foil and leave in the oven at 225°F/110°C/Mark ¼. Pour the excess fat into the bowl of duck fat.

To make the sauce, place the roasting pan over a medium heat on top of the cooker. Add wine and brandy to the pan. Scrape the coagulated juices at the bottom of the pan and stir vigorously. Simmer for 5 minutes, add the duck broth and reduce slightly over high heat. Set aside for later use.

One hour before the party, mix the beaten eggs into the stuffing and pour into the terrine. Cover with foil and a lid (or just foil), bake at 350°F/180°C/Mark 4 for 40 minutes, and then keep covered in the warm oven.

Just before you begin the first course of the dinner, heat in a frying pan the duck fat you have stored in a bowl and sauté the whole chestnuts, lemon rind and spring onions on all sides until lightly coloured. (Whole canned chestnuts are fragile and break easily if not carefully stirred.) Sprinkle with salt and pepper. Keep covered in a warm oven.

Place the roasting pan with the cooking juices, wine and broth on the cooker over a high heat. Twirl in the softened butter and correct the seasoning. Take the duck out of the oven and add all the pieces to the warm juices, stirring for 1 minute. Arrange on a serving dish and add the chestnuts and spring onions around them. Pour the rest of the juices over the whole dish. Cover with foil and keep warm in the oven.

When you are ready to serve Canard Farci, take the dish of stuffing out of the oven. Place it on the tea-trolley with the warm dishes and the Ratatouille or Purée. Take the plate of duck out of the oven. Add a bunch of parsley or a little bunch of watercress at one end and roll your trolley into the dining-room.

Each guest should have 2 or 3 pieces of duck with a little sauce over them, 1 or 2 spoonfuls of the stuffing, 3 or 4 sautéd chestnuts, a piece of sautéd spring onion, a twig of parsley or watercress and a spoonful of either the Ratatouille or Purée. Place leftovers in the oven to keep warm.

Note: This recipe can be prepared with a young 6 lb/2.75 kg turkey.

WINE

A full-bodied red or an Alsatian white wine.

WHAT TO SERVE BEFORE AND AFTER CANARD FARCI

HORS D'OEUVRES

1. Gougère
2. Pissenlits aux Lardons
3. Pissaladière
4. Caviar d'Aubergines with warm toast and raw vegetables

DESSERTS

1. Grand Baba
2. Crêpes Normandes
3. Mousse au Chocolat Glacée with a purée of fruits

TABLE DECORATION

A patterned tablecloth with rich caramel, warm rust and mellow ivory colours would look well with such an opulent meal. Place brown, beige and green candles on the table. You may want to add a brass or green pottery vase in the centre, fill it with foliage and add a few blue and yellow irises for a cheerful note.

Wrap pretty coloured napkins round the wine bottles. Add 2 brown or green lacquered baskets for bread. Don't forget butter pots and pretty salt and pepper shakers. Slide green or beige napkins in wood, silver or china napkin-rings or wrap a piece of coarse beige string or raffia with a wide bow round each one and slide a card or a dry eucalyptus leaf with the guest's name under the string.

STRATEGY FOR THE SUGGESTED MENU

- Guests invited for 7.30 p.m.
- Meal served at 8.30 p.m.

- The day before the Feast or earlier: prepare Grand Baba and freeze; store the syrup and glaze in jars. Prepare the Cabbage (or Fennel) Purée and refrigerate it. Prepare stuffing and refrigerate it.

- On the day of the Feast: 3 hours before the Feast take everything out of the refrigerator. Sauté the diced bacon for the salad and put in a bowl. Wash and trim the dandelions or chicory.
- Warm the Babas at 325°F/160°C/Mark 3 for 5 minutes while you reheat the syrup. Pour half of the syrup slowly over the Babas. Allow them to rest and absorb the syrup. After a while pour the remaining syrup and allow to rest again until all is absorbed. Sprinkle a little brandy on top. Reheat the glaze and pour it on top of the two Babas.
- Bake the duck.
- Bake the stuffing.
- Reheat the Purée. Sauté the onions and chestnuts in the duck fat in the skillet.

7.30 Your first guests arrive.

8.25 Put pieces of duck into the warm sauce and keep warm in the oven, covered. Place dandelions or endive greens on each salad plate. Heat the vinegar and oil, and add the crisp lardons for 1 second. Pour the lardons over the greens and sprinkle with pepper. Bring the plates to the table. Light the candles. Ask your guests to be seated at the table.

8.30 Start the meal.

8.40 While your guests finish the Pissenlits, go to the kitchen and bring the Canard with spring onions, chestnuts, Purée and stuffing, and the warm plates, to the table.

8.50 Offer second helpings.

9.00 Change the plates. Bring the Grand Baba to the table.

LEFT-OVERS

1. Soup: a duck soup made with the left-over diced meat and the delicious broth.
2. Curried duck: chop or slice the left-over duck and sauté it in a little vegetable oil with 1 or 2 sliced onions. Sprinkle with curry powder, correct the seasoning and add 1 or 2 chopped tomatoes. Serve over steamed or boiled rice.
3. Salad: shred the left-over duck meat and serve it with boiled green beans seasoned with a lukewarm vinaigrette seasoning.
4. Gratin: chop the left-over meat and stuffing, add a little duck broth, or 2 diced tomatoes and a few diced boiled turnips. Spread in an ovenproof dish, sprinkle breadcrumbs on top, dot with butter and reheat for 30 minutes.

Cassoulet

A lavish version of stew that includes beans, pork, duck, lamb, onions, tomatoes and herbs baked under a fragrant breadcrumb crust.

> SUGGESTED MENU
>
> *Pissenlits aux Lardons*
>
> *Cassoulet*
>
> *Granité au Vin*
> *Thin Biscuits*
>
> *Cahors*

Over the centuries this earthy superdish, Cassoulet (the word comes from *cassole*, the earthenware pot in which it is baked and served), has inspired endless quarrels, much praise, and a fair amount of analytical evaluation.

Cassoulet involves a rather long process and many ingredients but is basically simple to prepare. By starting the shopping and cooking two days before the Feast you will have a spectacular *plat de résistance* and no problem whatsoever when entertaining.

Among the innumerable one-and-only cassoulets, three stand out. In Castelnaudary, a small city in the south-west of France where the dish may have been brought by the Arabs in some rough version around the seventh century, it is proudly and religiously prepared with dried white beans, garlic, ham, sausage and pork rind. The second-ranking 'authentic' version is that of Toulouse. In the city of aeronautics, where the Airbus and the Concorde are made, pieces of *confit*, preserved goose or duck, are added. Finally, in Carcassonne the 'genuine' recipe includes lamb and an occasional partridge. In fact, the dish was prepared in all three places with dried broad beans for centuries until other varieties of beans, including the traditional white beans, were introduced to Europe by Columbus in the fifteenth century.

The secret of this legendary dish is that it is made in three steps. The beans are first blanched, which makes them easier to digest. Then they are cooked with lean salt pork, raw ham and sausages in a white wine broth made with very flavourful herbs and vegetables. Meanwhile, the lamb is cooked apart, with tomatoes, onions, wine and herbs, and the duck is pan-roasted. It is the final fusion of all these elements, slowly baking together and mingling their flavours, that turns this velvety stew into a triumphant dish crowned by its golden crust.

There is agreement in all three important versions that the crusts on the top of the Cassoulet *must* be broken and 'buried' in the beans and meats at least three, but preferably seven, times during the baking. The crust thus thickens as it develops flavour and seals the aromatic mixture underneath. This may well be the single most important and typical characteristic of Cassoulet.

Cassoulet is a very hearty, very substantial, quite heavy dish. As tastes and needs have evolved in the last decade, Cassoulet has likewise been altered for more conservative contemporary taste. This is for the better, I think, since I frankly don't see anyone around today able to eat, digest and survive the kind of Cassoulet served at my grandparents' table a few decades ago. Then it took days of herb broth and mineral water to recover from an 'authentic' Cassoulet.

The following recipe is, I think, a perfect arrangement. I have clung fiercely to what makes Cassoulet unique, discarding only the amount of fat involved in the preparation. There is lean salt pork, sausage, raw ham and lamb cooked one day in advance, which makes it easy to discard the fat. The duck thighs, cooked slowly, give out their fat into the fragrant cooking juices, which later add to the dish's seasoning. The cooking juices of the lamb, pork and beans are very highly seasoned; altogether they make for a very tasty, varied, spectacular Cassoulet but not an overwhelmingly rich one. We can enjoy it to our heart's content without transgressing any sensible rule of nutrition.

Organization is again of the essence. Cassoulet must be prepared calmly one or two days in advance. It improves as it reheats, and left-overs are a treat, so make an abundant, spectacular display. Prepare it in a 10 pt/5 l gratin dish or large casserole, deep enough so Cassoulet does not dry out and wide enough so each guest has a good portion of the delicious crust.

By having the time to remove bones, fat and gristle, to slice the meats carefully, to correct the cooking broth and all the cooking juices, your Cassoulet will be a true masterpiece and an easy one to enjoy. Fit and fully contented, you will notice once more how good times and good food enjoy each other's company.

A Cassoulet has to be very abundant, but remember that it freezes beautifully.

FOR ABOUT 12 PEOPLE

DUCK

> *6 fresh duck legs (drumsticks and thighs) or 5 pieces of confit of duck*
>   *or 5 pieces of confit of goose*
> *Sea salt*
> *Dried thyme*

BEANS

> *3 lb/1 .25 kg dried white beans*
> *Several duck, chicken, veal or meat bones (to improve the broth)*
> *2 lb/900 g lean salt pork or unsmoked bacon, rind removed, cut into*
>   *1-in/25-mm pieces*
> *2 onions, peeled and studded with cloves*
> *3 carrots, peeled and finely chopped*
> *2 stalks celery, finely chopped*
> *3 tsp dried thyme or 4 sprigs fresh thyme*
> *10 peppercorns*
> *3 bay leaves*
> *Bunch of parsley, including stem*
> *8 cloves garlic, peeled*
> *3½ pt/2 l boiling broth or water (approximately)*
> *About 1 lb/450 g Toulouse or similar garlic cooking sausages*
> *1 lb/450 g cured ham in one piece*

LAMB

> *6 lb/2 .75 kg lamb (leg or stewing meat), boned*
> *4 tbsp (or more as needed) olive or vegetable oil*
> *6 onions, peeled and chopped (to make about 4 cups)*
> *2 stalks celery, thinly sliced*
> *10 tomatoes, peeled, seeded and chopped, or 1 lb 12 oz/794 g can of*
>   *tomatoes with the liquid*
> *8 cloves garlic, peeled*
> *6 tsp dried thyme or several sprigs of fresh thyme*
> *3 bay leaves*
> *1⅔ pt/900 ml dry white wine*
> *16 fl oz/450 ml broth or water*
> *Salt*

ASSEMBLING THE CASSOULET

> *Freshly ground pepper*
> *6 tsp dried thyme*
> *2 tbsp chopped fresh mint leaves (optional but lovely)*
> *3 cups breadcrumbs, preferably home-made*
> *1 cup minced parsley*
> *4 cloves garlic, peeled and minced*
> *½–1 oz/12–25 g butter or 1–2 tbsp walnut oil*
> *Chicken stock, if necessary (to cover the beans and meat before*
>   *baking or to moisten the Cassoulet in the oven)*

Since confit of duck or goose is very expensive, the following way to prepare duck makes for a reasonable yet delectable Cassoulet.

One day before the party rub the duck legs with coarse salt and dried thyme. Leave overnight to marinate.

Meanwhile, prepare the beans. (*Note*: Make sure you don't use stale beans; they will burst while cooking. In fact, the dried beans should be this year's crop.) Unless the instructions on the packet are different, soak them in cold water for 2 hours. Drop in a saucepan of lukewarm water, bring gently to a boil, simmer for 2 minutes, remove from the heat and let stand in the water for 1 hour. The beans should double in volume. Drain and discard the water.

Put the beans in a saucepan with the bones, if any, the pieces of lean salt pork, onions, carrots, celery, thyme, peppercorns, bay leaves, parsley and garlic. Cover with boiling broth or water and bring back to a boil slowly. Lower the heat and simmer, covered, for 1½ hours, until the beans are cooked but not mushy. Add the sausages for the last 30 minutes. Add cured ham for the last few minutes.

Drain the beans, reserving the broth for later use. Put the beans into a large bowl and add salt and pepper to taste. Place the meats – salt pork, ham and sausages – on plates and cover with cling film.

Meanwhile, prepare the lamb; remove the gristle and fat, and dry with a paper towel. Cut into 2-in/50-mm cubes (to make about 8 cups). Heat the oil in a large frying pan and brown the lamb cubes on all sides. Remove the lamb from the pan and pour off all but 1 tablespoon of the fat. Add the onions and celery. Lower the heat and cook about 3 minutes, until the onions are translucent. Add the tomatoes, garlic, thyme, bay leaves, white wine, broth and salt. Return the browned lamb to the pan. Bring to a boil, then lower the heat and simmer for 1 hour, partially covered.

Remove the meat and set aside for a few minutes. Strain the broth, pressing down on the vegetables to extract as much juice as possible.

Bring to a rapid boil and reduce, uncovered, until the liquid measures about 1⅔ pt/900 ml. Return the meat to the broth and cool to room temperature. Cover with cling film and refrigerate.

Refrigerate the beans and other meats.

On the morning of the party, take everything out of the refrigerator. Wipe the pieces of duck with a dry paper towel. In a heavy frying pan pan-roast the duck legs in a little vegetable oil for 1½ hours, covered, on a low heat, turning them from time to time while you prepare the rest of the Cassoulet. When the duck is cooked, remove it from the frying pan and add a little white wine or water. Scrape the bottom to melt the coagulated juices and set the pan aside. When the duck is cold, cut each leg into 2 parts.

Remove all fat from the lamb pieces and from its broth. Remove the fat from the top of the beans.

Slice the sausages into 1-in/25-mm slices. Cut the cured ham into 1-in/25-mm cubes. Check the taste of the bean and pork cooking broth, and season with salt and pepper if necessary.

Put a layer of cooked beans on the bottom of the casserole. Sprinkle with a little pepper and a little thyme. Add the lamb, pieces of salt pork or bacon and cured ham, more beans, a little pepper and thyme, then the pieces of duck, sausage slices and finally the rest of the beans. Season with pepper and thyme. Add mint leaves if you have them. Carefully pour the juices of the duck and the lamb, and enough of the broth that the beans cooked in, to cover the ingredients in the Cassoulet dish. The level of the liquid should reach ½–¾in/12–18mm below the rim.

Keep the remaining broth to add to the Cassoulet as it bakes. Sprinkle the breadcrumbs and all but 6 teaspoons of minced parsley over the surface of the Cassoulet. Dot with butter. Cover with foil and refrigerate.

Set aside the remaining parsley and minced garlic in a piece of aluminium foil for sprinkling at the last minute before serving.

Two and a half hours before the dinner is to be served, preheat the oven to 350°F/180°C/Mark 4. Take the Cassoulet out of the refrigerator. Place the broth near the oven. Unwrap the casserole and set it in the upper third of the oven. As soon as a golden crust forms – about 15 minutes – lower the temperature to 300°F/150°C/Mark 2 and break the surface of the crust with the back of a spoon. Push it down into the beans and baste with the casserole liquid. Carefully add some of the reserved broth at the edges of the dish so the beans remain moist and the liquid remains always just under the level of the crust.

Break and baste the crust 3 to 7 times depending on your patience

(I think 3 breakings of the crust is sufficient). The beans must be very moist at all times. Allow the last crust to form and turn gold and crisp before serving.

Wrap the Cassoulet dish in a beautiful tea-towel. Add the minced parsley and garlic on top and bring it to the table with the warm plates.

Place the large Cassoulet dish on a side table, and either ask your guests to come and help themselves or place a generous ladleful of Cassoulet on each warm plate with a bit of juice to moisten and a piece of crisp crust.

After serving, return the Cassoulet dish to the oven at once and keep it warm until your guests are ready for second helpings. This must be an unhurried meal, so make sure your Cassoulet arrives at the table piping hot so you can linger to your heart's content.

WINE

A light red wine, such as a Cahors or Beaujolais, a strong chilled rosé, a dry chilled white wine, or a full-bodied red wine, such as Bordeaux or a Burgundy.

WHAT TO SERVE BEFORE AND AFTER CASSOULET

HORS-D'OEUVRES TO BE SERVED WITH THE DRINKS

For this hearty, solid dish, experts recommend very little before and a very light dessert. In France raw oysters or clams on the half shell are often served with sliced lemons and buttered country bread.

1. Crudités en Panier with one sharp sauce
2. Pissenlits aux Lardons
3. Beef or chicken broth with thin warm toast

DESSERTS

1. Granité au Vin with two plates of thin biscuits
2. Mélange de Fruits
3. Cervelle de Canut
4. Lemon, coffee or mint sorbet

TABLE DECORATION

Such a generous superlative country feast needs a warm and rich table setting. Everything on the table is useful and also lovely and interesting enough to contemplate for a long time.

You may, of course, use the predictable rustic red-and-white chequered cotton tablecloth, but for a more interesting combination you may prefer a quilted cotton tablecloth in shades of rich brown. Or you may like a dark red, deep blue and cream paisley fabric. A brass, copper or silver tureen in the centre filled with dahlias, plump roses, anemones or peonies and an abundance of blue, ivory and red candles of different heights all over the table may be lovely.

Make sure there are at least 3 bottles of wine on the table. Wrap their necks with little table-napkins. Choose big off-white or coloured cotton napkins. Add a soup spoon to each place setting.

STRATEGY FOR THE SUGGESTED MENU

- Guests invited for 7.30 p.m.
- Meal served at 8.30 p.m.

- One day before the Feast: prepare the first part of Cassoulet. Prepare the Granité au Vin.

- On the morning of the Feast: prepare the remaining part of the Cassoulet.

- On the evening of the Feast:
  6.00 Preheat the oven. Bake the Cassoulet in the oven. Break the crust and add broth and juices from time to time. Prepare the salad.
  7.30 Your first guests arrive.
  8.15 Light the candles. Bring water, bread and butter to the table. Take the dandelions for the Pissenlits out of the refrigerator and divide on to individual salad plates. Sauté the bacon for a minute. Add vinegar and pour on top of each plate of greens. Bring plates to the table.
  8.30 Ask your guests to be seated at the table. Meal starts.
  8.40 Wrap the Cassoulet dish in a tea-towel, bring it to the table and serve.
  9.00 Clear the table and change plates. Bring the Granité au Vin and biscuits to the table.
  Later After this sumptuous meal an old brandy, preferably an Armagnac or cognac, is welcome.

LEFT-OVERS

1. Add a little broth and some breadcrumbs on top, then reheat in the oven.

2. Make a robust peasant soup by chopping the left-over pieces of meat and adding them to some broth.

3. Cassoulet freezes beautifully. Stir in a few tablespoons of canned tomatoes before reheating.

Chou Farci

Stuffed cabbage.

It is served in bistros, in *guinguettes* and in country inns, but Chou Farci remains essentially a jewel of family cooking and a pillar of festive gatherings. Like all traditional festive dishes it was invented to react against the monotony of daily cooking by transforming inexpensive and easily available ingredients in imaginative and original ways. Consequently, Aunt Marie's or Cousin Jeanne's Chou Farci was always a shared event worth remembering in the family patrimony of good things.

> SUGGESTED MENU
>
> *Pissenlits aux Lardons*
>
> *Chou Farci*
>
> *Compote de Poires*
>
> *A Full-bodied Rosé*

There are innumerable interpretations of Chou Farci because each region, each bistro and each cook is confident that he or she follows the very best version. Many combinations have been tried, eliminated, selected, adopted and improved in the course of the years, and as a result the choice is wide. The cabbage may be stuffed with pork, lamb, beef, chicken or ham and also with peas, chestnuts, mushrooms, olives, apples, prunes, rice and moistened bread. It may be seasoned with garlic, herbs, shallots or spices. Generally the meats are braised or boiled (left-over Pot-au-Feu is superb) since roasted meats are often too lean for stuffing that must remain tasty and unctuous after its long cooking. Chou Farci may be braised with vegetables or simmered in broth, or it can be steamed.

Chou Farci may be served with a sauce of cream and fresh herbs, a fresh tomato sauce or a sauce made with wine and puréed vegetables. Whatever recipe is finally chosen the variations on this theme are numerous, from hearty to truly refined. Calmly prepared a day in advance, the Chou improves in flavour, is easy to reheat and easy to serve. It is not quick to prepare, but this is one of those cases in cooking when the longest way is the best in the long run. The cabbage leaves are first blanched in boiling water to make them pliable, then a rich stuffing is spread between them and finally the whole cabbage is reshaped and placed in a large piece of cheesecloth to cook. It is fun to create a Chou Farci.

The recipe offered here has been proven and has been used as the centre of many generations of family Feasts. I have tried my Alsatian cousin's version with apples, my Provençal aunt's rendering with Swiss chard, peas and artichokes, and my northern neighbour's variation, where the cabbage is stuffed mostly with a variety of meats. But mine, which is the version offered here, seems to gather a consensus among friends and relatives for a hearty, highly spirited and wonderfully satisfying festive meal. Once 'reconstituted', the stuffed leaves make for a spectacular and majestic plump cabbage.

Note that although one stuffed cabbage is plenty, two is more fun if you want an extravagant, truly memorable meal.

FOR 8 PEOPLE

INGREDIENTS

> *2 cabbages (about 3 lb/1.25 kg) trimmed*
> *1 oz/25 g butter*
> *1 tbsp vegetable oil*
> *2 large onions, peeled and coarsely chopped (about ½ cup)*
> *8 oz/225 g lean salt pork or lean bacon rind, cut into ¼-in/6-mm cubes*
> *1½ cups of the centre leaves of your parboiled cabbage, coarsely chopped*
> *1 lb/450 g boiled ham, chopped*
> *4 cloves garlic, peeled and finely chopped*
> *3 eggs, lightly beaten*
> *1 cup cooked rice (⅓ cup raw rice)*
> *1 cup chopped parsley*
> *1 tsp freshly ground coriander*
> *Freshly ground pepper*
> *Salt*
> *Fresh herbs such as parsley, chives and tarragon, finely minced*

ACCOMPANIMENTS

> *3 long stalks celery, peeled and cut into 2-in/50-mm pieces*
> *2 courgettes, sliced lengthways and cut into 2-in/50-mm pieces*
> *3 fennel bulbs, trimmed, no strings and cut in half lengthways*
> *4 small turnips (about 1 lb/450 g), peeled, halved or quartered*
> *4 carrots, peeled, cut lengthways, and then cut into 2-in/50-mm long pieces*
> *2 large garlicky or very spicy sausages, pricked with a fork before cooking*

SAUCES

The cold sauce is passed round, the warm sauce is spooned over each portion of Chou Farci to moisten it as you serve it.

COLD

> *8 fl oz/225 ml olive oil*
> *Salt to taste*
> *1 tsp freshly ground coriander*
> *2 tbsp minced fresh herbs such as thyme, marjoram, chervil and*
>   *parsley*
> *1–2 tomatoes, plunged in boiling water for easy peeling, deseeded*
>   *and diced*

WARM

> *1 bowl warm cabbage broth*
> *Minced parsley*

GARNISH

> *3 tbsp finely minced fresh herbs: parsley, basil, chives, tarragon*

The day before the Feast, wash and trim the vegetables, then store them in the refrigerator. (The sausages and vegetables are served with the Chou Farci. Add them to the pan during the last 30 minutes of cooking.)

Cook the cabbage leaves. Remove and discard the core and tough outside leaves. Bring a large saucepan of water to a boil and parboil the cabbage, uncovered, for about 10 minutes. Remove the cabbage to a colander and refresh under cold water. When cool, peel off the leaves and drain them on paper towels; keep the small centre leaves for stuffing.

Heat the butter and oil in a large frying pan. Add the onions and sauté until soft. Add the cubed pork and cook 5 minutes more. Transfer to a mixing bowl and allow to cool. Chop the centre leaves of the cabbage (to make 1½ cups). Add to the bowl with the ham, garlic, eggs, rice and parsley. Stir all the ingredients until well combined. Season with coriander and pepper, and add salt if needed. The stuffing should be rather coarse.

Line a bowl with a large piece of cheesecloth or a thin tea-towel. Spread a few cabbage leaves on the cheesecloth to line the bowl. Sprinkle the leaves with salt and pepper, then spread on a layer of stuffing. Cover with 2 or 3 cabbage leaves, another layer of stuffing, and so on until you have used all your ingredients. Cover with the final 2 cabbage leaves. Gather up the top of the cheesecloth and tie it with string. You will have a neat, compact ball. Leave it in its bowl in the refrigerator until ready to cook.

Prepare the cold sauce. Mix the olive oil, salt, coriander and herbs in a bowl. Stir in tomatoes. Cover with cling film and refrigerate.

You will prepare your bowl of warm broth at the last minute.

On the day, 2 hours before the dinner, take the Chou Farci, raw sausages, trimmed vegetables and bowl of sauce out of the refrigerator.

Fill the bottom part of a steamer with water and bring it to a boil. (A multi-tiered steamer is most useful here. It makes for firm vegetables; it enables you to cook three things at once; and it keeps everything warm if your guests are late.) Place the Chou Farci in the first tray of the steamer. After 1 hour add the trimmed vegetables on the second tray and place the 2 sausages in the boiling water in the bottom of the pan. Cook for 30 minutes more on medium heat. Check once to make sure there is enough water boiling in the bottom compartment. The cabbage, vegetables and sausages will be ready at the same time and can wait for about 1 hour if you turn off the heat but keep the lid on the saucepan.

If you are not using a steamer, fill a large saucepan with water and bring to a boil. Place the stuffed cabbage in the boiling water, lower the heat and simmer for 30 minutes. Add the vegetables and sausage. Cook 30 minutes more.

When ready to serve the meal, carefully place the cabbage in a bowl. Cut open the strings with scissors and push away the cheesecloth. Tip the bowl to drain off the excess liquid. Place a large serving plate on the top and, holding on tight to the plate and bowl, turn them together in a decisive gesture. Peel away and discard the cheesecloth. Turn the cabbage upside down once more on to another plate in order to have it top side up.

Pour some of the warm cooking broth in a bowl and sprinkle a little parsley on it before you take it to the table. You will spoon it over each helping of Chou Farci.

When all your guests are seated, bring the warm plates, Chou Farci, sauces, bowl of finely minced fresh herbs, cooked vegetables and sliced sausages to the table.

When everyone has seen the glorious green Chou, take a modest bow and then a deep breath: this is no time for maybes. Armed with a big knife, a wide spatula, a big spoon and the good wishes of the whole assembly, you are now ready to officiate. Cut 2 wedges of Chou Farci and lay them on their sides on each warm plate. Arrange some vegetables and a slice or two of sausage alongside the Chou. Spoon a little broth over everything and sprinkle some minced fresh herbs over all. Pass the plates and the 2 bowls of sauce to your guests.

WINE

A full-bodied rosé or hearty red wine.

WHAT TO SERVE BEFORE AND AFTER CHOU FARCI

With such a rich dish, nothing too distracting or excessive is needed before or after.

HORS-D'OEUVRES TO BE SERVED WITH THE DRINKS

- Pissenlits aux Lardons
- A salad of rocket, slivers of fennel and chicory with a sharp vinaigrette dressing
- Crudités en Panier, with a pungent sauce
- Pissaladière
- Warm almonds and Olives Sautées

DESSERTS

- Compote de Poires
- Mélange de Fruits
- Crémets aux Fruits
- Granité au Vin
- Panier de Frivolités
- Poires, Pruneaux, Oranges au Vin Rouge et aux Épices
- Ripe fruit such as grapes, with a good ripe cheese, such as Roquefort, served with a Sauternes or any good sweet wine

TABLE DECORATION

Your *plat de résistance*, your glorious superdish, will give the tone of the meal, and you may like your table to reflect some of the quiet opulence and informal provincial charm of your Chou Farci. Use natural elements: cotton, straw, wood, terracotta, ivory-coloured candles. In the centre of your table place a basket filled with chubby red geraniums or a short-flowered shrub or an exuberant pyramid of fruits and vegetables with Queen Anne's Lace tucked in. The setting should suggest nature at its most generous.

Since the plates are kept warm in the kitchen, place a folded napkin between the forks and knives as you set the table.

STRATEGY FOR SUGGESTED MENU

- Guests invited for 7.30 p.m.
- Meal served at 8.30 p.m.

- One day before the Feast: prepare the dandelion greens, diced bacon, stuffed cabbages, cold sauce, trimmed vegetables and cooked pears.

- On the day of the Feast:
  6.30 Take everything but the pears out of the refrigerator.
  7.30 Start cooking Chou Farci. Your first guests arrive.
  8.10 Add vegetables and sausages to the steamer.
  8.30 Turn off the heat under the Chou and the steamer. Keep covered. Light the candles on the table. Ask your guests to be seated. Heat vinegar in the frying pan and pour dressing on Pissenlits aux Lardons. Bring Pissenlits to the table.
  8.50 Prepare Chou Farci for the table and serve as described.
  9.10 Bring dessert and a plate of thin biscuits to the table.

LEFT-OVERS

1. Chou Farci is easy to reheat with a little broth, but it will not be too presentable.
2. Gratin: chop all the left-overs, pour into a gratin dish, and cover with single cream. Season the cream with a little broth and a little tomato. Sprinkle breadcrumbs on top. Dot with butter and bake for 30 minutes at 375°F/190°C/Mark 5.
3. Farcis: stuff halves of tomatoes and onions with the chopped left-overs moistened with a little broth or tomato sauce. Sprinkle the top of the vegetables with grated Gruyère or Parmesan cheese before baking for 30 minutes.

Coq au Vin

A splendid marinated chicken seasoned with red wine, vegetables and herbs.

SUGGESTED MENU

Jambon Persillé

Coq au Vin
Celeriac Purée
Watercress and Chicory Salad

Compote de Poires

Côtes du Rhône

This is one of the most popular of traditional dishes. In serious bistros, in country inns and in homes throughout France, Coq au Vin is served for big occasions. All the variations of this potent sauce and moist chicken dish are interesting, whether cooked with white wine or red wine, whether thickened with rooster blood, with egg yolk and cream, with puréed chicken livers or with a *beurre manié*.

Apparently it all started when the prosperous Gauls, under siege by Roman troops, sent Julius Caesar a thin, old rooster wearing round its neck an ironic message: '*Bon Appétit!*' As we came to learn, Caesar was big enough to take a joke and turn it to his advantage. He responded by inviting the leaders of the Gauls to dinner. They accepted and were served a Gallic chicken simmered with herbs in Roman wine. They loved it, and they saw the Gallo-Roman relationship with a new eye. According to the legend, this Coq au Vin marked the beginning of a long civilization and the beginning of a cautious but lasting friendship.

Today it is easy to find full-bodied wine and good vegetables when we prepare our Coq au Vin, but a year-old rooster is difficult to come by if you are not raising it yourself. The following recipe takes into account the shortcomings of our times and compensates for them. We heat the marinade first and, for concentrated flavour, marinate the chicken overnight. We cook the legs and thighs of the chicken, which need longer cooking, first and add the breasts later because they are fragile but absorb the juices wonderfully. We cool the chicken in its sauce. Later the sauce is thickened with chicken livers and a small amount of butter and flour mixed and puréed together to form a pasty mixture (*beurre manié*).

By the time it is served, the young chicken has absorbed as much flavour from the herbs, vegetables and wine as possible; the sauce is potent and velvety, the meat aromatic.

Prepared one or two days ahead, this is a foolproof dish that keeps improving when reheated and needs no attention before the meal. You can serve Coq au Vin with a basket of boiled potatoes. The following menu includes Celeriac Purée because it is made entirely in advance, is easy to reheat and adds a little extra charm. A tossed green salad is also suggested, but, of course, Coq au Vin needs no trimmings and can be served by itself.

FOR 8 PEOPLE

BROTH

> *Chicken necks, bones and innards*
> *1 onion, stuck with 3 cloves*
> *Bouquet garni*
> *Salt to taste*
> *Thyme*
> *Peppercorns*
> *24 fl oz/675 ml water or 16 fl oz/450 ml very good stock*

MARINADE

> *1⅔ pt/900 ml hearty, young, tasty red wine*
> *2 onions, sliced*
> *1 carrot, peeled and sliced*
> *Bouquet garni*
> *2 cloves garlic, peeled and crushed*
> *4 tsp dried thyme*
> *10 peppercorns*
> *3 tbsp olive oil*

CHICKEN

> *8 large chicken thighs*
> *8 chicken breasts*
> *6 drumsticks*
> *20 mushroom caps, or more if tiny*
> *24 pearl onions or 12 shallots, peeled*
> *4 large carrots, peeled and cut into thick slices*
> *3 celeriac*
> *7 stalks celery, trimmed and cut into 1-in/25-mm pieces*
> *3 tbsp vegetable oil*
> *2½ oz/65 g butter*
> *Salt*
> *Freshly ground pepper*
> *3 tbsp dried thyme*
> *1–2 tbsp flour*
> *4 oz/100 g lean salt pork or bacon, rind removed, cut into ¼ × 1 in/*
> * 6 × 25 mm pieces (about 2 cups)*
> *16 fl oz/450 ml chicken broth*
> *8 fl oz/225 ml red wine (if meat is not covered by liquid when it starts*
> * cooking)*

Bouquet garni (1 bay leaf, 2 sprigs parsley, 1 sprig thyme)
2 large onions, peeled and sliced
3 tbsp flour
1½ oz/40 g butter, softened
2 tbsp cream
2–3 chicken livers, trimmed
4 cloves garlic, peeled and crushed
Pinch of freshly grated nutmeg
Juice of 1 lemon
3 tbsp good brandy: Marc or Plum brandy or cognac

GARNISH

3 slices of buttered bread, crustless and cut into 24 triangles
3 tbsp parsley or chives, finely minced

ACCOMPANIMENTS

Choose from the following:
Basket of potatoes boiled in their skins
Celeriac Purée
Rice
Fennel Purée
A tossed green salad

For the chicken broth, put the ingredients into a large saucepan and cook for 30 minutes, uncovered. Correct the seasoning.

For the marinade, combine the red wine and other ingredients in a saucepan. Bring to a boil, lower the heat and simmer for 5 minutes. Let cool to room temperature.

Place the chicken pieces in a roasting pan or dish large enough to hold them all flat in one layer. Pour the cooled marinade over the chicken pieces. Cover with cling film and leave in the refrigerator overnight, turning 2 or 3 times.

Meanwhile, trim the mushrooms, onions, carrots, celeriac and celery. Cover and refrigerate.

On the morning of the Feast, remove everything from the refrigerator. Remove the chicken from the marinade. Reserve the liquid.

Heat 3 tablespoons of oil and 1½ oz/40 g of butter in a large frying pan. Pat dry each piece of chicken with paper towels. Sprinkle each piece with salt, pepper and thyme, and brown on all sides for 5 minutes, starting with the thighs and the drumsticks, which require longer cooking. Cook the breasts only 2 minutes on each side. Then sprinkle each piece lightly with flour and cook 1 minute more. You will have to make several batches so all the pieces are crisp and golden. Remove the chicken from the pan and set aside.

Add the salt pork or bacon to the warm frying pan over a low heat. When the pieces are crisp and brown, remove and put aside. Pour off the extra fat. Add the pearl onions, carrots and celery to the pan for a few minutes, turning them with a wooden spoon. Remove the vegetables and set aside. Sauté the mushrooms in the pan for a few minutes. Sprinkle them with salt, remove from the pan and set aside.

Remove as much fat as you can from the liquid left in the frying pan and pour any remaining cooking juices into a large casserole with about 1 oz/25 g of butter. Heat the juices and oil, add the browned chicken thighs and drumsticks, the reserved marinade liquid with the vegetables, and the chicken broth. Bring to a boil, lower the heat and add the bouquet garni and sliced onions. Simmer for about 30 minutes, until the juices of the chicken run pale yellow when you prick it with a fork. Add the chicken breasts to the casserole, making sure they are submerged in the liquid. Cool the Coq au Vin to room temperature and then refrigerate.

Cook and purée the celeriac, then cool, cover and refrigerate.

Preheat the oven to 400°F/200°C/Mark 6. Spread the bread triangles with butter, toast in the oven for 2 minutes on each side, then turn off the oven. You will reheat the *croûtons* at the last minute.

Note: These foods don't need refrigeration if kept in a cool spot; otherwise refrigerate.

One hour before the meal take everything out of the refrigerator: Celeriac Purée, chicken in its sauce, mushrooms, onions, bacon and sautéed but uncooked onions, carrots and celery. Remove the skin and any gristle you see from the chicken. With a spoon remove the fat from the surface of the chicken cooking juices and taste the broth; it should be highly aromatic.

Pour the cooking juices from the chicken into a large casserole and bring to a boil. Make the *beurre manié* by working the flour and softened butter into a paste. Whisk it bit by bit into the hot sauce. Cook for a minute or so, uncovered. Add the onions, carrots and celery. Lower the heat and cook for 10 minutes. Add the chicken, cover and simmer 10 to 15 minutes more.

Cook the potatoes in a separate pan of salted water.

Reheat the Celeriac Purée on a low heat in a covered pan with 2 tablespoons of cream.

Meanwhile, cut the chicken livers into very small pieces with scissors and add to the casserole. Slide in the mushrooms, bacon, onions, garlic, nutmeg and lemon juice. Cover and cook 2 or 3 minutes more.

Discard the bouquet garni. Check the seasoning. Add the brandy, turn off the heat and keep the casserole covered in a warm spot.

Reheat the bread *croûtons* for a few minutes in the oven. Make sure the guests are seated.

Pour the potatoes into a basket or dish. Pour the Celeriac Purée into a side dish. Place the salad greens in a bowl over the dressing and on top of the crossed serving spoon and fork. Take the *croûtons* out of the oven. Rub them with a clove of garlic and dip one corner of each bread triangle into the Coq au Vin sauce, then into the minced parsley. Place them on a side dish. Put the remaining parsley in a bowl on the table.

At the table, serve a breast and a thigh or a drumstick, a few onions, a few mushrooms, some celery and carrots and a few pieces of bacon on each plate. Spoon the sauce over, sprinkle with the chopped parsley and add 2 *croûtons* on the side. Add 1–2 spoonfuls of Celeriac Purée to each plate. Pass the basket of boiled potatoes round the table. Toss the green salad and pass it round.

WINE

A red Burgundy, Beaujolais or Côtes du Rhône, or a hearty, young, full-bodied red wine. Best to use the same wine in cooking and with the meal.

WHAT TO SERVE BEFORE AND AFTER COQ AU VIN

HORS-D'OEUVRES TO BE SERVED WITH THE DRINKS

1. Jambon Persillé, served with toast fingers
2. Poireaux Tièdes Vinaigrette
3. Terrine aux Herbes

DESSERTS

1. Compote de Poires
2. Grand Baba
3. Crémets aux Fruits

TABLE DECORATION

This is a hearty, colourful dish but not a messy one. A tablecloth in various shades of ochre, yellow or peach would be pretty. You might choose a rich paisley or a bold flowery print for your tablecloth, and in the centre of the table you might place a wide terracotta or pottery bowl filled with large Granny Smith apples, some thin green pears and tiny clusters of black and white grapes, in which you can put a few fluffy yellow and pink roses (in little glasses stuck between the fruit). If you can find them, add a few twigs of foliage or, better still, a few twigs of those small black and dark blue berries that grow wild along roads and in garden hedges.

You may want to use an assortment of pale green, ochre or yellow candles and wrap napkins round the necks of your wine bottles. Set out individual butter pots, or two larger ones for the boiled potatoes, big cotton napkins and two green or ochre lacquered bread-baskets. If you serve tossed salad, it may be wise to provide separate plates; little crystal half-moons are nice for this.

STRATEGY FOR THE SUGGESTED MENU

- Guests invited for 7.30 p.m.
- Meal served at 8.30 p.m.

- The day before the Feast: cook the marinade (or on the day before or even earlier). Marinate the chicken for at least 12 hours. Prepare the Jambon Persillé. Trim all the vegetables. Cook and purée the celeriac. Prepare the bacon. Mince the parsley and chives and put in a bowl. Cook the pears and ginger. Cover and refrigerate everything.

- On the morning of the Feast: sauté the chicken, bacon, mushrooms, pearl onions or shallots, carrots and celery, and set aside. Add the marinade and its vegetables and cook for about 30 minutes. Cool.

- One hour before the Feast: remove the fat from the chicken juices. Remove the skin from the chicken. Toast the *croûtons* and leave them in the turned-off oven. Prepare the salad dressing and salad bowl.
  7.30 Your first guests arrive.
  8.00 Finish the Coq au Vin according to the recipe. Reheat the Celeriac Purée on a low heat. Boil the potatoes.
  8.30 Turn off the Coq au Vin, Celeriac Purée and potatoes. Light the candles. Ask your guests to be seated at the table. Bring the Jambon Persillé to the table.
  8.45 Reheat the toast for a minute and finish according to the recipe. Wrap the covered Coq au Vin casserole in a pretty tea-towel. Pour the potatoes into a basket. Pour the Celeriac Purée into a dish. If possible, place these on a tea-trolley along with the bowl of minced parsley, the plate of *croûtons*, tossed salad and warm plates.
  9.00 Take everything to the dining-room and serve.
  9.30 Clear the dinner plates. Bring the cooked pears. Pass the crème fraîche bowl round the table with 2 plates of thin biscuits.

LEFT-OVERS

1. Omelette: drain the pieces of chicken. Debone and chop up the meat. Mix it with a few tablespoons of parsley, a few eggs, and salt and pepper. Cook as an omelette and dot with butter before serving.

2. Croquettes: chop up the left-over chicken. Mix with the left-over Celeriac Purée and a few left-over potatoes, mashed. Mix in salt, pepper and 2 eggs. Make some flattened little balls, roll them in breadcrumbs and fry until golden crisp.

3. Reheat gently all the Coq au Vin left-overs. Add a cup of boiled sliced carrots and boiled sliced potatoes at the last minute and serve sprinkled with chives or parsley.

4. The left-over chicken meat with the mushrooms, onions and bacon can be gently reheated in their own sauce and used as sauce over hot pasta.

Couscous

A fragrant meat and vegetable stew.

SUGGESTED MENU
Olives Sautées
Roasted Almonds
Couscous
Compote de Poires
Rosé

Steamed vegetables, crisp herb-seasoned shish kebabs, warm chick-peas and a spicy tomato sauce are served with the fluffy, steamed, hard wheat couscous grain.

It is, of course, a celebrated North African dish, but sunny, spicy, exotic Couscous has in the last decades become one of France's national dishes, as much as Pot-au-Feu or Onion Soup. Couscous is one of the choices whenever a spectacular extravaganza is needed. Everyone – including grandmothers, infants and the most severe nutrition-minded guests – can indulge happily in Couscous because it is made with the best wheat grain and offers a variety of fresh vegetables. The chick-peas are full of nutritive qualities; the grilled lamb in the stew is meticulously lean and tasty; the tomato sauce is barely cooked. In short, all the ingredients of a major Couscous Feast are thoroughly healthy.

Far from a fickle fashion or a silly experiment, this traditional dish is as satisfying as it is exalting. It is the kind of meal you leave quoting the old proverb: 'Fate cannot harm me; I have dined today.'

The word 'couscous' probably comes from the sound made by the steam passing through the perforated tray and the bubbling of the broth. Like Pot-au-Feu, Cassoulet and Bouillabaisse, it is one of those great dishes that can be done in a more or less elaborate way. A large variety of vegetables may be included: courgettes, broad beans, chilli peppers, artichoke bottoms, aubergines, leeks, turnips, carrots. A few highly seasoned meatballs may be cooked in the broth. A large piece of lamb ribs sprinkled with herbs and grilled, a few fiery *merquez*, the thin, spicy sausage, onions, bacon and peppers, shish kebabs or a cumin-flavoured beef, lamb and vegetable stew may be added to the steamed vegetables and the couscous grain for an opulent display.

The only drawback of this truly sumptuous dish is that it can be very messy to eat. Along with the pile of couscous grain, there are many vegetables on the plate. Then, when the various stews are added, the plate tends to turn into a mushy battlefield full of lamb, beef and chicken bones. It can make for a difficult situation to tend to with grace at a dinner table.

And so I have selected my favourite rendering of Couscous. The flavours, variety and abundance are there, but the bones, fat and gristle are not. The steaming pyramid of fluffy grain can be enjoyed as a gentle counterpoint to the fragrant dishes of meats and vegetables and the fiery sauce. There is diversity in colour: red, green, orange, white. For variety of texture there is boiled as well as grilled meat, crisp vegetables and soft vegetables. For complements of flavour there are bland grain and bland vegetables, fiery stew and fiery sauce.

A philosopher once declared that life was an effort that deserved a better cause. The following preparations may also seem like an elaborate effort, but to all Couscous food groupies, such an end amply justifies the means. If you do not have a couscoussière – a pottery or stainless-steel pot with a perforated top – use a multi-tiered steamer or a colander fitted on top of a saucepan of boiling water. The main thing is for the steam to escape through the perforated tray and the couscous grain not to touch the boiling water.

FOR 8 PEOPLE

CHICK-PEAS

> 1 lb/450 g chick-peas
> 4 shallots or young onions, minced (about 3 tbsp)
> 2 fl oz/50 ml olive oil
> Salt
> Freshly ground pepper to taste

MEAT AND VEGETABLE STEW

4 tbsp olive oil
1 oz/25 g unsalted butter
3 lb/1.25 kg beef, chuck or round, cut into 2-in/50-mm pieces and
    trimmed of fat
3 lb/1.25 kg beef short ribs, trimmed of fat
3 lb/1.25 kg lamb shank, trimmed of fat
2 onions, peeled and sliced
1 large green pepper, seeded and cut into 1-in/25-mm squares
1 aubergine (1–1½ lb/450–675 g) cut into 2-in/50 mm chunks
2 courgettes (approximately 8 oz/225 g), cut lengthways and sliced
    into 2-in/50-mm chunks
3 cloves garlic, peeled and sliced
2 large beef bones (ask the butcher to cut into 4- or 5-in/100- or
    125-mm long pieces)
3 bay leaves
Sprig of thyme
1⅔–2 ¼ pt/900 ml/1.4 l water or beef broth
1–2 tbsp cumin powder
Salt
Freshly ground pepper
Tabasco
2 tbsp minced fresh coriander or parsley

SHISH KEBABS

7–8 lb/3–3.5 kg leg of lamb, trimmed and boned (approximately 4
    lb/1.8 kg of meat remain)
5 slices (about 8 oz/225 g) lean bacon ¼-in/6-mm thick, with rind
    removed and cut into 1-in/25-mm pieces
5 small onions, peeled and quartered
2 green peppers, seeded, trimmed and cut into 1-in/25-mm pieces
2 tbsp mixed dried herbs (such as thyme, oregano, rosemary)
3 tbsp olive oil
Juice of 2 lemons

TOMATO SAUCE

1 medium onion, peeled and finely chopped
2 tbsp olive oil
1 lb 12 oz/794 g can tomatoes with their juices
2 cloves garlic, peeled and crushed
3 bay leaves
Salt
Freshly ground pepper
For flavouring the sauce:
2 cloves garlic, peeled and finely chopped
½ tsp ground cumin

½ tsp ground coriander
½ tsp powdered ginger
1 tsp Tabasco sauce
4 fl oz/100 ml virgin olive oil
3 tbsp finely chopped parsley
Salt
Freshly ground pepper

STEAMED VEGETABLES

4 small onions, peeled and halved
8 carrots, peeled and cut into 4-in/100-mm sticks
2 turnips, peeled and quartered
3 stalks celery, cut into 4-in/100-mm sticks
4 courgettes, cut lengthways and then into 1-in/25-mm slices
4 large leeks (white only), cut in half lengthways and then into
  4-in/100-mm long pieces; tie together with string in a neat bundle
  for easy handling
4 bulbs fennel, cored and quartered

COUSCOUS GRAIN

2 lb/900 g hard wheat medium or fine couscous grain (fine is generally
  more delicate and makes for a fluffier dish, but I find medium safer
  and more interesting in texture and taste)
12 fl oz/350 ml water
2 tsp salt
2 oz/50 g butter (approximately)
5 tbsp olive oil (approximately)

GARNISH

Watercress

Begin to prepare the Couscous elements the day before the Feast.

To prepare the chick-peas, soak them overnight in cold water. Drain and place the chick-peas in a large saucepan with enough cold water to cover. Bring the water to a boil, lower the heat, and simmer for 1½–2 hours, until tender but not mushy. Drain and discard the water. Cool. Add the minced shallots, olive oil, salt and pepper. Cover and refrigerate until ready to reheat for serving. (The chick-peas can be prepared to this point up to 3 days in advance.)

To prepare the stew, heat the oil and butter in a large frying pan and sauté the pieces of meat in small batches for about 5 minutes, making sure they brown on all sides. Drain the browned meat on paper towels and transfer the pieces to a deep casserole. Reserve.

To the same pan, add the onions, green pepper, aubergines and courgettes. Cook over medium heat about 10 minutes, until all the vegetables are soft. Remove the vegetables with a slotted spoon to paper towels to drain. When cool, transfer to a bowl, cover and refrigerate.

Add the garlic, beef bones, bay leaves, thyme and water or broth to the pieces of sautéd meat in the casserole. Sprinkle with cumin. Cover, bring to a boil, then simmer for 2 hours, removing the lid for the last hour. Cool, cover and refrigerate.

To prepare the shish kebabs, alternate pieces of lamb, bacon, onion and green pepper on 10 or 12 large skewers. Set the kebabs in a shallow dish and season with the herbs. Pour over the olive oil and lemon juice. Cover and set aside in the refrigerator until ready to cook.

To prepare the tomato sauce, cook the chopped onion in the oil for about 10 minutes, until soft. Add the tomatoes, garlic, bay leaves, salt and pepper. Bring the liquid to a boil, then lower the heat and simmer for 5 minutes, uncovered. Remove the bay leaves, put the sauce in a blender and process until smooth. Set aside to cool.

Meanwhile, prepare the flavouring for the sauce. In a small bowl, combine the garlic, cumin, coriander and ginger. Stir in the Tabasco, olive oil and parsley. Season with salt and pepper.

Add to cooled tomato sauce. Cover with cling film and refrigerate.

Prepare the vegetables, cover with cling film and refrigerate.

On the day of the Feast, 2 hours before the meal, take the chick-peas, sautéd meat, cooked vegetables, shish kebabs, tomato sauce and prepared raw vegetables out of the refrigerator. At this point you can begin to assemble the meal. First, spread the couscous grain into a wide shallow bowl or on to a big round tray. Sprinkle with 8 fl oz/ 225 ml of water to which has been added 2 teaspoons of salt. Toss with your hands and make sure all the grains are wet. Let it rest for 30 minutes.

Meanwhile, remove the fat from the top of the meat stew and all visible gristle and fat on the meat. Discard the bones and bay leaves. Bring to a boil, then add the sautéd vegetables. Lower the heat and simmer, covered, for 30 minutes. Check and correct seasoning with salt, pepper and cumin. Set aside and keep warm.

Place all the trimmed raw vegetables in the first perforated tray of a multi-tiered steamer. Cover and steam over boiling water for 30 minutes, or until tender.

Heat the plates. Reheat the meat and vegetable stew in one saucepan, and the chick-peas with some broth in another saucepan.

Fill the bottom part of the steamer (or couscoussière) with water again and bring it to a boil.

Line the top tray with a piece of folded cheesecloth. Spoon the couscous grain on it, fold the four corners of the cloth together loosely and steam for 20 minutes.

Turn off the heat, open the cheesecloth and with a fork break any lumps of couscous. Sprinkle with the remaining water, a little salt, 1 tablespoon of olive oil and 1 tablespoon of butter. Toss with 2 forks so each grain is coated. If you see any lumps, roll the grain between your fingers quickly and lightly so you don't burn yourself. Grains should be separated. Cover and let it rest for 20 minutes.

Grill the shish kebabs for about 5 minutes on each side.

Pour some of the cooking broth from the meat and the vegetable stew into a serving bowl, then pour the meat and vegetables into a deep serving dish. Sprinkle with fresh coriander or parsley. Cover and place on the tea-trolley.

Take the vegetables out of the steamer tray and place them in a long serving dish. Pour a spoon of hot stew broth over them, cover and place on the trolley.

Remove the couscous grain from the steamer tray. Open the cheesecloth, toss in the remaining butter and oil, and roll with your fingers or with 2 forks, making sure all is fluffy and there are no lumps. If it is too warm, roll the grain in a clean tea-towel.

Pour the couscous grain into a wide bowl, spoon a little hot broth over it. Cover and place on the trolley. Place the chick-peas in a dish and then on the trolley.

Place the shish kebabs in a narrow dish so it fits on your trolley and place some watercress in a corner. Place the tomato sauce in a bowl on a tray along with a bowl of steaming cooking broth and a bowl of Tabasco mixed with broth.

Light the candles. Ask your guests to be seated at the table.

Remove the covers from all the dishes, add the warm plates to the tea-trolley and roll it into the dining-room.

Make sure everybody sees the splendid display, then either ask your guests to help themselves or serve them yourself, placing on each warm plate 2–3 tablespoons of fluffy couscous, a shish kebab, a twig of watercress, a few steamed vegetables, some chick-peas and 2 tablespoons of the meat and vegetable stew.

Pour a little broth over everything. Sprinkle some coriander or parsley over the meat and pass a plate to each guest. Pass round the tray with the hot broth and spicy tomato sauce. Meanwhile, return the left-over meat, vegetables and broth to the kitchen to keep warm until you offer second helpings. This time pass the serving dishes round the table along with the 2 bowls of seasonings.

WINE

A very chilly rosé wine or a hearty red wine.

WHAT TO SERVE BEFORE AND AFTER COUSCOUS

HORS-D'OEUVRES TO BE SERVED WITH THE DRINKS

1. A few Crudités and warm nuts
2. Pissaladière
3. Olives Sautées

DESSERTS

1. Compote de Poires
2. Granité au Vin
3. Mélange de Fruits with Panier de Frivolités, if you have time to prepare them
4. Tarte Tatin aux Poires et aux Pommes

TABLE DECORATION

Couscous, with its golden dome of grain, its stews and its sauces, will make for a busy table even if you use a tea-trolley to serve from, so make the centre-piece as visible and as attractive as possible but keep it quite small.

A pyramid of oranges, tangerines and kumquats piled on a flat basket and then dotted with streams of winding greenery or cut flowers would be lovely. You may also like to use a glass bowl filled with branches of candied dates, litchis on their twigs and kumquats, all very airy and light in the centre of your table. Position white candles round the centre-piece.

Choose a busy pattern with warm colours for the tablecloth; tomato sauce and the various stews will be passed round with more abandon and insouciance by your guests if you don't have a delicate, pristine cover. Choose big, dark, red, rust or brown cotton napkins. Place the bottles of wine in terracotta coolers or with a rust or brown napkin round their necks.

One basket of bread is enough because couscous grain takes its place in such a meal, but butter is needed on the table to use on the grain or on the steamed vegetables as a gentle counterpoint to the fiery sauces. Make sure there are enough butter pots round the table.

STRATEGY FOR THE SUGGESTED MENU

- Guests invited for 7.30 p.m.
- Meal served at 8.30 p.m.

- The day before the Feast: prepare the meat and vegetables, tomato sauce, marinated shish kebabs and chick-peas. Refrigerate. Trim the raw vegetables and cook the pears. Refrigerate.

- Early on the day of the Feast: prepare the olives, almonds and a few long-stemmed young onions or radishes. Leave to be warmed later.

- On the evening of the Feast:
  6.00 Take everything out of the refrigerator.
  6.15 Prepare and spread the couscous grain according to the recipe.
  7.30 Put the hot water in the bottom of the steamer. Your first guests arrive. Sauté the olives. Reheat a few almonds in the oven.
  7.40 Bring olives, almonds and onions along with a stack of paper napkins to your guests.
  Arrange the couscous grain in the steamer. Grill the shish-kebabs, turning once. Reheat the chick-peas. Gently reheat the meat stew with its aubergines, courgettes and peppers.
  8.00 Place the couscous grain in steamer.
  8.20 Finish steaming the couscous grain, cover and let it rest.
  8.30 Light the candles. Ask your guests to be seated at the table.
  Prepare the serving trolley. Add the final touches to the couscous grain and pour into a bowl. Pour steamed vegetables into a dish. Pour meat into another dish. Pour warm chick-peas into a third dish. Place broiled shish-kebabs on a narrow, flat dish or round the meat stew. Place the bowls of sauce and warm plates on the trolley and then roll the trolley into the dining-room.
  8.45 Bring one or two plates of second helpings of Couscous and leave on the table for easy serving.
  9.00 Change plates. Serve the cooked pears, crème fraîche and a plate of thin biscuits. You may add a bowl of store-bought bitter chocolate ice cream.

LEFT-OVERS

1. Reheat Couscous left-overs by steaming them or simmering them in broth. They improve and are better than on the first day.
2. Hachis Parmentier with the chopped left-over meats and a good potato purée.
3. A rich soup: chop up all the left-over vegetables and meats. Add a little water to the broth to reach the desired consistency.

4. Gratin: dice the left-over meats and vegetables. Add tomato sauce (⅓ spicy tomato sauce and ⅔ plain tomato sauce, or 3 canned tomatoes, drained and chopped) and stir. Check and correct the seasoning, cover with breadcrumbs and a little olive oil and bake at 325°F/160°C/Mark 3 until crisp (about 20–25 minutes).

Daube de Boeuf en Gelée

A highly seasoned, marinated and simmered pot-roast of beef served cold in its natural jelly.

The word 'daube' comes from the oval-shaped covered casserole tradionally used in Provence to prepare stews. This marinated and slowly cooked beef makes a splendid summer dish at an alfresco meal, but for best results you must prepare it at least a day and night ahead.

SUGGESTED MENU

*Crudités à la Tapenade
and à la Rouille*

*Daube de Boeuf en Gelée
Gratin Dauphinois
Green Salad*

Grand Baba

Bordeaux

An even simmering plus vibrant herbs and a carefully chosen piece of beef, at once a bit gelatinous and lean, will make for a splendid Daube. And since it is cooked many hours before you taste it, its flavours will have time to mingle and enhance one another, and the unmoulded dome of *gelée* will stand firmly.

The counterpoints of the fragrant Daube de Boeuf en Gelée are a crisp and bitter Green Salad (endive, rocket or dandelions mixed with other greens) and a luscious Gratin Dauphinois. This menu is so effective and so glorious that your guests will leave your table convinced that the world is a perfect place created only to provide them with endless ineffable pleasures.

Don't forget that if you prepare the dish too late and the *gelée* is too runny, you may, of course, serve it as a warm dish. And for your singing tomorrows, the left-over Daube can be reheated again and again for everyone's happiness.

FOR 8 PEOPLE

MARINADE

> *1 ⅔ pt /900 ml dry white wine*
> *8 fl oz/225 ml red wine vinegar*

2 tbsp cognac or *eau de vie* or *brandy* or gin
2 tbsp olive oil
2 tsp dried thyme or *a few sprigs fresh thyme*
1 carrot, peeled and sliced
2 cloves garlic, peeled and crushed
2 bay leaves
10 juniper berries (optional but lovely)

MEAT

5 lb/2.25 kg lean, trimmed rump roast, cut into ½ × 1 in/12 × 25 mm
   pieces (make sure meat has no nerve, fat or gristle)
Salt
Freshly ground pepper
4 fl oz/100 ml olive oil and vegetable oil, approximately (enough to
   sauté meat)
8 oz /225g lean salt pork or lean slab bacon, with rind removed and
   diced into ¼-in/6-mm pieces
3 cups onions (about 2 lb/900 g), peeled and sliced
4 cloves garlic, peeled and crushed
5 bay leaves
2 sage leaves
2 tsp dried thyme or 1 large sprig fresh thyme
2 cloves
1 veal bone, cracked (optional)
2-in/50-mm piece dried orange rind or 4-in/100-mm piece fresh
   orange rind
Bundle of parsley stems and leaves tied with a string
1 tsp ground ginger or 2-in/50-mm chunk fresh ginger
10 peppercorns
Salt
3 cups carrots (about 1 lb/450 g), peeled and thickly sliced
5 large tomatoes (about 2 lb/900 g), peeled, seeded and chopped
4 fl oz/100 ml Madeira, port or a good sweet sherry
½ cup firm green olives
½ cup black olives, pitted
3 tbsp chopped flat parsley
Tiny stems of parsley leaves

SAUCE

3 anchovy fillets
2 firm tomatoes, peeled, deseeded and diced
2 tbsp capers
Pinch of freshly ground pepper
8 fl oz/225 ml olive oil
1 tbsp parsley, basil or chives, cut with scissors (not too fine)

ACCOMPANIMENTS

> *Gratin Dauphinois*
> *Green Salad with a vinaigrette dressing*

Start the cooking on the morning of the day before you have your Feast. Combine all the ingredients for the marinade. Place the cut meat in a large bowl, sprinkle it with salt and pepper, add the marinade, cover with cling film, and keep in the refrigerator at least 4 hours or overnight, turning the pieces 3 or 4 times.

When you are ready to start cooking, drain the meat and reserve the marinade. Carefully dry each piece of meat with a paper towel. Heat 3 tablespoons of olive and vegetable oil in a thick-bottomed frying pan and sauté the pieces of meat over high heat on all sides to brown. Lower the heat and cook a few minutes more. You will have to do this in 2 or 3 batches. Pour the sautéed meat into a bowl and set aside.

Add a little oil to your frying pan and sauté the diced pork and onions for a few minutes; pour into the enamelled cast-iron casserole. Add the sautéed pieces of beef, garlic, 2 of the bay leaves, sage, thyme, cloves, veal bone, orange rind, bundle of parsley stems, ginger, peppercorns and salt to the casserole. Cook for a few minutes, stirring once, and then add the marinade. The liquid should barely cover the meat. Bring slowly to a boil, uncovered, lower the heat, cover and simmer for 2 to 2½ hours.

Add the carrots and tomatoes, cover and cook 1 hour more, or until a fork easily pierces the beef. Add the Madeira or sweet wine. Cook for a few minutes uncovered and then turn off the heat. Let cool completely.

Remove as much of the fat floating on the top as you possibly can. Correct the seasoning. Discard the bay leaves, peppercorns, bundle of parsley and orange rind.

Rinse a large bowl or 2 charlotte moulds with cold water. Place the 3 remaining bay leaves in the bottom of the dish. Surround the bay leaves with a circle of cooked carrot slices from the pot, followed by a wider circle of green olives and another of black olives. Finally use 1 tablespoon or more of chopped parsley to cover any open space on the bottom of the bowl or mould. Press gently against these garnishes with your hands so they will adhere to the dish. Taking great care not to disturb the decorative layer, place the pieces of beef, cooked vegetables and cooking liquid in the bowl. Press gently against the surface with your hand so any trapped air escapes. Cover the top of the mould with a piece of cling film and refrigerate overnight or longer (up to 2 days).

A few minutes before serving the Daube de Boeuf en Gelée, dip a tea-towel in hot water, squeeze it and spread it round the bottom and sides of the bowl for a second. Pass a knife round the edges to loosen the jellied meat. Place a wide plate on top of the bowl (or moulds) and, holding tight to the edges of the bowl and the sides of the plate, turn them upside down in one decisive and steady movement. Your dome of jellied Daube should detach easily and stand proudly on the plate. If you are using the charlotte moulds, proceed in the same calm way with one after the other, placing each dome on its own plate.

Prepare the cold sauce. Crush the anchovy fillets with a fork. Mix the tomatoes, capers, pepper and oil in a bowl. Add the fresh herbs and stir gently.

Take the Gratin Dauphinois out of the oven and wrap it in a tea-towel. Surround the base of the Daube with a wreath of tightly gathered parsley leaves. Stick three 1-in/25-mm pieces of parsley on top like little flags and bring the Daube, Gratin, cold sauce and bowl of salad to the table.

Toss the salad with a vinaigrette dressing and leave it on the table with the cold sauce for your guests to help themselves when they choose.

When all the guests have seen the beautiful Daube dome, serve every plate yourself very carefully, using a wide spatula and a big spoon, and placing a section of crisp, mellow Gratin on each plate alongside the Daube. Have your guests help themselves to the sauce and tossed salad.

WINE

Any generous, full-bodied red wine, not a light one, preferably a Bordeaux, a Bourgogne or a Côtes du Rhône.

WHAT TO SERVE BEFORE AND AFTER DAUBE DE BOEUF EN GELÉE

HORS-D'OEUVRES TO BE SERVED WITH THE DRINKS

1. Crudités à la Tapenade and à la Rouille
2. Pissaladière
3. Two or three small, flat, cold omelettes made with tomato and basil, onions, and herbs or chopped spinach and cheese, cooled, then cut into little pieces and presented on a bed of small lettuce leaves
4. Paper-thin slices of sausage and Parma or good country ham with slivers of toast and thin breadsticks
5. A tray of cucumbers, peeled, cut lengthways and filled with Tapenade, then sliced into 1-in/25-mm pieces

DESSERTS

1. Grand Baba
2. Cervelle de Canut
3. Crémets aux Fruits
4. Granité au Vin
5. Mélange de Fruits
6. Flan au Caramel and a plate of thin biscuits

TABLE DECORATION

Daube de Boeuf en Gelée can be served as an outdoor informal dish or as the core of a more elegant indoor meal. Outdoors you may like to use a brown or faded green quilted tablecloth. A basket of crisp and enticing vegetables punctuated with long-stemmed spring onions or radishes makes a perfect centre-piece. Or place a piece of wicker filled with fruit in the centre for a simple, lived-in, drowsy, informal country feeling. Three pretty jugs for the wine, wood or terracotta salt and pepper shakers and candleholders, and a plain wooden tray for sliced bread would create a nice, lazy, summery feeling. You may also like to use some faded green baskets for the bread. *Note*: Let Monet, Renoir or Colette be your good angel and inspire you as you set your table – and your mood.

If you eat indoors, you may want to create a rhapsody in yellow: a sunflower yellow tablecloth, yellow butter pots, yellow crockery, yellow candleholders and a yellow basket filled with yellow fruit – grapes, plums, lemons, pears. And perhaps here and there a touch of blue or brown to counterpoint the dazzling yellow symphony. Set an engaging table, serene, cheerful and warm, and remain vigilant to avoid the very worst of sins in a Feast: overdoing things and looking pretentious and fussy.

STRATEGY FOR THE SUGGESTED MENU

- Guests invited for 7.30 p.m.
- Meal served at 8.30 p.m.

- Two days or one day and a night ahead: marinate the meat.

- The day before the Feast: prepare the Crudités, sauces, Daube, chopped shallots for the Gratin, greens for the salad, salad dressing and Grand Baba. Refrigerate.

- On the day of the Feast:
  6.45 Preheat the oven. Remove everything from the refrigerator.

Heat the milk, peel and slice the potatoes and prepare the Gratin Dauphinois and put it in the oven. Pour salad dressing into the bottom of a salad bowl and put the serving spoon and fork on top, and the salad greens on them, ready to be tossed later. Place wine, · water, bread and butter on the table. Place the basket of Crudités and bowls of sauces on the sitting-room table with drinks.

7.30 Your first guests arrive.

8.25 Unmould Daube on a plate. Light the candles. Ask your guests to be seated at the table.

8.30 Take the napkin-wrapped Gratin, tossed green salad, Daube and its bowl of sauce to the table.

8.50 Bring Babas to the table along with a small decanter of good rum.

LEFT-OVERS

1. Omelette: sauté a chopped onion in a little oil or butter in a large frying pan. Add the chopped left-over Daube and cook for 1 minute, stirring. Pour the beaten eggs (according to how much left-over Daube you have), salt and pepper, and cook a rich country omelette. Dot the top with some cold left-over sauce.

2. Croquettes: beat 2 or 3 eggs. Add the chopped left-over Daube and a boiled potato if you feel the mixture is too liquid. Form 2-in/50-mm balls, roll them in flour and fry in oil until golden.

3. Pasta and beef: dice the left-over Daube meat and reheat it gently in its sauce, correcting the seasoning. Cook the pasta and toss the warm Daube into the pasta. Sprinkle with a few drops of olive oil and grated Parmesan or Gruyère cheese. Serve at once.

4. Farcis: parboil aubergines, courgettes and tomatoes. Scoop out the flesh of each and chop the vegetables roughly. Add the chopped left-over Daube and correct the seasoning. Fill each vegetable shell with a teaspoon or so of the mixture. Sprinkle with breadcrumbs, dot with butter or olive oil, and bake for 30 minutes at 375°F/190°C/Mark 5.

Fondue Bourguignonne

Marinated diced pieces of beef and chicken dipped in a pan of hot oil and served with a variety of sauces.

SUGGESTED MENU

Pissaladière

Fondue Bourguignonne

Madeleines Tièdes aux Fruits

A Full-bodied Red Wine

The ultimate convivial dish – a cheerful gathering round a fire and a joyous ritual – Fondue will please all ages and will ensure a lively and friendly Feast. Generally, one burner will do for eight people if you have a round table, but you should have two burners if you have a long table. Prepare a variety of breads, many bowls of capers, pickles, sliced onions and gherkins, a plate of sauces and a set of long forks. Remember to warn your guests: anyone who lets a piece of meat fall into the oil deserves to pay a fine – a bottle of champagne, a bottle of good wine or the rendering of a song.

The following 'peasant' version of Fondue Bourguignonne includes marinated diced chicken breasts as well as diced pieces of beef. You may also want to include diced lamb.

The Fondue is served with a large bowl of tossed salad, a dish of warm potato crisps and a basket of tiny new boiled potatoes. It may be followed by a mixture of egg and grated cheese that each guest dips into the boiling oil until golden (see page 137).

Once more you will notice how a meal executed at the table brings joy and lively participation by all the guests sharing the good-natured ceremony.

FOR 8 PEOPLE

MEATS

> *3 lb/1.25 kg tender beef, with no fat or gristle, cut into 1-in/25-mm dice*
> *2 chicken breasts, cut into 1-in/25-mm dice*

MARINADE

> *Olive oil*
> *Peppercorns, coarsely cracked*
> *Thyme*

COOKING OIL

> *16 fl oz/450 ml vegetable oil*
> *Sprig of thyme*
> *1 clove garlic*
> *1 bay leaf*

GARNISH

> *1 cup gherkins*
> *1 cup onions*
> *1 cup capers*
> *1 cup black* or *green firm olives with pits* or *stuffed with anchovies* or *peppers*
> *1 raw onion, peeled and sliced*

CRUDITÉS *Select from list on page 25*

Place all the diced pieces of meat in a bowl. Sprinkle with olive oil, cracked peppercorns and thyme, and stir. Cover with cling film. Keep refrigerated and marinate for a few hours.

SAUCES

Meanwhile, select and prepare 3 of the following sauces.

1. Pistou: prepare according to the recipe on p. 47. Add a little oil or half a crushed tomato to make it more unctuous when you dip the meat in it.

2. Mayonnaise: make 3 bowls, using:

> *3 egg yolks*
> *1 tsp Dijon mustard*
> *18 fl oz/500 ml olive and peanut oil at room temperature*
> *Juice of 1 large lemon (about 4 tbsp)*
> *Salt*
> *Freshly ground pepper*

Put the egg yolks and mustard in a bowl. Beat with a whisk for 1 minute, until sticky, and slowly add the oil. Make sure the egg yolks are absorbing the oil.

When all the oil is absorbed, stir in the lemon juice to thin it. Season with salt and pepper. Divide among 3 different bowls and season each one differently.

Stir 1 tsp of curry powder into the first bowl of mayonnaise. Add salt to taste and more curry powder if wanted. Cover with cling film and refrigerate.

Prepare a Rouille, adding garlic and Tabasco to your second bowl of mayonnaise.

Add 4 tbsp fresh basil, chives, or flat parsley to the third mayonnaise.

3. Mix 6 tbsp soured cream, 1 tbsp Dijon mustard and the juice of 1 lemon until smooth. Correct the seasoning.

4. Dip 2 large tomatoes into a bowl of boiling water, remove the skin, deseed and place the tomatoes in a blender or food processor with 3 cloves garlic, 5 anchovy fillets, 10 pitted olives, 1 tsp capers, 1 tbsp fresh herbs, and some pepper. Blend. Correct the seasoning, cover with cling film and refrigerate.

5. Mix ½ cup pitted black olives, 2 tbsp olive oil and the juice of 1 lemon in a blender. You should have a smooth paste.

6. In a bowl, mash with a fork 2 hard-boiled egg yolks and 2 tbsp Dijon mustard until you have a smooth paste. Beat in 4 tbsp oil slowly, stirring so the yolks absorb the oil and turn into a thick cream. Add the juice of 1 lemon. Squeeze 1 tbsp chopped gherkins and 1 tbsp capers in a piece of cheesecloth to eliminate excess moisture. Add to the sauce. Stir in 1 tbsp minced herbs and 2 egg whites passed through a sieve. Correct the seasoning, adding salt and pepper to taste.

Cover the bowls of sauce you have prepared with cling film and refrigerate. Place the garnish – gherkins, onions, capers and olives – into little bowls. Cover with cling film and refrigerate. Peel and slice raw onion, cover and refrigerate.

Two hours before the meal take the marinated meat out of the refrigerator and place it on two plates surrounded with a few small leaves of lettuce or some parsley stems. Keep it covered with cling film.

Cook the tiny new potatoes in a saucepan of salted water.

Prepare the raw vegetables and place them in a basket or two.

Prepare the dressing for the tossed salad. Pour it in the bottom of a bowl, cross the salad utensils above it and place the prepared salad on top. Pour a bag or two of potato crisps on a baking-sheet and heat them for 15 minutes in the oven at 325°F/160°C/Mark 3.

When you are ready to serve dinner, heat the ingredients for the cooking oil in a heavy-bottomed saucepan on a high heat. When bubbling, discard the thyme, bay leaf and garlic and pour the oil into the fondue dish – over the burner (the oil level must never reach higher than two-thirds of the dish). You are now ready to start the meal.

Place on the table the two plates of diced beef and chicken, baskets of Crudités, bowls of garnish, baskets of bread, bowl of warm potato crisps, basket of boiled potatoes, bowls of sauces and the large bowl of untossed salad.

Each guest will have a long-handled fork to cook his meat. He will then transfer the cooked piece to a regular fork so he can dip it in the various sauces he has spooned on to his plate and not burn his lips in the process.

During the meal the plates of meat, Crudités, sauces, bread, garnish and potatoes are constantly passed round the table with the salad. Keep the flame at medium and add about 4 fl oz/100 ml of warm oil to the fondue dish in the middle of the meal.

WINE

A good red wine. People drink a lot with fondue, so prepare many jugs of water and many bottles of wine.

WHAT TO SERVE BEFORE AND AFTER FONDUE BOURGUIGNONNE

Since there is no first course served while at the table, offer the hors-d'oeuvres with the drinks.

HORS-D'OEUVRES TO BE SERVED WITH THE DRINKS

1. Gougère
2. Pissaladière
3. Sautéd warm almonds and hazelnuts
4. A plate of very small Farcis, to eat with the fingers
5. For an extravagant all-fondue Feast: Fondue Savoyarde, so the same setting is used twice.

DESSERTS

1. Madeleines Tièdes aux Fruits
2. Tray of cheese (but not if Fondue Savoyarde is a first course)
3. Grand Baba
4. Crémets aux Fruits
5. Tarte au Citron et aux Amandes or Tarte Tatin aux Poires et aux Pommes
6. Mélange de Fruits

TABLE DECORATION

It will be a very crowded table, so use a simple, bright cotton tablecloth or a brightly coloured American or vinyl-coated cloth but no synthetic fabric. Choose large, bright cotton napkins as well as some paper napkins, large simple glasses, a metal tray to place under the burners (just in case), lots of water jugs and wine decanters, a variety of pretty bowls for the sauces and accompaniments, and handsome baskets for the bread. Make sure your table is totally cleared before you bring the dessert, which should be substantial and pretty. Since there is no centre-piece, the colour has to come from the crockery and the tablecloth. No flowers and no candles, of course, with a Fondue.

STRATEGY FOR THE SUGGESTED MENU

- Guests invited for 7.30 p.m.
- Meal served at 8.30 p.m.

- On the morning of the Feast: prepare the Pissaladière, vegetables, salad; bowls of sauces; bowls of gherkins, onions, capers and olives; cubes of meat; Madeleines and fruit purées.

- On the evening of the Feast:
  7.30 Just before your first guests arrive, take everything out of the refrigerator: Pissaladière, meat, vegetables, Crudités, condiments, sauces and salad greens. Add the bread baskets, cold water, wine and butter to the already set table.
  Cook the potatoes.
  Reheat the Pissaladière in the oven at 350°F/180°C/Mark 4.
  8.00 Lower the oven temperature to 250°F/120°C/Mark ½. Bring the Pissaladière along with the drinks to your guests in the sitting-room. Heat the potato crisps in the warm oven.
  8.20 Heat the prepared cooking oil, pour it into a fondue dish over the burner, and place it in the middle of the dining-room table. Turn off the oven, remove the potato crisps, and place the Madeleines in the oven. Transfer the warm potato crisps to a side dish. Pour the boiled potatoes into a basket and bring them both to the table along with the plates of meat, baskets of Crudités, bowl of tossed salad, and bowls of gherkins, onions, capers and olives.
  8.30 Ask your guests to be seated and start the meal.
  9.00 Bring warm Madeleines along with fruit purées to the table.

LEFT-OVERS

1. Meat and green omelette: chop the left-over meat in small pieces. Sauté 1 chopped onion in 1 tablespoon of oil. Add the meat and when it is golden, pour a few beaten eggs, chopped parsley, salt and pepper over it. Cook on a high heat. Dot with butter before serving.
2. Meat sauce for pasta: make a thick tomato sauce. Sauté chopped left-over meat and 1 onion. Add to the sauce. Serve with spaghetti and a bowl of grated Parmesan.

3. Gratin: mix chopped pieces of meat with cooked rice, cheese and a little tomato sauce or 2 chopped, seeded and peeled tomatoes. Cover with breadcrumbs and a little olive oil, and bake about 30 minutes at 375°F/190°C/Mark 5.
4. Hachis Parmentier, page 147.
5. White gratin: make a thick white cream sauce and add left-over finely chopped meat. Pour the mixture between two layers of cooked macaroni. Cover with grated cheese, dot with butter and breadcrumbs and bake.
6. Farcis: mix cooked rice, 1 egg, a little chopped parsley and the finely chopped left-over meat. Sauté with 1 chopped onion. Fill parboiled courgettes and onions and halves of raw seeded tomatoes. Sprinkle breadcrumbs on top and bake.
7. Soup: add some left-over diced vegetables, 2 cloves garlic, a sprig of sage or thyme, and a bay leaf to the left-over meat. Cook with water, salt and pepper for 30 minutes. Serve with grated cheese or sautéd diced croutons.

Fondue Savoyarde

A cheese, wine and brandy fondue served with diced bread and a variety of vegetables.

Fondue Savoyarde is a warm mixture of cheese melted in white wine into which guests plunge cubes of crisp bread. This dish traditionally follows active recreation, but there is no need to ski a slope or climb a mountain to earn it.

There are some new things under the sun, at least in this realm. Besides the cubes of bread we could, for a lighter, more diverse and healthier fondue, prepare a basket of carefully cut raw vegetables and dip them in the cheese sauce. Since the Fondue is shared from a communal dish and kept warm at the table, you will need one large burner for eight people at a round table, and two burners if you use a long table. Custom dictates that whenever a guest drops his piece of bread or vegetable in the Fondue, he has a fine – generally a song or a bottle of champagne for the whole gathering to share the following week.

SUGGESTED MENU

Terrine aux Herbes
Toast and Gherkins

Fondue Savoyarde

Mélange de Fruits

Fruity White Alsatian

Note: The traditional cheeses for fondue are Emmenthal, Comté and Fribourg. A good quality Gruyère cheese is fine. You may add a little Cantal or even some Roquefort or blue cheese. You may also add a little mustard, a tablespoon of chopped chives or a pinch of curry powder. This 'varies the pleasures', as the French put it.

FOR 8 PEOPLE

ACCOMPANIMENTS

BREAD

> *Good white bread cut into ½ × 1 in/12 × 25 mm dice; about 10 dice per person*

VEGETABLES

> *1 large cauliflower, cut into florets, raw or parboiled*
> *4 carrots, peeled, cut into thick slices, raw or parboiled for 5 minutes*
> *2 heads broccoli, cut into florets and parboiled for 5 minutes*
> *Bunch of radishes, with 2 in/50 mm of stems on, if possible*
> *Bunch of spring onions, with green stem on and trimmed*
> *Several stalks of celery, trimmed and cut into 1-in/25-mm pieces*
> *10–15 new potatoes, boiled in their skins*

TOSSED SALAD

> *4 fl oz/100 ml vinaigrette dressing*
> *1 bunch watercress or a few leaves of chicory, washed and trimmed (about 4 cups)*
> *½ cup coarsely chopped walnuts*

FONDUE SAUCE

> *2 cloves garlic, peeled and crushed*
> *1 oz/25 g butter*
> *1 tbsp oil*
> *2½ lb /1.1 kg cheese, all or mostly Gruyère, grated (about 8 cups)*
> *16 fl oz/450 ml (approximately) dry white wine or fruity white Alsatian, such as a Gewurztraminer*
> *Salt*
> *Freshly ground pepper*
> *2 tbsp cornflour*
> *1 tbsp cold water*
> *Pinch of freshly grated nutmeg*
> *3 tbsp kirsch (optional)*
> *2 eggs*

Prepare 1 or 2 baskets of vegetables, setting red radishes, creamy white cauliflower, green broccoli and bright orange carrots side by side in a colourful display.

Divide the bread into 2 baskets.

Make the dressing for the salad. Pour the dressing in the bottom of a large bowl. Cross the salad utensils above it, then place the washed and trimmed watercress or chicory and a handful of walnuts on top. You will toss this later.

Thirty minutes before you serve your meal, place the cubes of bread in the oven at 250°F/120°C/Mark ½. Check the bread from time to time; it should become dry but not too crisp. Lower the temperature if necessary. Boil the potatoes in a saucepan of salted water.

Ten minutes before the dinner is served, prepare the sauce. Rub the fondue dish with the garlic cloves, then add them and the butter, oil, grated cheese and wine to the dish. Cook over a low flame, lifting and folding – never *stirring* – the mixture with a wooden spoon until it is totally homogeneous. The mixture is smooth, unctuous and fragrant; it must have the consistency of a warm custard. Simmer the Fondue for a few minutes, then season to taste with salt and pepper. Dissolve the cornflour in the water and add it. Add the nutmeg and brandy. Check the taste, then transfer the Fondue dish to the brazier in the centre of the table.

Each guest will spear a cube of bread or piece of cut vegetable with his long-handled fork, dip it in the hot Fondue, coat with the cheese mixture and then transfer it to a regular fork to avoid burning his lips. It is best to peel and slice a potato and pour a little Fondue over. The salad can be eaten with the Fondue.

After 5 minutes or so, add a little wine at room temperature if the Fondue sauce gets too thick.

In the middle of the meal serve *le coup du milieu*, a tiny glass of kirsch, to all the consenting adults at the table.

At the end of the meal, when there are only 2 tablespoons of Fondue left, add 2 eggs to the mixture, stir and ladle a bit of this soft mixture on to each guest's plate.

WINE
Have plenty of cold water on hand as well as fruity Alsatian or dry white wine and kirsch.

WHAT TO SERVE BEFORE AND AFTER FONDUE SAVOYARDE

HORS-D'OEUVRES TO BE SERVED WITH THE DRINKS

1. Terrine aux Herbes with an assortment of toasted bread and a bowl of gherkins

2. Caviar d'Aubergines
3. Pissaladière
4. Plate of Parma ham and spicy sausage slivers with a bowl of olives sprinkled with thyme.

DESSERTS

1. Mélange de Fruits
2. Granité au Vin
3. Poires, Pruneaux, Oranges au Vin Rouge et aux Épices
4. Assortment of sorbets piled in halved melon shells along with Panier de Frivolités

TABLE DECORATION

Since you cannot use any centre-piece or candles, and since your table will be very crowded, you should have a very bright and cheerful cotton tablecloth (not synthetic, it is too dangerous), large cotton napkins as well as a stack of paper napkins, pretty plates, and an assortment of lovely natural or spray-painted baskets for the bread, the boiled potatoes and the vegetables.

Note: A metal tray under the burners is a good idea for safety's sake and to catch drips.

STRATEGY FOR THE SUGGESTED MENU

- Guests invited for 7.30 p.m.
- Meal served at 8.30 p.m.
- The day before the Feast: prepare the terrine and the vegetables for the Fondue and greens for salad.
- On the day of the Feast: prepare the fruit salad in the morning. Refrigerate.
  7.30 Your first guests arrive. Toast the bread. Place the terrine and gherkin bowl on a tray.
  8.00 Boil the potatoes. Dry the bread cubes. Add the warm toast to your terrine tray and bring it to your guests with the drinks.
  8.20 Prepare the Fondue and bring it with baskets of bread and vegetables, salad, cold water and chilled wine to the table.
  8.30 Ask your guests to be seated.
  9.00 When the Fondue is eaten, clear the table completely.
  Bring the Mélange de Fruits and a tray of thin biscuits.

LEFT-OVERS

1. Hors-d'oeuvres: gently reheat left-over Fondue and pour over triangular pieces of toast. Sprinkle with lemon juice and a little chopped parsley before serving.
2. Cook some potatoes in a pan of salted water. Slice them, place them in an ovenproof dish and sprinkle with crushed coriander and a little salt. Reheat the Fondue, thinning it with 4 tablespoons of milk, if necessary. Pour over the potatoes and bake for 30 minutes at 325°F/160°C/Mark 3.

Gratin de Poulet au Fromage

Chicken fricassée seasoned with mustard, ginger and cream, cooked with leeks topped with cheese, and baked to golden.

Although this wonderful dish seems to be handed down by the gods to give meaning and pleasure to our Feasts, it is in fact just a present given from man to man.

The ingredients – mustard, cream, ginger, wine – Burgundian in spirit, are readily available. Because the chicken, prepared in advance, cools in its juice and is reheated later in its sauce, all flavours are enhanced to result in a truly delectable dish. Leeks and celeriac are a superb addition, but if they are not available, use chicory and turnips with the celery. This luscious preparation must include a variety of vegetables.

> SUGGESTED MENU
>
> *Poireaux Tièdes Vinaigrette*
>
> *Gratin de Poulet au Fromage*
>
> *Mousse au Chocolat Glacée Orange Sauce*
>
> *A Light Red Wine*

FOR 8 PEOPLE

FRICASSÉE

> *3 frying chickens, each cut into 8 pieces*
> *6 tbsp vegetable oil*
> *3 oz/75 g butter*
> *Salt*
> *Freshly ground pepper*
> *24 fl oz/675 ml dry white wine, or more if needed*
> *2 cups peeled and diced celeriac or turnips (approximately)*

*6 leeks or heads of chicory, white only, cleaned, quartered
    lengthways and then cut into 2-in/50-mm sticks (about 5 cups)
2 cups celery stalks, trimmed and cut into 2-in/50-mm long sticks
3 tbsp Dijon mustard
16 fl oz/450 ml double cream
Pinch of nutmeg
3 tbsp freshly grated ginger
8 oz/225 g Gruyère cheese, grated (about 2 very full cups)
Cayenne pepper
6 tbsp breadcrumbs
1 cup grated Gruyère cheese*

ACCOMPANIMENTS

*Fennel Purée or Broccoli Purée
Watercress salad*

On the day before the Feast prepare the chicken: discard the wings, lower part of the back, and extra bits of bones, gristle or skin (these can be used for broth). Keep only about 19 to 20 attractive, smooth pieces so when the meat is served in a thick sauce it does not hold any bad surprises for your guests. Dry each piece of chicken with a paper towel. If your guests are finicky, use only chicken breasts.

Heat 2 tablespoons of oil and 1 oz/25 g of butter in a wide frying pan and sauté the pieces of chicken, skin side down first, for about 10 minutes. Do not over-crowd the pan; the chicken should fit comfortably in a single layer. Turn the pieces to the other side with a pair of tongs so they brown evenly. Sprinkle with salt and pepper and set aside. Continue to sauté the chicken in batches.

Place the golden pieces of chicken in the casseroles in which 1 oz/25 g of butter and 2 tablespoons of oil are heating and cook on a low heat, uncovered, for 40 minutes, turning with a long-handled wooden spoon from time to time so all the pieces cook evenly. Pour out excess fat. Add a little white wine or a little water to the pans and scrape the bottom once or twice.

Meanwhile, prepare the purée you have selected. When it is cool, cover it with cling film and put it in the refrigerator.

Place the diced celeriac in a saucepan of cold water, bring to a boil and cook for 10 minutes. Drain and keep for later use.

Wash the watercress, wrap it in a clean tea-towel and keep in the refrigerator.

Heat 1 oz/25 g of butter and 2 tablespoons of vegetable oil. Add the leeks and celery. Sprinkle with salt and cook on a low heat until soft. Set aside for later.

Pierce the meat with a fork to check when it is done. When it is ready, transfer all the pieces of chicken to a bowl. Discard the fat in both casseroles. Add the rest of the white wine and with a fork vigorously scrape the coagulated cooking juices in the bottom of both casseroles. Transfer all the juices into a saucepan. Beat the mustard, cream, nutmeg and grated ginger in a bowl and add to the pan. Stir in the wine and cooking juices, then add the grated cheese, stirring slowly. Simmer for 1 minute; your sauce should be quite thick.

With a pair of kitchen scissors cut and discard any piece of loose skin or gristle left on the chicken. Place the pieces of chicken back in the casserole, sprinkle with salt and cayenne pepper, and pour the cream and cheese sauce over them, stirring delicately with a long-handled wooden spoon. Add the leeks and celery, and stir gently. Check the seasoning. This should be a pungently flavoured dish. Pour into 2 buttered gratin dishes. Cover with aluminium foil and put in the refrigerator.

On the day of the Feast, 40 minutes before you sit down to dinner, take the salad greens, purée and 2 gratin dishes out of the refrigerator. Sprinkle breadcrumbs and the cup of grated cheese on top of the gratins. Cover loosely with lightly oiled foil and bake at 350°F/180°C/Mark 4. A few minutes before serving, remove the foil so the top becomes crisp.

Warm the plates. Pour the purée into a saucepan and place it in a larger pan partly filled with water to prevent the bottom from burning while you reheat it. Or reheat it very carefully over a low heat, stirring the whole time.

Toss the watercress salad with the oil and vinegar dressing.

Bring the purée, salad bowl and warm plates to the dining-room. Wrap the 2 gratin dishes in tea-towels and present them to your guests to admire. Each guest should be served 2 pieces of chicken with its sauce and vegetables, then a portion of the purée and a little bunch of watercress salad.

WINE

A light red wine or a rosé.

WHAT TO SERVE BEFORE AND AFTER GRATIN DE POULET

HORS-D'OEUVRES

1. Poireaux Tièdes Vinaigrette
2. Crudités à la Tapenade, au Saussoun

3. Halved tomatoes and halved hard-boiled eggs stuffed with Pistou sauce
4. Pissaladière

DESSERTS

1. Mousse au Chocolat Glacée
2. Flan au Caramel
3. Granité au Vin
4. Washed and drained strawberries flavoured with lemon juice and sugar and served with a plate of Crémets aux Fruits
5. Grand Baba
6. Panier de Frivolités
7. Poires, Pruneaux, Oranges au Vin Rouge et aux Épices
8. Tarte au Citron et aux Amandes

TABLE DECORATION

The two generous gratins, the bowl of watercress and the purée will be most inspiring, so you don't need to search for effects. You may like to have a fresh *déjeuner de soleil* feeling and give a wink to the painter Claude Monet, his taste for great simple dishes and for the colours he chose in his Giverny house: blue, yellow and white. Some of the no-iron solid blue or yellow or flowered sheets are wonderful to cover your table. Avoid a decorated look; the room should have a nonchalant charm. There is no need for everything to match or comply with a scheme. You might want to use a nice polished wooden bowl or plain basket filled with a pyramid of pears as a centre-piece. If you own an old wire wine bottle carrier, you might fill it with glasses of irises, narcissi, daffodils. You could scatter blue, white and yellow candles all round, wrap a white napkin on the wine bottles' necks, fold the napkins in a fan shape and place a leaf or flower on each one. You might write the name of each guest on a dry eucalyptus leaf, too. Cocteau said that elegance is the art of not astonishing, so keep it good-natured and cheerful.

STRATEGY FOR THE SUGGESTED MENU

• Guests invited for 7.30 p.m.
• Meal served at 8.30 p.m.

• Two days ahead, prepare Poireaux.

• The day before the Feast: prepare the Gratin de Poulet, Broccoli or Fennel Purée and Mousse au Chocolat Glacée.

- On the day of the Feast:

  6.50 Take the Gratin out of the refrigerator.

  7.30 Your first guests arrive.

  7.50 Reheat Gratin in the oven. Reheat the Purée on a low heat. Prepare the salad and dressing, and place in a bowl ready to toss later.

  8.30 Light the candles. Bring cold water to the table and ask your friends to be seated. Bring in Poireaux Tièdes.

  8.50 Bring the Gratin, the Purée and the salad to the table.

  9.10 Bring Mousse au Chocolat and fruit to the table.

LEFT-OVERS

1. Croquettes: add an egg and a little fresh herbs to the chopped left-overs. Make small balls, flatten them a little, roll them in a little flour, fry in hot oil and serve piping hot with chopped parsley.
2. Crêpes: fill the crêpes with boned, chopped left-over Gratin. Add a little of the sauce. Dot the top of the folded or rolled crêpes with butter and bake in the oven at 350°F/180°C/Mark 4 for about 30 minutes.

Gratinée Lyonnaise

A sumptuous onion soup enriched with cheese, eggs, port and crisp croûtons.

Onion soup usually evokes sentimental or vagabond nights, racy late suppers where bons vivants rekindle their forces for new pleasures ahead. Yet in France onion soup traditionally is a family dish, the blessed solution to festive Sunday gatherings, because it is a splendid meal by itself.

> SUGGESTED MENU
>
> *Terrine aux Herbes*
> *Toast and Gherkins*
>
> *Gratinée Lyonnaise*
>
> *Tarte au Citron et aux Amandes*
> *Fresh Fruit*
>
> *Dry White Wine*

There are countless 'unique and authentic' renderings of this dish. Some cooks like only the flavour of onion and discard it from the broth after it is cooked; some like to see and taste the slices of onion; some like it puréed, and others, grated. Some like onion soup thin and light; some like it rich and thick. Some serve it in individual tureens; some from a large one. Some grate on a bit of raw onion; some add a little grated cheese; some spread a little onion purée on toasted bread before placing it on top of the soup. Some add a poached egg just before serving; some a chopped tomato. Generally Gruyère cheese is used, but some use Parmesan, and in some regions blue cheese is chosen for a more potent variation. Some add a little milk; and some a splash of white wine; some a tablespoon of cognac or port; some a drop of vinegar. Some alternate slices of toasted bread and layers of cheese and then pour the hot broth through a funnel into the pot. Each variation has its virtues.

My favourite version, which is both unctuous and crisp, comes from Lyon, the gastronomic capital of France. This is the one to serve whenever an extravagantly rich onion soup is chosen as the core of a festive meal.

The secret here is the browning of the onion in butter and oil, the slow simmering in broth, the addition of cheese (half slivered inside, half grated on top) and the final addition of egg, port and cognac just before serving.

In France a plate of raw oysters served with a shallot and wine vinegar sauce or a plate of thinly sliced Parma ham, hot sausages and a tossed green salad are the favourite counterpoints to this heady sweet and mellow soup.

Here again the proportions are for eight people, but since this is the main dish it should be abundant and left-overs are always welcome.

FOR 8 PEOPLE

GRATINÉE

> *4 pt/2.25 l home-made chicken, beef or veal broth; use water if you*
> *   have no broth and correct the seasoning later*
> *Twig of thyme*
> *2 bay leaves*
> *3 lb/1.25 kg yellow onions, peeled and thinly sliced (about 12 cups)*
> *1½ oz/40 g butter*
> *2 tbsp vegetable oil*
> *Salt*
> *1 tsp sugar*
> *1 tbsp flour*
> *16 fl oz/450 ml dry white wine*
> *24 slices of French bread (baguette), 1 in/25 mm thick, toasted on*
> *   both sides*
> *1 lb/454 g Gruyère cheese (3 cups grated, 1 cup cut in slivers)*
> *4 egg yolks*
> *3 tbsp cognac (optional)*
> *4 tbsp Madeira, port or sherry*
> *Freshly ground white pepper*

Heat the broth. Add the thyme and bay leaves.

Cook the sliced onions in the butter and oil in a large, covered frying pan until soft and golden. Sprinkle with a pinch of salt, the sugar and flour, and cook 5 minutes more on a medium heat, uncovered, stirring, until the onions and flour are brown. Do not let the onions burn. Pour the wine into the onions, stirring carefully. Pour the onion mixture into the broth pan and simmer 30 minutes more. Correct the seasoning. Cool. Cover with cling film and refrigerate.

An hour before the meal, preheat the oven to 400°F/200°C/Mark 6. Place the slices of bread on a baking sheet and brown on both sides until crisp. Sprinkle the toast with a little grated cheese and bake for 1 minute.

Spread the bottom of the tureens or soufflé dishes with the slivers of cheese. Pour the soup over them, cover with the toasted bread slices and the remaining grated cheese and dot with a little butter. Bake in a 350°F/180°C/Mark 5 oven for about 20 minutes. To brown the top, place under the grill for a second just before serving.

Beat together the egg yolks, cognac and port in a bowl with a pinch of white pepper. Bring it to the table with the tureen of Gratinée wrapped in a tea-towel.

Call your guests to attention: Gratinée Lyonnais, golden and crisp and preceded by a potent heady aroma, is a breathtaking sight. Then comes the ritual for all your guests to watch as you officiate. Lifting an edge of the cheese-and-bread crust with a fork, pour the egg yolk mixture into the hot soup and beat it gently to blend with the rest of the soup. This ritual is called *touiller*, and it has been known for years to soften the hardest hearts and wet the driest eyes.

WINE

A dry white (red is not advisable).

WHAT TO SERVE BEFORE AND AFTER GRATINÉE LYONNAISE

HORS-D'OEUVRES TO BE SERVED WITH THE DRINKS
1. Terrine aux Herbes
2. Crudités à l'Anchoyade
3. Caviar d'Aubergines with a basket of trimmed raw vegetables and breadsticks as a dip
4. A plate of thinly sliced Parma ham and thinly sliced Hungarian or Italian dry sausage wrapped round breadsticks or served with small slivers of toasted bread

DESSERTS

1. Tarte au Citron et aux Amandes
2. Cervelle de Canut
3. Crémets aux Fruits
4. One large ripe cheese such as Brie or Camembert, or three perfect Coulommiers or fresh *chèvres*, with one or two ripe fruits such as pears, figs, grapes or apples; or a large piece of Roquefort with black grapes, walnuts or pecans and a bottle of old port
5. Tarte Tatin aux Poires et aux Pommes

TABLE DECORATION

This rich meal deserves a lively and cosy setting. You may choose a thick, coloured tablecloth in shades of ivory, faded rose or green, with wide cotton napkins tied with green ribbons and a shallow bowl filled with fluffy ivory and tea roses. Scattered round the table should be a collection of small antique baskets or small antique boxes and plenty of faded green and beige candles. You might have pretty individual butter pots, two baskets filled with a variety of bread, jugs of cold water and at least two wine decanters.

STRATEGY FOR THE SUGGESTED MENU

- Guests invited for 7.30 p.m.
- Meal served at 8.30 p.m.
- Two days before the Feast: prepare the Terrine aux Herbes.
- One day before the Feast or on the morning of the Feast: prepare the Gratinée and Tarte au Citron.
- On the day of the Feast:
  7.25 Heat the Gratinée on a low heat. Warm the toast. Place the terrine, toast and gherkins on the coffee table in the sitting-room. Brown the bread for the Gratinée in the oven for a few minutes.
  7.30 Your first guests arrive.
  8.00 Bake the tureens.
  8.30 Light the candles. Ask your guests to be seated at the table. Bring the Gratinée and the egg and cognac mixture to the table. Mix in front of your guests and serve.
  8.50 Bring Tarte au Citron and a bowl of fresh fruit to the table.

LEFT-OVERS

1. Soup: add a little broth and a few sliced potatoes to your left-over Gratinée. Reheat on a low heat.

Hachis Parmentier

A rich beef, parsley, garlic, potato and cheese gratin.

When Antoine Parmentier was promoting the use of the potato in French cuisine, he offered its pretty blue flower to Louis XVI, and Marie Antoinette wore it among the jewels in her headdress. The regimes have changed, but the panache of the potato remains high in French cooking.

Of all the culinary creations bearing his name, Hachis Parmentier, which is generally made with left-over beef moistened with broth and mixed with mashed potato, may seem to be one of the most humble. Easy and cheap though it may be to prepare, Hachis is absolutely irresistible, particularly this version. It is made with raw beef, potatoes, cheese and an inordinate amount of fresh parsley, and it truly represents family cooking at its best. For decades this has been one of the most perfect dishes to offer when children, hungry adolescents and older people are gathered. Hachis Parmentier may be one of the ultimate crowd pleasers, one of those simple dishes you can serve and enjoy for ever.

When you prepare Hachis, double what seems like a fair quantity, since nobody can remain either sensible or sober in front of this fragrant, crisp gratin. Prepared ahead of time and reheated at the last minute, it is served piping hot from its napkin-wrapped baking dish accompanied by a large bowl of watercress seasoned with an oil and vinegar dressing.

Some people prefer to spread a beaten egg and a few dots of butter on top of the dish, while others draw lines in the potatoes with the tips of a fork for a wave effect. I like to sprinkle on breadcrumbs, grated cheese and a little olive oil for a crisp, golden crust. Although you will not say what an arrogant cook once declared – 'We have done so well that there is no possibility of doing better or of doing otherwise' – you may let your friends whisper it.

Hachis looks better when served in two gratin dishes, so everyone can have some of the fragrant crust.

SUGGESTED MENU

Pissaladière

Hachis Parmentier
Watercress Salad

Flan au Caramel

A Full-bodied Rosé

FOR 8 PEOPLE

HACHIS

> 3 onions, peeled and chopped (about 1½ cups)
> 4 cloves garlic, peeled and crushed
> 2 large bunches flat parsley, chopped (about 2 cups)
> 2 tbsp vegetable oil
> 3 lb/1.25 kg lean beef, freshly chopped
> 8 oz/225 g lean salt pork or bacon or country ham, chopped
> Salt
> 3 bay leaves
> 1 egg, slightly beaten
> Freshly ground pepper
> 5 lb/2.25 kg potatoes
> 1½ oz/40 g butter
> 24 fl oz/675 ml warm milk (approximately)
> Freshly ground nutmeg
> 8 oz/225 g Gruyère cheese, grated (about 1½ cups)
> 3 tbsp breadcrumbs

GARNISH

> A tossed salad of bitter dandelions or endive with crisp bacon or a
> tossed salad of chicory and watercress seasoned with olive oil and
> vinegar

The day before the Feast prepare the onions and garlic. Rinse and chop the parsley. (If you don't find the flat variety of parsley, add some other fresh herbs such as basil, chives and thyme with the curly parsley.)

Heat the oil in a large frying pan and sauté the beef, stirring with a wooden spoon so it crumbles and cooks evenly. After a few minutes pour into a dish and set aside for later.

Add the salt pork or bacon to the pan. Cook for a few minutes, until crisp, then add to the dish with the beef.

Add the onions to the frying pan. Sprinkle with salt, add the bay leaves and cook for about 10 minutes, until soft. Pour into the beef and bacon dish, and mix in the chopped parsley, crushed garlic and beaten egg. Check and correct the seasoning, adding salt and pepper to taste. Discard the bay leaves.

Heat a large saucepan of salted water. Add the washed, unpeeled potatoes and cook for about 25 minutes, until soft. Drain. Wearing oven gloves or using a tea-towel to protect your hands, peel the potatoes and purée them in a food mill or mouli while they are warm. Whip in the butter and then some warm milk. The purée should be quite moist. Correct the seasoning, adding nutmeg, salt and pepper to taste.

Butter 2 gratin dishes. Pour a layer of potato purée, a layer of the meat mixture and a top layer of potato purée in each of the dishes. Pat the top of the dishes with your wet hands or the back of a spoon. Sprinkle on the grated cheese and breadcrumbs, and dot with butter. Cover with cling film or foil and place in the refrigerator until ready to bake.

On the day of the Feast, 2 hours before the beginning of the meal, prepare the greens for the tossed salad. Pour the dressing into the bottom of a bowl, cross the serving spoon and fork on top, and then pile the greens on top of them. You will toss it at the last moment.

Take the gratin dishes out of the refrigerator and remove the cling film or foil. Forty minutes before you sit down to dinner preheat the oven to 350°F/180°C/Mark 4. Ten minutes later, put the Hachis in the oven and bake for about 30 minutes. Lower the temperature for the last 10 minutes if you see the top getting too brown. If your guests are lingering over drinks, cover the gratin tops with foil, lower the temperature to 225°F/110°C/Mark ¼, and don't worry.

Wrap a large tea-towel round each gratin dish and bring them, piping hot, to the table for everyone to admire and enjoy. Bring the bowl of salad. Toss the salad, place it on the table so everyone can help himself when he chooses, and either serve each guest with some Hachis or pass the dishes, each on its own tray, round the table.

WINE

Any red wine or strong rosé.

WHAT TO SERVE BEFORE AND AFTER HACHIS PARMENTIER

HORS-D'OEUVRES TO BE SERVED WITH THE DRINKS

1. Pissaladière
2. Crudités à la Tapenade, au Saussoun and à l'Anchoyade
3. Caviar d'Aubergines with an assortment of Crudités

DESSERTS

1. Flan au Caramel
2. Mousse au Chocolat Glacée
3. Poires, Pruneaux, Oranges au Vin Rouge et aux Épices
4. Grand Baba
5. A tray of cheeses with three ripe fruits

TABLE DECORATION

A simple fabric in either pretty natural-and-white stripes or a red or bright blue and white mattress-ticking cloth is what you might want to use on your table with solid-coloured cotton napkins.

Hachis Parmentier is not a messy affair, and since you have one dish for each end of the table, serving is easy and neat. Make sure each dish is wrapped with a large, pretty tea-towel or napkin, and place each on a small tray for easy handling. Fill a large flat basket with three or four potted geraniums as a centre-piece or fill a large bright ceramic bowl with aubergines, peppers, artichokes and fruits. Insert a few twigs of leaves here and there in the bowl.

If you have a pretty collection of old boxes, tins or mustard jars, you may want to fill them with cut flowers. Natural beeswax candles set in a round country bread or thin, tapered candles set in the centre of artichokes or cauliflowers may be pretty. Set the table with cheerful crockery, three wine decanters, two or three bread baskets and a jug or two of water for an easy, informal and confident Feast.

STRATEGY FOR THE SUGGESTED MENU

- Guests invited for 7.30 p.m.
- Meal served at 8.30 p.m.

- One day before the Feast: prepare the Pissaladière, Hachis and Flan.

- On the day of the Feast:
  6.30 Take everything out of the refrigerator. Lay the table and set out the bread, butter, wine and flowers. Prepare the salad.
  7.25 Reheat the Pissaladière.
  7.30 Your first guests arrive.
  8.00 Serve Pissaladière in the sitting-room and place the Hachis in the oven.
  8.35 Light the candles and ask your guests to be seated. Bring in iced water, the Hachis and the green salad.
  9.00 Bring Flan au Caramel with a tray of biscuits.

LEFT-OVERS

1. Croquettes: stir 1 egg, a few mushrooms and a little fresh parsley into your left-over Hachis. Form small balls and flatten them slightly with the palm of your hand. Roll them in a beaten egg and then in breadcrumbs. Fry in vegetable oil.

2. Omelette: you can add a handful of chopped basil or parsley and a few beaten eggs to prepare a flat country omelette. When it is cooked, brush the top with a little butter or olive oil and serve with a tossed green salad.

3. Farcis: parboil courgettes or aubergines, cut them in half, scoop out most of the inside pulp, mix it with left-over Hachis and then stuff the vegetable halves. Sprinkle with grated cheese and bake for 30 minutes at 375°F/190°C/Mark 5.

Jambon en Saupiquet

A fresh ham seasoned and marinated with herbs cooked to crispness, and served with a light sauce of vinegar, shallots and juniper.

Saupiquet is a medieval dish that comes from Burgundy. Traditionally prepared with a light sauce flavoured with tarragon and juniper, and enriched with a little cream, it is both sweet and tart, and totally delicious.

> SUGGESTED MENU
>
> *Pissaladière*
>
> *Jambon en Saupiquet*
> *Gratin Dauphinois*
> *Tossed Green Salad*
>
> *Poires, Pruneaux,*
> *Oranges au Vin Rouge*
> *et aux Épices*
>
> *Beaujolais*

In the following recipe, a fresh, unsalted, unsmoked piece of ham – in other words, part of a leg of pork – is used.

A 6–7 lb/2.75–3 kg piece of fine-grained pork on the bone, from the leg fillet or knuckle end, firm to the touch with very white fat, is perfect for our Jambon en Saupiquet.

'Tell me what you eat, and I will tell you what you are,' goes for pigs, too. Even if the pig you buy has not fed on chestnuts like those in Corsica and parts of France, or on cheese as in parts of Italy, it will turn into a sumptuous offering after being rubbed with salt, marinated with fragrant herbs and seasoned with this tangy sauce.

Make sure you cook the pork sufficiently: when pricked with a fork the juices should be clear. When ready to eat, the meat must be uniformly white or pale grey, with no more than the slightest hint of pink.

Left-over cold pork is delicious as is, and can also be used in a great many wonderful dishes. So make a generous display of crisp Gratin Dauphinois, fresh tossed salad and the glorious *pièce de résistance*: the plate of sliced ham under its lively, velvety sauce, with, if you wish, a little paper collar wrapped round its bone and surrounded by tiny apples and herbs. After their first bite, your guests will turn into Militant Piggy Groupies and dismiss the everlasting question, 'Are the only true paradises the lost ones?' with a contented sigh and another bite of Saupiquet. To enjoy fully the pleasures of the moment is the only thing on their minds from now to dessert.

Note: If time is of the essence and you want to improvise a reasonable facsimile of this, prepare the sauce, pour it over thick over-lapping slices of cooked ham and place the dish, covered with foil, in the oven at 300°F/150°C/Mark 2 for 30 minutes or so, until the sauce is absorbed and the pork is warm.

FOR 8 PEOPLE

MEAT

> *6–7 lb/2.75–3 kg raw pork leg or fresh ham, not deboned, salted or*
>   *smoked*
> *½ cup sea salt (approximately)*
> *10 cloves garlic peeled and cut into slivers*
> *1 tbsp coarsely cracked peppercorns*
> *5 bay leaves, crumbled or cut finely with scissors*
> *3 tsp dried sage*
> *3 tsp dried thyme*
> *2 tsp coriander seeds*

SAUCE

> *24 fl oz/675 ml red wine vinegar*
> *10 shallots, peeled and finely minced*
> *10 juniper berries, crushed*
> *5 fl oz/150 ml dry white wine*
> *16 fl oz/450 ml single cream*
> *Cracked peppercorns to taste*
> *2 tbsp fresh tarragon leaves or 1 tbsp dried tarragon*

ACCOMPANIMENTS

> *Gratin Dauphinois or Gratin d'Aubergines*
> *Watercress, lettuce and chicory tossed salad seasoned with a*
> *vinaigrette and garnished with crumbled egg yolks and minced*
> *parsley*
> *If possible, small crab apples and cinnamon*

Prepare the ham the day before the Feast. Remove the rind and trim some of the fat to leave a layer about ¼ in/6 mm thick. Rub the whole surface of the pork leg with the sea salt. Leave to marinate for 2 hours.

Rinse under cold water until the salt is removed. Dry thoroughly with paper towels. Make deep slits with a small sharp knife all round the meat and round the bone. Insert the garlic slivers and some of the peppercorns, bay leaves, sage, thyme and coriander into the slits. Coat the surface of the ham with the rest, pressing with your palms to make it cling. Cover with a piece of foil. Refrigerate overnight.

On the day of the Feast take the meat out of the refrigerator 4 hours before the meal is to be served. Preheat the oven to 450°F/230°C/Mark 8. Place the pork, fat side up, on a rack in an oiled, not too large (so juices don't burn) ovenproof dish. Cook for 5 minutes, turn and lower the oven temperature to 350°F/180°C/Mark 4.

Meanwhile, prepare the Gratin Dauphinois and time it to cook for 1½ hours.

Turn the pork over after 40 minutes and cover loosely with a sheet of foil. If using crab apples, core and peel them, sprinkle them with a little cinnamon and place them round the pork for the last 30 minutes or so.

Meanwhile, warm the plates.

Prepare the sauce. In a large, non-reactive saucepan combine the vinegar, shallots and juniper berries. Bring to a boil and reduce over high heat until most of the vinegar has evaporated, about 10 minutes. Cool. Pour into a bowl.

Prepare the tossed salad. Pour the dressing into a salad bowl, cross the salad fork and spoon above it, and then arrange the salad on top and leave covered with a wet cloth.

The pork is cooked when its juices run clear and its flesh retains only the slightest hint of pink. Cover with foil and allow to rest for 10–15 minutes before carving. You may want to staple a piece of white paper around the bone.

Pour off the fat from the roasting pan. Place the pan over medium heat on top of the cooker and carefully pour in the wine. Scrape bits in the bottom of the pan with the back of a fork. Bring the deglazed juice to a boil and reduce slightly. Pour in the vinegar, shallot and juniper berry reduction. Remove from the heat.

Place the ham on a large cutting surface and trim away the fat. Going against the grain, cut slices ½–1 in/12–25 mm thick. Arrange the slices, overlapping, on a serving dish and keep warm while finishing the sauce.

Gently heat the shallot, vinegar and juniper berry reduction and deglazed juices mixture. Add the cream and cracked peppercorns and bring to simmer. Correct the seasoning. Pour over the sliced pork. Sprinkle with tarragon leaves. Cover with foil and keep warm in the oven at a low temperature until ready to serve.

Call your guests to the table. This dish must be served very warm.

Bring the warm plates, salad, Gratin and pork to the dining-room.

Arrange 2 slices of pork, a cooked apple and 2 tablespoons of Gratin on each warm plate. Place the tossed salad on the table so every guest may help himself.

WINE

A Beaujolais-type red wine, quite light and fruity, a dry white wine, a rosé, or a Madeira.

WHAT TO SERVE BEFORE AND AFTER JAMBON EN SAUPIQUET

HORS-D'OEUVRES TO BE SERVED WITH THE DRINKS

1. Poireaux Tièdes Vinaigrette
2. Caviar d'Aubergines with warm toast, and Crudités en Panier
3. Pissaladière

DESSERTS

1. Poires, Pruneaux, Oranges au Vin Rouge et aux Épices
2. Oeufs à la Neige et aux Fruits
3. Crêpes Normandes

TABLE DECORATION

This is an unfussy table since the slicing of the meat and the spooning of the sauce over it have been done in the kitchen. Once everything is served the meal can proceed in an uninterrupted flow, so you may use whatever table setting you want.

Ham is traditionally served for Easter and Christmas, so any heavy 'theme' decoration is to be avoided here. You could perhaps choose a multiflowered cloth that falls to the floor, and over it a piece of lace or macramé (square if your table is round, rectangular if your table is long), covering only the top of the table. In the centre you could fill a round white tureen with poppies, anemones or buttercups. Left in the water for a few hours before the party, their stems will bend into whimsical shapes. Select bright napkins to match one of the shades of the tablecloth and tie each folded napkin with a piece of bright ribbon in a contrasting colour, and perhaps a leaf or a cut flower stuck in it. Beware of acute cuteness, but let your table be cheerful and pretty.

You may want to use plain white or pressed glass, terracotta or coloured crockery accessories for a *festin campagnard* feeling. Use natural baskets for the bread and a little yellow, pink or red napkin round the necks of your three wine bottles. Make sure there are butter pots, bread in baskets and two jugs of cold water on the table.

STRATEGY FOR THE SUGGESTED MENU

- Guests invited for 7.30 p.m.
- Meal served at 8.30 p.m.

- One day before the Feast: season the pork as indicated. Prepare the Poires, Pruneaux, Oranges au Vin Rouge dessert, the cooked onions for the Pissaladière, and the greens for the salad. Cover each item and refrigerate.

- On the day of the Feast: 4 hours before the dinner, take the bowl of cooked onions, the pork and the salad greens out of the refrigerator.
  5.30 Preheat the oven and cook the pork. Meanwhile, prepare the vinegar and shallot sauce. Prepare the dough and the Pissaladière.
  6.30 Prepare the Gratin. Prepare the salad and place on crossed servers above the dressing in the bowl. Bake the Pissaladière.
  7.00 Bake the Gratin. Turn the pork, cover with foil and add apples.
  7.30 Your first guests arrive.
  8.00 Bring the Pissaladière to your guests.
  8.30 Slice the pork. Reheat the sauce. Light the candles. Ask your guests to come to the table.
  Bring the Gratin, tossed salad, Jambon and its bowl of sauce to the dining-room.
  8.50 Offer second helpings; they don't have to be piping hot.
  9.10 Change the plates. Bring the dessert.

LEFT-OVERS

1. Hachis Parmentier, page 147.
2. Wrap the sliced pork in a piece of foil. Place in the oven at 325°F/160°C/Mark 3 to reheat. Serve with a spirited Vinaigrette, page 249, and boiled potatoes.
3. A hearty winter soup: dice the left-over pork. Add some lentils, cooked beans or chick-peas. Sprinkle with fresh herbs.
4. Cold: slice and serve with mustard and cold boiled potatoes, spring onions and raw celery salad.

Marmite Dieppoise

A spectacular stew of mussels, fish, shrimp, leeks and onions seasoned with curry powder, white wine and fresh herbs.

Dieppe is France's oldest seaside resort and one of the most interesting towns in Normandy for seafood lovers. History and geography define this dish: fish, shellfish and cream abound in the province, and the spices brought by the merchant ships long ago have made curry powder and cayenne pepper part of the local cooking for centuries.

SUGGESTED MENU

Crudités en Panier

Marmite Dieppoise

Cheese and Fruit

Muscadet

Marmite Dieppoise, a lusty Norman creation, is a sumptuous chowder prepared with a dry white wine. It is a simple dish to serve all year round. Although sole, prawns and turbot are sometimes used in restaurant versions, the traditional ingredients are easily available and make for a delicious, luxurious, dramatic one-dish extravaganza.

Prepared a day in advance, Marmite Dieppoise will gain in flavour and will be easy to reheat at the last moment.

There are many variations of this dish, but the following one is my favourite. Instead of thickening the broth with flour and butter, I add puréed celery and leeks: this makes the dish lighter, more fragrant and quite unctuous.

If your broth is very tasty and you truly cannot find fresh fish, then frozen fillets may be used, but the mussels must be absolutely fresh.

FOR 8 PEOPLE

INGREDIENTS

> *5 oz/140 g butter*
> *7–8 leeks, washed, trimmed, split and chopped*
> *Head of celery, washed, trimmed and chopped*
> *3 onions: 1 peeled and sliced, 2 peeled and chopped*
> *2 lb/900 g mussels*
> *1⅔ pt/900 ml dry white wine*
> *Salt*
> *Freshly ground pepper*
> *1 carrot, peeled and sliced*
> *Parsley, washed and chopped*

2 bay leaves
10 peppercorns
About 2 lb/900 g fish bones and/or fish heads
1⅔ pt/900 ml hot water
10 pieces fresh cod or halibut or haddock, cut into 4-in/100-mm
  chunks
10 fillets flounder or sole
8 scampi or 16 shrimp
16 fl oz/450 ml double cream
1–2 tsp good curry powder
1 tsp cayenne pepper
8 large scallops, trimmed and dried carefully
Juice of 1 lemon
8 thin slices of French bread or 5 slices of good whole-wheat bread,
  cut into 4 triangles, buttered and ready to be baked
2 tbsp finely minced chervil or parsley

Prepare the Marmite the day before the Feast. Heat 4 oz/100 g of butter in a thick-bottomed frying pan. Add the leeks, celery and sliced onion. Cook over a low heat for a few minutes, until soft. Purée with a food processor or blender; pour into a bowl and set aside.

Pour the mussels into a large sink of cold water and add 1 tablespoon of salt. Leave for 1 hour. Scrub the mussel shells with a hard brush and remove the beards. Place the clean mussels in a large saucepan. Add half the white wine, 1 chopped onion, salt and pepper. Cover and cook over a high heat for 5 minutes, tossing occasionally, until the mussels open. Drain. Pass the liquid through a sieve lined with cheesecloth and reserve for later use. Remove the mussels from their shells. Reserve 10 shells and place them in a bowl with the mussels; cover with cling film. Discard the other shells.

Heat ½ oz/15 g of butter in a saucepan. Add the other chopped onion, carrot, parsley, bay leaves and peppercorns, and cook for 5 minutes. Add the fish bones and fish heads if you have any and stir. Pour in the rest of the wine and the hot water, and simmer for 20 minutes. Pass through a sieve into a larger saucepan, add the strained mussel liquid and simmer for a few minutes.

Sprinkle the fish with salt and add them to the hot broth to cook for about 4 minutes. Add the fish fillets. Add the scampi or shrimp 1 minute later and cook 4 minutes more. Turn off the heat and, using a slotted spoon, delicately transfer the fish and scampi to a dish. Cool, cover with cling film and place in the refrigerator.

Add the puréed leeks and celery to the warm fish broth, stir, bring to a boil and reduce for a few minutes; you should have about 7 pt/4 l of liquid. Stir in the cream, curry powder and cayenne pepper. Check the seasoning and add salt or spices to taste. The broth should be highly flavoured. Let it cool completely, transfer to a bowl, cover with cling film and place in the refrigerator.

Heat the remaining butter in a frying pan. Add the scallops and cook for a few minutes. Sprinkle with salt, turn on the other side, sprinkle with salt, pepper and the lemon juice, and then turn off the heat. Let the scallops cool, then add them to the bowl of mussels and mussel shells. Cover with cling film and refrigerate.

On the day of the Feast, 1 hour before your meal, take everything out of the refrigerator. Preheat the oven to 400°F/200°C/Mark 6. Place the buttered slices of bread on a baking sheet and bake until crisp. Remove to a basket and set aside.

Reheat the broth gently in a large saucepan. Place the chopped fresh herbs in a small bowl. Heat the soup plates and the tureen.

Ten minutes before sitting at the table, add the cooked fish, fillets and scampi to the warm broth and heat for a few minutes. Pour the cooked scallops, mussels and mussel shells delicately into the warm tureen. Pour about 2 cups of the hot broth on top and cover to keep warm. Do not reheat them. Bring the tureen to the table.

Wrap a pretty tea-towel round the large saucepan of broth and fish, and bring it to the table with the warm plates, chopped fresh herbs and bread *croûtons*.

Don't let your guests help themselves to the Marmite: it is messy, and they don't know the variety to be sampled. This is a dish over which you should officiate. Serve at the table in full view so the whole process can be watched and admired by all and the pleasure of this luxurious dish can be fully appreciated.

Place a chunk of fish, fillet of fish, some scampi, 1 scallop, some mussels and a mussel shell in each plate. Ladle some warm soup on top, sprinkle on chopped chervil or parsley and add a few buttered *croûtons*.

When everyone has been served, pour what is left of your tureen into the saucepan. Cover and keep warm for second helpings.

WINE

A cool Muscadet, a white Burgundy, a crisp Alsatian wine, or any dry white wine served very chilled.

WHAT TO SERVE BEFORE AND AFTER MARMITE DIEPPOISE

HORS-D'OEUVRES TO BE SERVED WITH THE DRINKS

1. Crudités à la Tapenade, à l'Anchoyade, au Saussoun or Pistou sauce

2. Gougère
3. Terrine aux Herbes served with triangles of crisp country bread

DESSERTS

1. A tray of selected cheeses with a few ripe fruits
2. Crêpes Normandes
3. Tarte Tatin aux Poires et aux Pommes
4. Oeufs à la Neige et aux Fruits, with a plate of thin biscuits

TABLE DECORATION

There should be no extra frills, no fussy display here. The charm will operate and the conversation will start the minute the steaming tureen of Marmite Dieppoise appears.

You may like to set the table with a deep blue or an ivory-coloured tablecloth. Place a few large shells filled with tiny shells or pebbles here and there on the table. Or make a lovely fluffy fresh bundle for your centre-piece: wrap the bottom parts of three little potted ferns or short geraniums with a large piece of white muslin or cheesecloth and tie the gathered fabric loosely with two thin blue ribbons.

If you have a blue tablecloth and if you own a Chinese red lacquered box, you may want to fill it with big greyish-blue pebbles as a centre-piece, then place ivory-coloured candles all round.

Place the dinner plates (the soup plates are kept warm in the kitchen), napkins, soup spoons, forks and knives – all three are needed for a Marmite – on the table along with a pretty water jug, three bottles or decanters of wine and two or three baskets lined with a napkin and filled with a variety of breads. If you are serving at the dinner table rather than from a tea-trolley, make sure it is not too crowded once the saucepan and the tureen are on it and that there is plenty of room for you to serve each plate and pass it along easily.

STRATEGY FOR THE SUGGESTED MENU

- Guests invited for 7.30 p.m.
- Meal served at 8.30 p.m.

- One day before the Feast: prepare the Crudités and sauces, or the Gougère or Terrine, and the Marmite.

- On the day of the Feast:
  7.25 Take everything out of the refrigerator. Bring the Crudités and the bowls of sauce with the drinks to the table in the sitting-room.

7.30 Your first guests arrive.

8.00 Reheat the soup on a low heat.

8.15 Add the fish to the soup.

8.30 Ask your guests to be seated. Light the candles. Bring the Marmite and the warm soup plates to the dining-room.

8.50 Bring the cheese tray and the fruit to the table.

LEFT-OVERS

1. This stew reheats wonderfully. You can either add a little wine and serve it with fresh *croûtons* or, if you don't have enough left-overs, add diced potatoes, a handful of mushrooms and a little milk for a light soup.
2. Ramekins: add sliced mushrooms to the chopped left-overs, fish and shellfish. Stir in a little cream sauce. Pour into individual ramekins, sprinkle with grated cheese, dot with butter and bake for 30 minutes at 350°F/180°C/Mark 4.

Moussaka Provençale

A chopped lamb, herb and vegetable mixture served with fried aubergines and a light tomato sauce.

Aubergines are native to India, but ever since Arabs brought them to Spain, they have become a staple of Mediterranean cuisine. In Greece, Moussaka is served with a white cream sauce, but the version we use here is part of the traditional Provence repertory, which is lighter and more pungent.

SUGGESTED MENU

Crudités en Panier

Moussaka Provençale

Tarte Tatin aux Poires et aux Pommes

White Burgundy

Prepared in advance, reheated 30 minutes before the meal and served in two different guises – as a glistening dome and as a crisp gratin with a bowl of fresh tomato sauce – it is a sumptuous dish.

Note: If you have a large group skip the unmoulded Moussaka and prepare only two large gratin dishes. They will go directly from the oven to the table and will be easier to serve.

FOR 8 TO 12 PEOPLE

MOUSSAKA

>*4 tbsp vegetable oil*
>*2 oz/50 g butter*
>*2 lb/900 g mushrooms, cleaned, trimmed and finely sliced*
>*12 elongated purple aubergines (avoid the seedy black ones, if*
>   *possible), total weight about 6 lb/2.75 kg sliced in half lengthways*
>*Salt*
>*Olive oil*
>*2–3 onions, peeled and finely chopped (2 cups)*
>*3 lb/1.25 kg minced lamb*
>*Freshly ground pepper*
>*3 bay leaves*
>*4 cloves garlic, peeled and minced*
>*8 tbsp chopped parsley*
>*2 tbsp dried thyme or savory or oregano*
>*1 lb 12 oz/794 g can tomatoes, drained, deseeded and coarsely chopped*
>*3 eggs, beaten*
>*1 cup chopped fresh mint leaves (optional but wonderful)*
>*½ cup breadcrumbs*
>*½ cup grated Gruyère or Parmesan cheese*

SAUCE

>*1 lb 12oz/794g can whole, peeled, deseeded tomatoes or about 6 large*
>   *fresh tomatoes, peeled, seeded and quartered*
>*2 bay leaves*
>*1 clove garlic, peeled and sliced*
>*2 tbsp coarsely cut parsley leaves*

ACCOMPANIMENTS

>*2 cups cooked rice*
>*1½ oz/40 g butter or 2 tbsp olive oil*
>*Bowl of cleaned, trimmed watercress*
>*Vinaigrette dressing*
>*Juice of 1 lemon*

You can prepare the Moussaka the day before or on the morning of the Feast.

Preheat the oven to 400°F/200°C/Mark 6. Heat 2 tablespoons of the oil and 1 oz/25 g of the butter in a frying pan. Add the sliced mushrooms, stir and toss on a high heat. When they become a little less stiff, lower the heat, add salt and after a minute remove from the heat. Cool and set aside.

With a sharp knife make slits in the flesh of the halved aubergines, making sure not to cut them down to the skin. Sprinkle salt over the surface of each half. After 15 minutes, rinse each piece under cool water, dry with a paper towel and rub a little olive oil all over. Fill a large baking dish with about 2 in/50 mm of water. Bring to a simmer on top of the cooker. Place the aubergine halves in the baking dish, skin side down. Bake for 30 minutes, or until tender but not mushy. You may have to do this in 2 batches.

Meanwhile, heat the remaining oil and butter in a deep frying pan. Cook the onions until transparent and golden but not brown. Add the lamb and cook over high heat, stirring often with a wooden spoon. Sprinkle with salt and pepper. Add the bay leaves, garlic, 5 tablespoons of parsley and the thyme. The meat should be evenly cooked and crumbly, without any big lumps. Add the canned tomatoes. Stir with the wooden spoon. After 5 minutes turn off the heat.

Remove the aubergines from the oven. With a large spoon remove the flesh and place all the skins on a plate. Coarsely chop and sauté the flesh for 2 minutes in a frying pan with a little olive oil. Add the cooked mushrooms, the onion-lamb-herb mixture and the beaten eggs, and stir carefully. Correct the seasoning with salt, freshly ground pepper or a little thyme. Discard the bay leaves. Add mint if you have some.

Oil the charlotte mould and the rectangular gratin dish carefully. Line them with the aubergine skins, dark side against the sides, pointing towards the top of the mould, and slightly overlapping one another. Save any trimmings for the top of the mould. Press with the palm of your hands against the sides to make sure it is well lined, then carefully add the meat and vegetable mixture with a spoon.

Place a few aubergine slices or some of the trimmings over the top of the filled mould and cover with a piece of foil, making sure it is tightly closed. Place in the refrigerator.

Sprinkle the top of the rectangular gratin dish with breadcrumbs and cheese. Sprinkle a few drops of oil on top, cover with foil and place in the refrigerator.

Prepare the sauce. Place the tomatoes in a medium-sized, non-reactive saucepan. Add the bay leaves and garlic, cook for about 5 minutes, then cool. Check and correct the seasoning. Whip to a smooth purée in a blender or food processor. Add the parsley. Cover with cling film and place in the refrigerator.

Cook the rice. Add a little olive oil, cover with cling film and set in the refrigerator.

On the day of the Feast, 1½ hours before the dinner, remove the Moussaka mould and gratin dish, tomato sauce and cooked rice from the refrigerator and remove the cling film. Chop remaining fresh parsley and keep in a little bowl for later use.

Preheat the oven to 350°F/180°C/Mark 4. Place both dishes in a large pan containing about 2 in/50 mm of simmering water. Cover loosely with a piece of foil and cook for 45 minutes to 1 hour, until warm. Remove the foil for the last 5 minutes. It may be necessary to use 2 pans of water to hold the moulds.

Thirty minutes before the meal, reheat the rice in a saucepan or sauté pan with a little butter and a little cold water. Stir with a fork. Or, if you have space in the oven, spread the rice on a baking dish, dot with butter or sprinkle with olive oil, and leave in the oven at 300°F/150°C/Mark 2 for about 10 minutes, until ready to use.

Make the vinaigrette in a large bowl. Add the watercress and place the crossed serving tools on top to use for tossing later.

Place a large plate upside down over the charlotte mould and, holding the edge of the serving plate and the handle of the mould with both hands, turn them over together in a decisive movement. Let the mould sit for a few minutes while you pour the rice into a serving dish and sprinkle it with the lemon juice. Pour the tomato sauce into a serving bowl and wrap a tea-towel round the gratin dish.

Remove the charlotte mould very carefully. Pour a small line of tomato sauce all round the purple dome of Moussaka and place 3 parsley leaves on top.

Bring the moulded Moussaka to the table with the Moussaka gratin dish, rice, tomato sauce, chopped parsley, salad and warm plates.

Make sure everyone has time to admire the beautiful purple dome of Moussaka as well as the crisp golden gratin of Moussaka, then start serving. It is a dramatic and beautiful dish that must be seen whole before you begin to give each guest a little white rice, a ladleful of the Moussaka gratin, and a part of the Moussaka dome, sprinkled with a little chopped parsley over all. Pass the bowl of tomato sauce round for everybody to help himself.

Place the bowl of salad on the table, toss the salad carefully and let each guest help himself.

WINE
A robust red wine or dry chilled white wine from Burgundy.

WHAT TO SERVE BEFORE AND AFTER MOUSSAKA PROVENÇALE

HORS-D'OEUVRES TO BE SERVED WITH THE DRINKS

1. Crudités à l'Anchoyade, au Pistou, à la Mayonnaise Curry
2. Poireaux Tièdes Vinaigrette

3. Mouclade
4. Lentilles ou Pois Chiches en Salade
5. Olives Sautées

DESSERTS

1. Tarte Tatin aux Poires et aux Pommes
2. Flan au Caramel
3. Tarte au Citron et aux Amandes
4. Crémets aux Fruits

TABLE DECORATION

Follow your feelings and use what you have at hand. This is a very spectacular dish, especially when it comes in two different attires, and you should not worry too much about the rest. A flowered or paisley tablecloth with dark red or dark blue napkins would be pretty with the colours of the aubergine and tomato in the Moussaka.

In the centre of your table you may like to place a large copper, silver or brass dish filled with blue and red and ivory anemones, or a beautiful arrangement of dark grapes, red apples and yellow peaches with some foliage stuck among them and winding down the sides. Place dark red or ivory-coloured candles round it. Make sure the two baskets of bread are lined with a fresh napkin and that you have at least two decanters or bottles of wine and a water jug on the table. Once more, a trolley or a side table is useful when you serve the two Moussakas so that the table remains neat and peaceful. Make sure everyone sees the Moussakas before you start serving.

STRATEGY FOR THE SUGGESTED MENU

- Guests invited for 7.30 p.m.
- Dinner served at 8.30 p.m.

- One day ahead or on the morning of the Feast: prepare the Crudités, sauces, Moussaka, salad greens, cooked rice, crème fraîche, and Tarte Tatin.

- On the evening of the Feast:
  6.30 Take the Moussaka, rice, tomato sauce, salad greens and Tarte Tatin out of the refrigerator. Leave the crème fraîche in the refrigerator until you are ready to serve it.
  7.25 Place the Crudités and bowls of sauces on the coffee table in the sitting-room. Preheat the oven to 300°F/150°C/Mark 2.

7.30 Your first guests arrive. Heat the Moussaka gratin and the Moussaka mould in the oven.

8.25 Reheat the rice. Lower the oven temperature to 250°F/120°C/ Mark ½ and, after you take the Moussaka out of the oven, slide in the Tarte Tatin to warm. Reheat the tomato sauce. Prepare the bowl of salad.

8.30 Ask your guests to sit at the table. Light the candles. Bring the warm plates, rice, tomato sauce and two Moussakas to the table with the bowl of tossed salad.

9.00 Bring the warm Tarte Tatin and the crème fraîche to the table.

LEFT-OVERS

1. Gratin: put all the left-over Moussaka into a baking dish. Add a little tomato sauce to thin it, sprinkle with breadcrumbs and grated cheese, and then reheat in the oven at 350°F/180°C/Mark 4 for 30 minutes.

2. Croquettes: add 1–2 eggs and a little chopped parsley to the left-over Moussaka. Make into small balls, roll them in flour, and fry in a little oil until crisp.

Paella

A lusty dish of meat, chicken, fish, shell-fish, a variety of vegetables and rice seasoned with saffron and lemon.

With its lavish profusion of colours, textures and flavours, Paella is a perfect party dish, a perfect summer dish, a perfect buffet dish. Always popular in the regions of France bordering Spain, its appeal has spread throughout the country, and Paella, pushing back boundaries, has for the last forty years been totally assimilated into the French patrimony.

SUGGESTED MENU

Tomatoes and Eggs filled with Pistou

Paella

Mélange de Fruits

Sangria

No room for discretion or measure here, but a vital exuberant experience. Originally cooked outdoors and eaten with wooden spoons directly out of the pan, Paella is likely to include a wide variety of ingredients: snails, eels, duck, chicken, rabbit, cod, crayfish, frogs, pork, artichoke hearts, green beans. A less fierce and exotic recipe is now a fixture on most Parisian and country restaurant menus as well as in festive family gatherings. No exotic ingredients, but the *tour de main*, the know-how, makes for its quality, which is the story of a successful integrated marriage. Fish, meat, vegetables and spices mingle happily, and the rice absorbs and combines all the tastes.

Paella gets its name from the pan it is cooked in, and if you can find one, do buy it at once – it has dozens of uses. A very large porcelain or enamelled cast-iron ovenproof dish will do, but make sure it fits in your oven.

This extravagant dish brings great immediate excitement to the table. Intrigued and baffled by such variety and such abundance, your guests will sail through the meal under its charm and become part of the Feast. The proliferation of ingredients is essential, and you can vary them according to your taste and what your market offers.

Paella seems more appealing in spring and summer, and is one of my favourite outdoor meals. Small fresh artichokes, green beans and tiny peas are delicious with Paella. For a hungry group I would include chicken breasts, sausage, shrimp, prawns, hunks of monkfish, and peas, green and yellow peppers, onions and tomatoes.

It takes a bit of time and organization to get all the ingredients ready, but it is easy to prepare and serve, and truly impossible to ruin. One of the most joyous dishes to offer for a festive gathering.

FOR 8 PEOPLE

INGREDIENTS

    8 tiny baby artichokes, trimmed, parboiled, and cut in half
    3 large onions, peeled; 2 sliced, 1 chopped
    1 green pepper, washed, trimmed, seeded and cut into strips
      ¼ × 1½ in/6 × 35 mm
    1 large red pepper, washed, trimmed, seeded and cut into strips
      ¼ × 1½ in/6 × 35 mm
    2 tomatoes, peeled and chopped
    8 oz/225 g green beans, cut in half
    1⅔ pt/900 ml mussels
    Vegetable oil
    Butter
    5 breasts of chicken, halved
    Salt
    2 cloves garlic, peeled and crushed
    Freshly ground pepper
    4 fl oz/100 ml dry white wine
    1 lb/450 g fillet of monkfish, cubed
    1 lb/450 g chorizo (hot) or garlicky smoked sausage diced
    ½ cup peas

10 large raw shrimp in their shells
10 raw prawns in their shells
3 cups rice
½ tsp saffron
2¼ pt/1.4 l boiling water
2 lemons, cut into wedges

You can prepare the Paella the evening before the Feast.

Prepare the vegetables. Scrub and wash the mussels.

Parboil the artichokes for 5 minutes until tender, and place in a bowl. Heat a little oil and butter in a frying pan and sauté the chicken breasts on all sides. Sprinkle with salt and cook 5 minutes more. Sprinkle the crushed garlic on top and cook 1 minute more. Add salt and pepper. Remove to a side dish.

Add a little wine to the pan. Scrape the coagulated juices at the bottom of the pan and pour the liquid on to the cooked chicken.

Add 2 tablespoons of oil to the pan and sauté the hunks of fish on all sides, until cooked. Sprinkle with salt and pepper and set aside. Add a little oil to the pan and cook the sliced onions until golden. Add the peppers and cook until barely tender. Place in chicken dish.

Add the sausage to the pan and cook on a medium heat for a few minutes. Discard the fat and pour the sausage into the bowl with the chicken and vegetables.

Add a little oil to the frying pan and sauté the chopped onion until soft. Add the rest of the white wine and mussels. Cook for 1 minute on a high heat until the shells open (see Mouclade, page 36). Shake and remove from the heat. Cool, discard the shells (keep 6 pretty ones for decoration), and pour the mussels into the bowl with the chicken.

Cook the peas and pour into the bowl with the chicken and mussels. Cover the bowl with cling film and place in the refrigerator.

Heat 2 tablespoons of oil. Cook the shrimp and prawns with their shells on over high heat for 1 minute on each side, until the shells turn pink. Place on a dish, cool, then cover with cling film and refrigerate.

On the day of the Feast, 40 minutes before you are ready to serve the Paella, preheat the oven to 350°F/180°C/Mark 4 and take all the prepared ingredients out of the refrigerator.

Heat a little oil in the frying pan. Add the rice and stir with a wooden spoon so the rice is coated on all sides, then pour it into a large ovenproof paella baking dish. Add the chicken mixture, saffron and boiling water. Bake, uncovered, for 30 minutes. Turn off the heat and stir in the mussels and peas delicately with a fork. Place the artichoke hearts, prawns and shrimp all round and leave in the oven 5 minutes more. The grains of rice should be separated and dry.

Sprinkle a little oil and place lemon wedges and a few mussel shells all round. Sprinkle lemon juice on top of everything. Wrap a tea-towel round the paella or baking dish and bring straight to the table. All your guests must have time to admire this splendid display of colours. Serve each guest because the dish is too large to pass round.

WINE

If you want a Spanish flavour, mix a large jug of chilled Sangria from a strong red wine, sparkling water, orange juice, a bit of Cointreau or brandy and sliced peaches – a refreshing and treacherous drink. Alternatively, serve a hearty, full-bodied red wine.

WHAT TO SERVE BEFORE AND AFTER PAELLA

HORS-D'OEUVRES

1. Four tomatoes and 4 hard-boiled eggs halved lengthways and filled with Pistou sauce. Top each with a small black olive and serve on a plate lined with watercress or rocket and tiny lamb's lettuce leaves.
2. Terrine aux Herbes
3. Watercress, rocket and chicory tossed salad
4. Pissaladière

DESSERTS

1. Mélange de Fruits
2. Flan au Caramel
3. Cervelle de Canut
4. Granité au Vin (doux)
5. Coffee ice cream with a bowl of ginger-flavoured whipped cream

TABLE DECORATION

This is a summery, joyous meal, so you may like to use a warm rust, a rich brown or a deep yellow tablecloth. Place a large basket of mangoes, oranges, grapes and yellow peaches in the centre of your table. Then form a loose wreath round the glasses with pieces of vine, wistaria, honeysuckle or ivy.

Pass finger-bowls, wet towels or a stack of paper towels as well as placing pretty wide cotton napkins on the table – shrimp and prawns can be messy. Set the table with forks, knives and soup spoons – a *must* for Paella *aficionados*.

STRATEGY FOR THE SUGGESTED MENU

- Guests invited for 7.30 p.m.
- Meal served at 8.30 p.m.

- The evening before the Feast: prepare the Pistou-filled tomatoes and eggs, Paella ingredients and fruit salad.

- On the day of the Feast:
  7.30 Your first guests arrive.
  8.00 Reheat the Paella.
  8.25 Light the candles. Ask your guests to be seated.
  8.30 Bring the plate of tomatoes and eggs to the table.
  8.50 Take the Paella out of the oven. Wrap it in a large tea-towel and bring it to the table.
  9.15 Remove the Mélange de Fruits from the refrigerator and bring it to the table with a plate of thin biscuits.

LEFT-OVERS

1. You can reheat the left-overs easily. Scatter a diced tomato on top, sprinkle a little olive oil, cover with a loose sheet of foil, and bake for 20 minutes at 350°F/180°C/Mark 4.
2. Stuffed peppers: trim and parboil large fleshy green or red peppers. Stuff them with the chopped Paella left-overs. Sprinkle breadcrumbs on top, dot with a little olive oil and bake for about 30 minutes at 375°F/190°C/Mark 5.
3. A flat omelette: stir 2 beaten eggs into the chopped Paella left-overs. Add a handful of chopped fresh herbs (parsley, basil, chives) and make a large flat omelette. When both sides are golden and firm, slide on to a plate and sprinkle with a little olive oil. Serve with a tossed green salad.

Pietsch

A veal or lamb breast stuffed with vegetables, ham, cheese and herbs, sautéd, and then cooked with vegetables in white wine.

I think Thurber was wrong when he said that the undisciplined mind was far better adapted to the confused world in which we live than the organized one. Had he known about Pietsch, he might have had another opinion. Here, organization makes for an easy, smooth process leading to a superb dish.

SUGGESTED MENU

Mouclade

Pietsch
Gratin d'Aubergines
Tossed Green Salad

Flan au Caramel
Thin Biscuits

Full-bodied Red Wine

This can be served cold or warm. Have the butcher remove all the bones and cut the pocket in the veal breast. The veal breast may be boned, flattened, filled and rolled for a more elegant presentation, but it will lose so much of its charm. Serve Pietsch with a side dish of Gratin d'Aubergines and perhaps a tossed salad of rocket, lamb's lettuce, watercress and chicory.

It will be the focus of your meal, so make sure all may savour the sight and the aroma of this plump and golden bundle before you slice it. Pietsch is the best antidote to stress, exhaustion, annoyance and anxiety.

As soon as the masterpiece appears, there is exultation, a sense of coherence and happiness round the table. The radiant faces are confident for a moment that their main activity is enjoying life to the fullest.

FOR 8 PEOPLE

PIETSCH

> *3 lb/1.25 kg Swiss chard* or *spinach, cooked and chopped (3 cups)*
> *2 onions, peeled and sliced*
> *Olive oil*
> *4 oz/100 g lean belly of pork* or *country ham, coarsely chopped*
>   *(1½ cups)*
> *1 cup chopped flat parsley*
> *Salt*
> *Freshly ground pepper*
> *5 cloves garlic, peeled and thinly sliced*
> *Pinch of freshly grated nutmeg*

¾ *cup grated pecorino* or *Parmesan cheese mixed with Gruyère cheese*
2 *tbsp moistened bread, well squeezed*
2 *eggs*
5–6 *lb/2.25–2.75 kg breast of veal*
1 *tsp cracked peppercorns*
4 *fl oz/100 ml white wine*
4 *stalks celery, trimmed and cut into 1-in/25-mm pieces*
3 *carrots, peeled and thickly sliced*
2 *bay leaves*
1 *clove garlic peeled*
4 *fl oz/100 ml water* or *broth*

SAUCE

3 *tbsp chopped fresh herbs*
3 *tbsp pitted and chopped black olives*
3 *tbsp olive oil*
2 *tomatoes, peeled, seeded and diced*
Salt
1 *tbsp coarsely ground coriander*

ACCOMPANIMENTS

Gratin d'Aubergines
Tossed green salad

The Pietsch can be prepared the evening before the Feast.

Bring a large pan of water to a boil. Add the green part of the Swiss chard or spinach leaves. Cook for 15 minutes, until tender. Drain and chop.

Sauté the onions in a little oil until golden. Add the chopped lean pork and sauté for a few minutes. Pour into a bowl. Add the parsley, cooked Swiss chard, salt, pepper, garlic, nutmeg, cheese and moistened bread. Stir well and then add the eggs and mix in.

Dry the veal breast with a paper towel. Sprinkle the inside and outside with salt and cracked peppercorns. Fill with the mixture and carefully close the opening with a trussing needle or skewers and string. With the tip of a very sharp knife cut some shallow criss-cross lines on top of the Pietsch. They will open and make for an attractive design when cooked.

Heat 2 tablespoons of olive oil in a large frying pan. Sauté the stuffed veal breast on both sides for about 20 minutes. Turn carefully with 2 wide spatulas. Add the white wine and scrape the bottom of the pan with a fork. Transfer the meat to an enamelled cast-iron casserole.

To the frying pan add the celery, carrots, bay leaves and garlic. Bring to a boil, add the water, bring back to the boil, then lower the heat and simmer, covered, for 2 hours. Uncover for the last 30 minutes. You may serve Pietsch at once or let it cool in its broth, cover with foil and refrigerate.

To prepare the tomato sauce, add the herbs and chopped olives to the olive oil. Stir in diced tomatoes. Season to taste with salt and coriander. Cover with cling film and refrigerate.

Prepare the Gratin d'Aubergines but do not bake it yet. Keep it in the refrigerator.

On the evening of the Feast, 1 hour before dinner, preheat the oven for the Gratin. Remove the fat from the surface of the broth in which the Pietsch has cooked. Slowly bring the veal breast and its broth to a boil and simmer until warm. Meanwhile, bake the Gratin.

When all is ready, bring the Gratin to the table with the bowl of cold tomato sauce, a bowl of warm broth from cooking the veal and the vegetables that were cooked with the veal. Place the veal breast on a wide, flat platter. Remove the trussing, surround the veal with parsley and bring it to the table with a large serving spatula and a large knife.

Note: A small board is useful to place against the meat or the stuffing as you slice the Pietsch. You can make one yourself by wrapping a piece of cardboard with two layers of foil.

Make sure all your guest have a chance to admire the splendid golden plump 'tummy', the gorgeous Pietsch, then place it on a serving trolley or side table. Cut slices from the Pietsch and serve on to a plate with a wide spatula. Pour a little of the cooking broth over each portion and add some celery, carrots and a sprig of parsley. Each person will then help himself to some of the tomato sauce and the Gratin.

WINE

A full red wine.

WHAT TO SERVE BEFORE AND AFTER PIETSCH

HORS-D'OEUVRES

1. Mouclade
2. Finely sliced fennel salad seasoned with coarsely cut walnuts and a dressing of olive oil, mustard and vinegar.
3. Pissaladière
4. Panier de Crudités with a few sauces

DESSERTS

1. Flan au Caramel and a plate of thin biscuits
2. Cervelle de Canut
3. Tarte au Citron et aux Amandes
4. Grand Baba
5. Poires, Pruneaux, Oranges au Vin Rouge et aux Épices

TABLE DECORATION

The main thing, to avoid trouble, is not to slice your Pietsch on the table. You will present it, let everyone admire it, and then place it on a serving trolley or side table for cutting. In this way your tablecloth and table setting can remain quite pretty.

Choose a warm-coloured tablecloth, perhaps a simple Indian patterned spread, a rich dark red and blue quilted cotton. You may wish to place an old wicker basket filled with grapes and red apples in the centre, or else a piece of crockery surrounded with coloured candles, and then scatter some short-stemmed cut flowers on the tablecloth. Remember that the gratin dish and the bowl of tomato sauce will have to be passed round and that you must make room for them as well as for the bread basket, wine decanters and water jug, salt, pepper and butter accessories. Keep the centre-piece bright and distinctive but small.

STRATEGY FOR THE SUGGESTED MENU

- Guests invited for 7.30 p.m.
- Meal served at 8.30 p.m.

- The night before or on the morning of the Feast: prepare Mouclade, Pietsch, Gratin d'Aubergines, salad and Flan au Caramel.

- On the day of the Feast:
  7.25 Preheat oven to 400°F/200°C/Mark 6 and take everything out of the refrigerator. Reheat the broth and Pietsch, as described. Place the Gratin in the oven.
  7.30 Your first guests arrive.
  8.00 Reheat the Mouclade broth over a gentle heat. Bring wine, water, bread and butter to the table.
  8.30 Light the candles. Ask the guests to sit at the table. Add mussels to the Mouclade. Pour into the tureen and bring to the table with warmed plates.
  8.50 Bring the Pietsch to the table with the Gratin and bowls of cold and warm sauces.

9.20 Bring Flan au Caramel and tray of biscuits with dessert plates to the table.

LEFT-OVERS

1. Cold sliced Pietsch is delicious served with a tossed salad. It is easy to slice and, served with cold tomato sauce, makes for a delicious buffet or picnic meal.
2. Farcis: chop everything and fill halved tomatoes and halved par-boiled courgettes. Sprinkle breadcrumbs on top, dot with olive oil and bake for 20–25 minutes at 375°F/190°C/Mark 5.

Plat de Farcis

A platter of peppers, tomatoes, onions, aubergines and courgettes stuffed with vegetables, ham or chicken, lean pork, parsley, garlic and cheese, and sprinkled with breadcrumbs and olive oil.

A bountiful display of light, lean and tasty Farcis is part of all Provence's summer *festins*. Because Farcis can be served hot, lukewarm or cold, the meal is ready whenever you wish and is perfect for a large family gathering, a buffet or a picnic.

SUGGESTED MENU

Soupe au Pistou

Plat de Farcis
Tossed Green Salad

Oeufs à la Neige
et aux Fruits

A Fruity Rosé

Far from the ready-made pleasures, the processed or frozen, convenient but boring preparations, Farcis feel and taste like real food; their flavours derive from healthy and intense products; they are pretty, colourful and at once moist and crisp. There is variety as well as quantity on the platter, and it delights the eye as much as the palate. In the highly evocative theatrical language of Provence, it is said that when Farcis are well prepared, they make guests think they have died and are already in heaven.

You can trim and fill the Farcis the night before your party and bake them while your guests are having drinks, then serve them piping hot, or you can cook, cover and refrigerate them to serve cold later. Make sure you have at least four different kinds of vegetables and that they are always small, firm and the freshest you can find.

FOR 8 PEOPLE

INGREDIENTS

3 lb/1.5 kg raw, chopped Swiss chard (green part only) or spinach
8 small red, yellow or green bell peppers, stems removed, cut in half
  lengthways and seeded
8 firm, shiny aubergines, stems removed and cut in half lengthways
Olive oil
10 onions; 8 peeled and whole, 2 peeled and chopped
8 firm courgettes, unpeeled, stems removed
8 firm, fleshy tomatoes
1 cup chopped lean belly of pork or lean bacon
2 cups chopped meat – a good cooked ham or boiled chicken
3 tsp dried thyme
4 cloves garlic, peeled and crushed
5 eggs, lightly beaten
3 cups freshly grated Parmesan and Gruyère cheese
1 cup chopped parsley
Salt
Freshly ground pepper
1½ cups (approximately) home-made breadcrumbs

ACCOMPANIMENTS

Tossed green salad (rocket, endive or watercress)
Vinaigrette dressing

Farcis can be prepared the day before the Feast.

Bring a large saucepan of salted water to a boil and cook the Swiss chard or spinach until tender. Drain and squeeze to extract as much water as possible. Chop and set aside.

Preheat the oven to 350°F/180°C/Mark 4. Place the pepper and aubergine halves on the baking pans. Put a little oil on the surface of the vegetables and bake for about 15 minutes, until soft. Remove from the oven, scoop out the flesh of the aubergines – leaving only ½ in/12 mm of flesh round the skin for a shell – with a spoon, and put in a bowl. Set aside.

Meanwhile, bring a large saucepan of salted water to a boil. Cook the whole onions and courgettes for 10 minutes. Cool and then cut the vegetables in half. Scoop out the pulp of the courgettes, leaving about ½ in/12 mm of flesh so the shell is firm enough to hold the filling. Take out the inner layers of the onions, leaving the outer three as shells. Put the courgette flesh and centre layers of the onions in the bowl with the aubergine flesh.

Cut the tomatoes in half. Scoop out and discard the seeds, and squeeze the excess juice. Don't peel the tomatoes.

Heat 2 tablespoons of oil in a large frying pan and sauté the chopped onions for a few minutes. Add the pork and other meats for 1 minute, then the pulp of the aubergines, courgettes and onions that you kept in a bowl. Add a little of the thyme and cook for a few minutes over a low heat. Turn off the heat, add the Swiss chard greens or spinach, the rest of the thyme, the garlic, eggs, grated cheese, parsley, salt and pepper. Check and correct the seasoning.

The stuffing should be firm and smooth. If it is too dry, add a few chopped tomatoes. Place all the vegetable shells – halved peppers, aubergines, courgettes, onions and tomatoes – on 3 or 4 oiled baking pans, or however many it takes to hold them. Fill each shell with 1 or 2 spoonfuls of the stuffing. Sprinkle the top of each vegetable Farci with some breadcrumbs, using up half of them. Do not overstuff. Cover with foil and refrigerate until ready to bake.

Note: This seems like much too much Farcis as you prepare it – 5 different vegetables for each guest. Because of the diversity of colours, textures and tastes, and because it is basically a very light vegetable-based filling, you should be prepared for this surprising fact: at the end of your Feast there will be very few Farcis left for your next picnic.

On the day of the Feast, 50 minutes before you serve your meal, while you lay the table and prepare the hors-d'oeuvres, preheat the oven to 375°F/190°C/Mark 5 and take the Farcis out of the refrigerator. Sprinkle them with the remaining breadcrumbs and dribble a little olive oil on top.

Place the tomatoes, onions and peppers on the same tray: they need about 30 minutes. Bake the aubergines and courgettes on another tray: they need about 45 minutes. They should be brown and crisp.

Prepare the tossed salad and dressing.

Transfer the cooked Farcis on to a large serving platter with a spatula and take piping hot or lukewarm to the table with the salad. Toss the salad and leave it on the table for your guests to help themselves when they want.

Serve 5 stuffed vegetable halves on each plate, using a wide flexible spatula and a big spoon. Farcis are made mostly with vegetables; they are lean and light, and the proof is in the eating. The left-over Farcis will not be there for long. Gather them on a plate, wait for about 10 minutes after the first serving and the passing of the salad, and then offer the Farcis once more.

WINE

A fresh rosé or a light red wine.

WHAT TO SERVE BEFORE AND AFTER PLAT DE FARCIS

HORS-D'OEUVRES TO BE SERVED WITH THE DRINKS

1. Gougère
2. Pissaladière

AND AS A FIRST SEATED COURSE

1. Soupe au Pistou, for vegetable fans
2. Jambon Persillé
3. Terrine aux Herbes
4. Lentilles ou Pois Chiches en Salade, also for vegetable fans

DESSERTS

1. Oeufs à la Neige et aux Fruits
2. Mélange de Fruits
3. Panier de Frivolités served with cooked fruits or a fresh fruit salad
4. Grand Baba
5. Mousse au Chocolat Glacée
6. Compote de Poires

TABLE DECORATION

The table must spell summer abandon, so you may want to choose a pretty Provençal-inspired or fresh country print cotton for your table-cloth with terracotta or bright crockery accessories. As a centre-piece you may fill a shallow crystal bowl with water and float a few coloured candles, along with stemless pansies, roses, daisies or geraniums, on top. Cut flowers will last for several hours, so you can prepare this decoration before you lay your table.

Or you may fill a bowl with fruits and put long pieces of ivy or vines between the fruit and winding down on to the tablecloth. You may want to fill glass candleholders with coloured candles and surround each of them with a twine of greenery, then make a serpentine wreath of flowers and leaves round the glasses.

Offer two baskets of bread, two or three wine decanters and a jug of cool water. But remember that you can depend on the freshness and variety of your platters of Farcis to make your Feast a cheerful one, so don't worry too much about the setting; what matters most is what is on the plate.

STRATEGY FOR THE SUGGESTED MENU

• Guests invited for 7.30 p.m.

- Meal served at 8.30 p.m.

- One day before the Feast: prepare Soupe au Pistou, Farcis, and Oeufs à la Neige. Prepare salad and dressing.

- On the day of the Feast:
  7.25 Take the soup and Farcis out of the refrigerator. Preheat the oven to 350°F/180°C/Mark 4. Reheat the soup on a medium heat, covered. Bake the Farcis in the oven.
  7.30 Your first guests arrive.
  8.30 Ask your guests to the table. Bring the soup plates, Soupe au Pistou, wine and cold water.
  8.40 Bring the Farcis from the oven to the table, along with the bowl of tossed salad.
  9.00 Reheat the caramel for a second and dribble it over the Oeufs à la Neige. Bring it to the table along with a plate of thin biscuits.

LEFT-OVERS

1. The left-overs can be eaten cold as they are and as hors-d'oeuvres, or with cold pork or beef.
2. Gratin: chop all the left-overs, vegetables, shells and stuffing. Add a little broth or tomato sauce for a moist mixture. Correct the seasoning, pour into a gratin dish, sprinkle with cheese, dribble with olive oil and bake for 30 minutes at 375°F/190°C/Mark 5. If you don't have enough left-overs to prepare a gratin, add 1–2 cups of boiled rice to the mixture.

Porc aux Herbes

A loin of marinated pork baked with spices and flavoured with a tangy red-currant sauce.

The festival of Saint John's Day in June celebrates the coming of summer and its many treasures: tender vegetables, berries of all kinds, peaches, apricots and plums. And when November comes, it is with Saint Cochon, Saint Piggy's, that the cosy, substantial, reassuring pleasures of winter are announced. On that day the pig is killed and relatives and friends gather to share the traditional preparations of fresh pork.

SUGGESTED MENU

Crudités with Sauces

*Porc aux Herbes
Sautéd Mushrooms
Celeriac Purée
Salad*

*Madeleines Tièdes
aux Fruits*

A White Wine

Like people, pigs eat meat as well as vegetables. Given a chance, a pig will feed on acorns, hazelnuts, chestnuts, mushrooms, blackcurrants, snails, frogs, roots of all kinds and, on the farm, on oatmeal, lean milk, beets and potatoes. This is what gives its meat a rich flavour, a firm texture and fragrant juices.

Throughout France pork is considered the king of animals; farmers still refer to it as '*le Monsieur*'. It is chosen for impressive festive occasions. Nothing in it is ever wasted; it all turns out into something delicious – pâtés, sausages and a variety of ham. When properly cooked even a pig that has not been taken to the woods to feed on delicious fruits and vegetables will give a mellow meat and fragrant amber-coloured cooking juices.

The following recipe of marinated pork flavoured with spices and vegetables is wonderful served with celeriac and mushrooms. We have chosen these and chicory and watercress salad, but you can select any of the accompaniments. The preparation is simple and the cooking mostly unattended. As always, remember to have a rich platter of foods on your table and that left-overs are welcome.

FOR 8 PEOPLE

MARINADE

> *3 onions, peeled and thinly sliced*
> *16 fl oz/450 ml red wine*
> *8 fl oz/225 ml port* or *red sweet vermouth*
> *10 peppercorns*
> *10 juniper berries*

2 cloves
2 bay leaves
1 tbsp grated orange rind
1 tbsp grated lemon rind

MEAT

5 lb/2 .25 kg boneless loin pork joint, trimmed of fat, rolled and tied
*   neatly to keep its shape during cooking*
Salt
A little vegetable oil

GARNISH

16 large prunes, pitted
1 cup port or sweet vermouth

ACCOMPANIMENTS

Choose 1 or 2 of the following:
Buttered celeriac: 2 celeriacs, peeled, diced, boiled and seasoned with
*   butter, salt and pepper*
Sautéd mushrooms: 2½ lb/1 .1 kg mushrooms, butter, oil, parsley
Purée of celeriac (buttered celeriac puréed and a few tablespoons of
*   double cream added before serving)*
Tossed green salad: 4 cups of trimmed watercress and chicory tossed
*   with a lemon and oil dressing*
Ratatouille
Gratin d'Aubergines
Gratin Dauphinois

SAUCE

4 tbsp Dijon mustard
1 tbsp grated fresh ginger
1 tbsp grated orange rind
4 tbsp redcurrant or cranberry jelly
1 tsp cinnamon

The day before the Feast, combine the marinade ingredients in a large saucepan. Bring to a boil, remove from the heat and let cool slightly. Meanwhile, dry the pork and rub it with salt. Place it in a bowl, pour the lukewarm marinade over it, cool, cover and refrigerate. Marinate overnight or longer (up to 2 days), turning a few times.

Place the pitted prunes in a bowl, add the cup of port, cover and let them soak for at least 4 hours, turning once, until ready to use.

Prepare the vegetables. Peel and cut the celeriac. Cook it for 20 minutes in a large saucepan of boiling salted water. When tender, drain, cool, cover with cling film and refrigerate. Wash, trim and cut the mushrooms. Sauté in a large frying pan with butter and oil. When they are still firm, turn off the heat. Cool, add salt, cover and refrigerate. Wash and trim the chicory and watercress, roll loosely in a tea-towel and refrigerate.

On the day of the Feast, 2 hours before the dinner, take the meat, celeriac and mushrooms out of the refrigerator. Preheat the oven to 375°F/190°C/Mark 5.

Lift the joint out of the marinade. Strain the marinade, keeping the liquid for later and reserving the onions. Dry the surface of the meat with a paper towel. The roasting pan should be quite narrow so the juices are not wasted or likely to burn during the cooking. Moisten the bottom of the pan with a little vegetable oil, place the pork on top, rub it with a little vegetable oil, and brown in the oven for about 20 minutes, turning it a few times.

Lower the temperature to 350°F/180°C/Mark 4 and cook for 15 minutes. Pour off any excess fat and add the reserved onions and half of the marinade round the roast, *not* on the meat itself.

Sprinkle the meat with salt and roast for about 1¼ hours, turning it a few times. Cover loosely with a piece of foil in the last 30 minutes. Check often and add a little marinade to the pan if necessary.

Reheat the diced celeriac for about 15 minutes on a low heat, adding a little butter, salt and pepper. Reheat the mushrooms for about 10 minutes, uncovered, on a low heat, adding salt and pepper, if needed, and freshly chopped parsley.

Place the olive oil, lemon, salt and pepper dressing in the bottom of a large bowl, cross the fork and spoon on top, and then place the watercress and chicory salad on top. Set aside for later.

After the pork has been roasting for 1½ hours, pierce with a fork. If the juices are red, it is not cooked enough; if they are white, the joint is overcooked; if pale pink, turn off, place the meat on a warm plate, cover with the foil and put in the warm oven. Tilt the roasting pan and remove as much fat as you can from the top of the cooking juices with a large spoon. Roll some paper towels and brush them across the top of the cooking juices to remove whatever fat is left. Deglaze the coagulated cooking juices in the bottom of the roasting pan with the rest of the marinade, scraping vigorously with a fork. Stir in the port in which the prunes were soaking (keeping the prunes for later). Pour the deglazed cooking juices into a saucepan. Bring to a rapid boil and reduce the liquid to 12 fl oz/350 ml. Add the mustard, ginger, grated orange rind, redcurrant jelly, cinnamon and, finally, the prunes. Cook on a low heat for 1 minute and then turn off. The prunes will absorb the flavour while you remove and discard the strings from the roast.

Slice the meat into pieces ½ in/12 mm thick. Sprinkle with salt and pepper, and place the slices overlapping on a warm serving dish. Pour the warm sauce you just prepared on top; it will mix with the juices that escaped from the meat as you sliced it. If there is too much sauce, pass it in a bowl separately. Cover the meat with foil to keep it warm and so that the sauce will permeate the meat. Pour mushrooms and celeriac purée in separate dishes. Toss the salad.

As soon as all your guests are seated, bring the pork, sauce, warm plates, celeriac, mushrooms, and salad to the table.

Give each guest 2 slices of pork and 2 prunes. Pour 2 spoonfuls of sauce on top and place 2 tablespoons of celeriac and 1 tablespoon of mushrooms on each side of the meat. Pass round the warm sauce and the bowl of salad.

You may leave all the dishes on the table so that the guests can have second helpings. Pork is very good lukewarm.

WINE

A white wine, but not too dry.

WHAT TO SERVE BEFORE AND AFTER PORC AUX HERBES

HORS-D'OEUVRES TO BE SERVED WITH THE DRINKS

1. Poireaux Tièdes Vinaigrette
2. Crudités with two sauces
3. Caviar d'Aubergines

DESSERTS

1. Madeleines Tièdes aux Fruits
2. Poires, Pruneaux, Oranges au Vin Rouge et aux Épices
3. Crêpes Normandes

TABLE DECORATION

This is a substantial winter meal, so your table should have a cosy and inviting feeling. You may like a large silver or copper bowl in the centre of the table, filled with a mixture of foliage or, if you collect them as I do, two birds' nests (there are pretty made-up ones in many shops now) filled with red berries, holly and other foliage. Place them at each end of the table. Perhaps you'd like a thick red quilted tablecloth and an abundance of green, red and cream candles in all sizes (but never too high), a few pretty lacquered baskets for bread, and bright napkins round the wine bottles. This is a cold-weather dish, so make the setting as warm and cheerful as you can.

STRATEGY FOR THE SUGGESTED MENU

- Guests invited for 7.30 p.m.
- Meal served at 8.30 p.m.

- The day before the Feast: marinate the pork. Prepare the celeriac, mushrooms, and salad dressing. Trim and wash all the Crudités. Prepare the two sauces, Madeleines and cooked fruits.

- On the day of the Feast:
  6.30 Take everything out of the refrigerator. Preheat the oven to 375°F/190°C/Mark 5.
  6.45 Brown the pork on all sides.
  7.05 Lower the oven temperature and cook the pork.
  7.30 Your first guests arrive.
  7.45 Serve the Crudités and the sauces with the drinks.
  8.00 Reheat the celeriac. Reheat the mushrooms.
  Slice the pork, deglaze the coagulated juices, reduce and finish the sauce. Cover with a piece of foil to keep warm. Pour the celeriac into a serving dish and season with butter. Pour the mushrooms into a dish and cover with a piece of foil. Cover the Madeleines with a piece of foil, and place them in the turned-off warm oven.
  8.30 Light the candles. Ask your guests to be seated. Bring the warm plates, sliced pork, mushrooms, celeriac, warm sauce and bowl of salad to the table.
  9.00 Change the plates. Bring the lukewarm Madeleines and the cooked fruit.

LEFT-OVERS

1. Mixed salad: diced left-over pork and cooked lentils served lukewarm with an oil, vinegar and mustard dressing and sprinkled with minced onion and minced basil or chives.
2. Pasta: chopped left-over pork mixed with chopped left-over mushrooms and seasoned with plain tomato sauce. Pour this over a dish of warm pasta and sprinkle with grated Parmesan and some olive oil.
3. Cold salad: diced left-over pork mixed with diced fennel and celery, and seasoned with a dressing of oil, crumbled hard-boiled egg yolk, mustard, and vinegar.
4. Sliced pork with a fresh tossed lettuce salad is delicious.

Pot-au-Feu

The glorious boiled dinner of meats and vegetables scented with herbs and served with an assortment of condiments and sauces.

SUGGESTED MENU

*Broth from the
Pot-au-Feu
Cheese Toasts*

*Pot-au-Feu
Chick-pea Salad*

*Oeufs à la Neige
et aux Fruits*

Red Bordeaux

Pot-au-Feu is France's national dish. It has been called the foundation glory of French cuisine and, according to Goethe, it is also the glory of home-cooking. Escoffier declared it the symbol of family life, and, in fact, whether it serves a real or an invented family, Pot-au-Feu truly stands against loneliness and division; it creates cohesion and warmth for a suspended moment while a group of friends gathered round a steaming pot share its procession of good things.

Pot-au-Feu is a reassuring and comforting dish. Faced with a pile of vegetables, bones, meats and a variety of sauces and condiments, man and woman, old and young, feel at once secure and confident. Once they have experienced this feeling for a few hours, they are, of course, likely to believe it can happen again and again, and spread this thought round and about. Hence, the importance of this invigorating dish in society, to the extent that Mirabeau declared that the foundation of empires lay in the common Pot-au-Feu. But Pot-au-Feu is not only a solid, heartwarming dish; it is a spectacular extravaganza, too.

At the beginning of the century the gourmet writer Marcel Rouff wrote an extraordinary novel about the most refined and gifted of gastronomes, Dodin Bouffant (*The Life and Passions of Dodin Bouffant*, 1925). After being lavishly entertained by the prince of Eurasia, who had overwhelmed him with a pretentious meal, Dodin Bouffant decided to serve a 'boiled beef garnished with its own vegetables'. The prince was insulted at first, thinking it a vulgar dish. But as soon as the splendid display of Pot-au-Feu appeared on the table, he 'wavered between the noble desire to create Dodin Bouffant a duke immediately, a wild urge to offer the gastronome half his fortune and half his kingdom and take over the rights of his gustatory administration, the irritation of being taught a lesson, and the haste to cut into the marvel which laid before him its intoxicating promises'. When asked to explain this apotheosis of simplicity and sophistication, Dodin simply replied with what is indeed the definition of and the key to all good food: 'A work of choice, demanding much love.'

All of France loves Pot-au-Feu, and each region has its variations, but no two villages, no two cooks agree on the ingredients. Of course, there may be meat, vegetables, bones and marrow bones. But some may add lamb, as in Provence, and some include veal or ham. Other possibilities may be a stuffed breast of veal, a stuffed goose neck, duck thighs, turkey legs, a piece of cured country ham or a preserved goose. Saffron, juniper berries or garlic may be added to the broth. A variety of vegetables can be selected. Although Pot-au-Feu is generally served with coarse sea salt and mustard, capers, olives, bitter cherries in vinegar and a variety of sauces may also be offered, with a salad of warm chick-peas as an accompaniment.

Alexander Dumas formally stated that French cooking owed its superiority to the excellence of French bouillon and advised that an old pigeon, a partridge, a rabbit could be added to the broth. He also firmly demanded seven hours of 'sustained simmering' for a Pot-au-Feu worthy of its name. He was excessive, but his claims went in the right direction.

Sensibly prepared, the true sophistication of this dish appears at once: it first announces its arrival on the table through the nose; it awakens everyone's appetite and then offers in abundance the means to satisfy it. It needs no introduction and its very presence at once overwhelms the senses.

This glorious meal – a heady broth, moist meats, a selection of well-cooked vegetables, crisp bread rounds spread with marrow – embodies everyone's idea of a good, healthy dish. In fact, it has been given for centuries to new mothers, melancholy adolescents and elderly people.

Preparing Pot-au-Feu also represents the precise orchestration of a great simple dish at its best. The slow simmering of the meat, herbs and bones requires no attention. The greatest challenges to the cook are the timing and the first-rate quality of the ingredients.

Pot-au-Feu must be prepared one day in advance, kept overnight in the refrigerator and the fat carefully removed the next day. In this way it is also easy to serve and most economical since nothing is lost of the broth, meat, bones and vegetables, and all can be used in a variety of preparations in the days to come.

And as you finish serving your guests, you will see them, as Dodin Bouffant observed, 'extract, in one stroke, between spoon and fork, the quadruple enchantment which is in their share' and later see the whole table 'abandon themselves, in all contentment, to the pleasures of taste, and to that sweet, confident friendship which beckons to well-born men after meals worthy of the name'.

You may select the sauces, vegetables and meats you wish from the lists given. Generally each guest should have 1 marrow bone, some sliced beef, some chicken, 1 carrot, 1 potato, 1 turnip, 1 leek and either a piece of celeriac or some green beans, along with one or two sauces, a few pickles, some good mustard and coarse salt. But you may add to this more vegetables, a stuffed breast of veal, a stuffed chicken, according to the party you have in mind.

Remember, left-overs will give you a week of delicious menus, so offer an opulent Pot-au-Feu to your guests.

FOR ABOUT 8 PEOPLE

MEATS

> *1 lb/450 g bones (approximately): a veal knuckle (have the butcher crack it) and some beef ribs*
> *2 lb/900 g ox tail, cut into 2-in/50-mm pieces (optional)*
> *8 pt/4.5 l water*
> *3 lb/1.25 kg brisket, neatly tied with a long piece of string so it can be lifted easily from the broth*
> *3 lb/1.25 kg rump pot roast, tied to hold its shape*
> *1 large piece about 4 lb/1.8 kg beef short ribs, trimmed*
> *2 onions, studded with cloves*
> *3 sprigs of fresh thyme*
> *3 cloves garlic*
> *Salt*
> *10 peppercorns*
> *Bouquet garni, composed of:*
>> *bunch of parsley*
>> *sprig of thyme*
>> *3 bay leaves*
> *1 leek, green part only*
> *1 carrot*
> *10 peppercorns*
> *1 bulb garlic, unpeeled*
> *4 lb/1.8 kg chicken*
> *8 marrow bones, sliced about 1 in/25 mm thick*
> *A peppery lean cooking sausage or a garlic sausage (saucisson à cuire)*

SAUCES

Choose 1 or 2 of the following:
1. *8 fl oz/225 ml mayonnaise seasoned with 1 tbsp mustard, 1 tbsp minced shallots, 2 tbsp capers, 1 tbsp crushed coriander and 2 tbsp minced parsley.*
2. *Tomato sauce: 2 sliced onions sautéd in oil into which 1 cup of drained canned tomatoes and a little pepper are stirred; cook for 30 minutes on a low heat and season to taste with salt and minced basil, chives or parsley at the last moment.*

3. *8 fl oz/225 ml olive oil, 3 tbsp minced fresh herbs (such as flat parsley, thyme, basil), 3 tbsp chopped capers, 5 tiny diced gherkins, 1 crushed clove garlic, 1 tsp Dijon mustard and 1 tsp red wine vinegar vigorously stirred together before serving.*
4. *8 fl oz/225 ml mayonnaise seasoned with 2 tbsp tarragon and 1 tbsp Dijon mustard.*
5. *Horseradish sauce: 5 tbsp freshly grated horseradish mixed with 8 fl oz/225 ml double cream, lightly whipped, 2 tsp mustard, and 2 tbsp red wine vinegar.*
6. *12 fl oz/350 ml double cream boiled slowly for 15 minutes to reduce, then enriched with 2 tbsp Dijon mustard and 2 tbsp tomato sauce (see No.2 above) and sprinkled with 2 tbsp chopped chervil or parsley.*
7. *8 fl oz/225 ml Aioli*

ACCOMPANIMENTS

Choose from the following:
Several types of mustards, but mostly Dijon
Sour gherkins or small dill pickles
Pickled onions
Sour black cherries in vinegar. Cover ripe cherries and part of their stems with wine vinegar, a few tarragon leaves, peppercorns and whole coriander; seal and keep for 2–12 months. The longer they are kept, the better they are. Can also be purchased.
Bowl of coarse sea salt
10 bread rounds, buttered, sprinkled with grated Gruyère cheese, and grilled for a few seconds before serving with the warm broth. These can be prepared in advance and reheated. Have an additional 8 rounds to be oven-dried later
8 bread rounds or triangles of oven-dried bread to be spread with the warm marrow and sea salt
Bowl of grated Gruyère and Parmesan cheese (for the guests who like it sprinkled on the broth)
Dish of grated celeriac seasoned with a mustardy mayonnaise, or a lukewarm salad of chick-peas

VEGETABLES

Choose a variety from among the following:
8 carrots, peeled, cut in half lengthways, then in half crossways, and tied in a bunch
1 large celeriac, peeled and quartered
6 white turnips, peeled and halved
2 fennel roots, cut in half, or whole if small
3 hearts celery, trimmed and quartered
Savoy cabbage, quartered (optional; cook separately or in the steamer)
8 leeks, white part only, leaving only 2 in/50 mm of green, cut in half lengthways, tied in a bunch and then wrapped in cheesecloth

10 small potatoes, peeled
1 lb/450 g green beans, trimmed

GARNISH

3 tbsp minced flat parsley and chives

Begin the day before the Feast. Place the veal and beef bones in a hot oven for a few minutes to brown them, then put them on the bottom of a very large saucepan. Add the ox tail. Cover with water and bring slowly to the simmering point, uncovered. The top of the water should just shiver. Add the brisket and rump pot roast. After a few minutes a brown scum will start rising; remove it from the surface continuously until it changes to white and frothy. Add a little cold water from time to time to make sure all the scum has risen to the surface. Continue to skim the broth as necessary.

Add the short ribs, clove-studded onions, thyme, unpeeled garlic, salt, peppercorns and bouquet garni to the hot broth. Bring almost to a boil and simmer gently for 2 more hours.

Meanwhile place the chicken (stuffed or plainly trussed with just an onion and a bay leaf inside) in an oven heated to 375°F/190°C/Mark 5, for 15 minutes to release some of the fat. Wipe the chicken carefully with a paper towel, add it to the broth and cook 1 hour more. The meat must cook for at least 3 hours and be very tender. Remove from the heat and cool to room temperature.

Place the meat and chicken on a large platter. Line a strainer with 1 or 2 layers of dampened cheesecloth, then pour the broth through it into a large bowl. Add salt or pepper to correct the seasoning of the broth. If the broth is weak-flavoured, place it in a saucepan on a high heat to reduce for a few minutes. Discard the bones, bouquet garni and onions. Add the cooked beef and chicken to the bowl, cover and refrigerate overnight.

Pat some sea salt into both ends of the marrow bones. Wrap them in a large piece of cheesecloth and tie with a long string. Refrigerate. Prepare the sauces and accompaniments you have selected. Cover with cling film and leave overnight in the refrigerator.

On the morning of the Feast, remove all the Pot-au-Feu elements from the refrigerator. The fat will be congealed on top of the dish and will be as easy to remove as a piece of wax. Discard any fat and gristle you can see on the cooked beef, mostly on the ribs. Cut the beef across the grain into slices ¼–½ in/6–12 mm thick. Wrap it in a large piece of cheesecloth and tie with a long string for easy removal and set aside. Cut the chicken, discarding any fat, gristle and skin. Place the pieces in a large piece of cheesecloth, tie with a long string and set aside.

About 1 hour before the meal place the broth in a saucepan. Add the sliced meat and cut-up chicken in their pieces of cheesecloth and bring to a boil, then lower the heat, and let it simmer gently, uncovered.

Place the cheesecloth-wrapped marrow bones in cold water and simmer for 20 to 30 minutes. Remove from the heat and set aside in hot water until ready to serve.

If you are using them, reheat the cheese bread rounds and plain bread rounds for a few minutes in the oven at 350°F/180°C/Mark 4. Turn off the oven and keep warm until the meal.

Fill the bottom of a multi-tiered steamer with boiling water. Prick the surface of the sausage with a fork and add it to the water. Place your selections of carrots, celeriac, turnips, fennel, celery hearts and cabbage on the steamer tray. Cover and cook for 10 minutes. Add a second tray with your selections of leeks, potatoes and green beans on top of the first one and cook 20 minutes more. It will be ready to serve, but if you need to wait, you can keep everything warm and firm for an hour in the tightly closed steamer removed from the heat.

If you don't use a steamer, cook the carrots, celeriac, cabbage, fennel and turnips in a large saucepan of salted water for about 10 minutes, then add the potatoes, green beans, sausage and leeks.

Ask one of your guests to help you. Warm the plates. Warm the large serving plates for a few minutes while you take the vegetables, meat, chicken and bones out of their saucepan. Remove the strings and cheesecloth. Place the sauces and accompaniments on a tray.

Bring cups or small bowls filled with hot broth to the table along with a bottle of port and a basket of warm cheese bread rounds. Your guests may add a drop of port to the broth and sip this delicious amber bouillon with the cheese rounds.

Meanwhile, bring in the sauces and whatever other condiments you have chosen to serve. Arrange the vegetables on 1 or 2 of the warm serving dishes and moisten them with the warm cooking broth. Also arrange the slices of beef and moisten with a little warm broth. Sprinkle with chopped chives. Garnish with some flat parsley.

Slide the sliced sausage and marrow bones on to a warm plate and add a little parsley for garnish. Serve it with oven-dried bread and a bowl of warm broth. It is good to have little spoons or forks for getting every bit of marrow from the bones; seafood forks or coffee spoons are good for this. This is one of those times when a tea-trolley or serving cart is very useful, so if you have one, load it up with the elements of Pot-au-Feu.

Present the platters in the dining-room so everyone can see the abundant colourful display. If you are set up for it, let each guest arrange his own combination of steaming vegetables, meats and sausage from a sideboard or serving table. Or arrange portions of Pot-au-Feu on each plate yourself, making a full selection of vegetables and meats moistened with a little broth.

The marrow should be extracted from its bones with the little spoons, spread on the warm bread rounds, and sprinkled with coarse salt by each guest. This is a delight to bite into. Pass the various condiments and sauces and a basket for discarded bones. The warm broth should be available throughout the meal.

Reassemble the remaining vegetables and meats on to 1 or 2 serving dishes. Add a bit of broth and pass round for second helpings. Lukewarm meat and vegetables from Pot-au-Feu are acceptable, but if you don't mind getting up and you want the second helpings to be piping hot, place the Pot-au-Feu left-overs back on the cooker and then bring them back for seconds.

WINE

A good red Bordeaux.

WHAT TO SERVE BEFORE AND AFTER POT-AU-FEU

HORS-D'OEUVRES TO BE SERVED WITH THE DRINKS

1. A bowl of warm broth with old port and cheese toasts. Use thin strips of oven-dried whole-wheat or white bread, or slices of French bread, spread lightly with butter and grated cheese. Grill to melt and slightly brown the cheese.
2. Pissenlits aux Lardons
3. Terrine aux Herbes
4. Poireaux Tièdes Vinaigrette

DESSERT

1. Oeufs à la Neige et aux Fruits
2. Crémets aux Fruits
3. Flan au Caramel
4. Mousse au Chocolat Glacée
5. Grand Baba

TABLE DECORATION

This glorious dish deserves a warm, festive table. You might like to choose a floor-length quilted tablecloth in a pretty shade of blue, and salmon-coloured cotton napkins. The table will be crowded, so keep the centre-piece small, with a distinctive colour and shape. A round lacquered basket filled with salmon petunias, or salmon-coloured geraniums or graceful tulips might be a suitable choice for the centre.

Choose pretty bowls for the various sauces and condiments, two baskets sprayed in blue and lined with white napkins for the oven-dried bread, and perhaps two plain ones for the discarded bones. Put a white or a salmon-coloured napkin round the necks of the red wine bottles and place salmon or white votive candles in front of each glass.

Remember to add tiny forks or spoons for the marrow when you lay the table.

STRATEGY FOR THE SUGGESTED MENU

- Guests invited for 7.30 p.m.
- Meal served at 8.30 p.m.

- The day before the Feast: prepare the vegetables of your choice, the sauces and condiments, the meat, bones and herbs, the chick-peas and dressing, and the Oeufs à la Neige. Cover and refrigerate them all.

- On the morning of the Feast: remove the fat from the top of the broth. Prepare the beef and chicken cheesecloth bundles.
  7.00 Preheat the oven to 300°F/150°C/Mark 2. Prepare the breads for the soup course and to serve with the marrow bones. Remove everything except Oeufs à la Neige from the refrigerator.
  7.20 Warm the plates. Reheat the meat and broth on a low heat in an uncovered saucepan. Prepare the steamer or saucepans for cooking vegetables, marrow bones and sausages. Turn off the oven, leaving the bread in it. Gently reheat the chick-peas.
  7.30 Your first guests arrive.
  7.50 Cook the vegetables, sausage and marrow bones according to the recipe. Arrange the serving dishes, sauces and condiments according to the recipe.
  8.00 Serve the broth, cheese rounds and port with the drinks.
  8.30 Light the candles. Ask your guests to be seated. Toss the chick-pea salad. Present the Pot-au-Feu.
  9.00 Take Oeufs à la Neige from the refrigerator at the same time as second helpings are served. Heat the caramel and pour it on top.
  9.30 Clear the table. Bring the dessert plates, Oeufs à la Neige and thin biscuits to the table.

LEFT-OVERS

1. Pot-au-Feu en Gelée: remove all bones, gristle and fat. Cut the meat in small pieces. Take a large wide bowl and spread it as prettily as you

can with one-third of the vegetables. Scatter some tarragon leaves on top. Spread half of the meat over the vegetables and scatter a few more tarragon leaves: add half of the remaining vegetables and the rest of the meat, and finally the rest of the vegetables. Press firmly with the palms of your hands. Remove any fat from the broth. Reheat the broth adding some minced chervil if you have it, and pour it over the meat and vegetables. Poke with a fork to make sure the broth has penetrated to the bottom of the bowl. Cool, cover with cling film or foil, refrigerate overnight, and then unmould. Surround the bottom of the dish with parsley.

2. Petite marmite: cut up the meat and vegetables in small pieces. Reduce the broth for 30 minutes. Check the seasoning, add the meat and vegetables, and reheat gently. Serve with crisp bread rounds or grated cheese. If you have left-over cabbage, chop it, sprinkle it with salt and place ½ tsp of it on crisp pieces of bread. Sprinkle cheese on top, pass them under the grill and float them in each soup plate.

3. Gratin: sauté a few sliced dry mushrooms, 6 finely chopped shallots, and 2 garlic cloves in a little oil and butter until soft. Add 1 cup of breadcrumbs, salt and pepper, and stir. Butter an ovenproof dish and spread half of the mixture in it. Add a layer of sliced left-over beef or chicken and then the rest of the mushrooms, shallots and breadcrumbs mixture. Carefully pour 4 fl oz/100 ml of dry white wine into the dish, dot with butter, and bake for at least 30 minutes at 375°F/190°C/Mark 5.

4. Boeuf en salade: thinly slice or dice the left-over beef and the boiled potatoes, and layer with a dressing of oil, vinegar, mustard, chopped capers, minced shallots and minced flat parsley. Place a few hard-boiled egg slices on top. Serve cold or at room temperature.

5. Hachis Parmentier, page 147.

6. Croquettes: add to the left-over beef and potatoes some chopped parsley and a few beaten eggs. Shape into balls and pan fry in butter and oil.

7. Mironton: peel and chop or slice a few onions. Sauté in butter and oil, and blend in some red wine vinegar and white wine, about 2 fl oz/ 50 ml for each person, and a little broth. Heat, stirring, and add chopped parsley, salt and pepper. Pour a little of the mixture into the bottom of a buttered ovenproof dish. Add the sliced left-over beef or chicken and spoon the rest of the sauce over. Sprinkle some bread-crumbs on top, dot with butter, and bake at 375°F/190°C/Mark 5. Tomato sauce and chopped watercress are sometimes added to the dish for a more pungent taste.

8. Serve the left-over broth with 1 poached egg per person and crisp bread rounds.

9. You can serve just the left-over broth, very warm, with the addition
of 8 tbsp port and 8 tbsp of double cream just before serving.
10. Left-over broth is the very best choice to precede Gratinée
Lyonnaise.
11. Stuffed Tomatoes, replacing ham with beef or chicken left-overs.

Potée

*A stew of white beans, cabbage, carrots,
leeks and pork seasoned with herbs and
spices.*

Once upon a time, because they needed
courage, reassurance and unity, and probably because they also were exceptionally
fond of pork and cabbage, the Gauls invented the Potée. They indulged in it for years,
and throughout the centuries this satisfying
superdish has warmed the hearts and souls
of every generation of Frenchmen.

SUGGESTED MENU

Pissenlits au Lardons

Potée

Granité au Vin

Graves

Potée – so-called simply because it is cooked in an earthenware pot –
still embodies the very idea of conviviality and cosy pleasures. There is
nothing more reassuring than a Potée simmering in a house, nothing
more evocative of home sweet home than family and friends gathered
round a lavish, generous and inviting Potée.

By tradition, this is a true country dish. The pork comes from the
farm, the vegetables from the garden, and they are prepared and
cooked in harmony; no ingredient upstages another. Everything simmers together and mingles for hours to give a moist and fragrant Potée.

Each regional version selects and clings to its very own ingredients,
so each Potée is unique. Lean salt pork, smoked bacon, rolled pork
shoulder, ham, quartered head of pig, spareribs, breast of lamb, stuffed
chicken, plain chicken, red beans, white beans, cabbage (of course),
garlic, clove-studded onions, carrots, turnips, leeks, brussels sprouts
and sometimes fresh peas, green beans and young onions all have their
place in a Potée. And when it appears on the table, toasted rye bread
may float on the broth while the meats and vegetables follow separately. Or the whole Potée may be presented on a single platter and the
broth kept for another day. In some regions one or two whole bulbs of
garlic (about eighteen cloves) cook in the broth and are spread, when

they are cooked and soft, on slices of country-style bread for a delicious nutty garnish.

The quality of this dish depends on the variety and, of course, the freshness of its ingredients, and on very careful cooking. Just like Pot-au-Feu, Potée should simmer and never be stirred in its slow cooking process. The steps are simple to understand and follow.

In the following recipe, handed down by generations of attentive cooks, there are a few tiny new tips: brown the vegetables before simmering them in the broth; blanch the beans and cabbage separately and add them later to the Potée; trim all the meats so there is little gristle and just enough fat; and sauté the sausage before adding it at the last moment. This Potée will then become very tasty and also highly digestible.

At the table you will have sliced meats on one serving dish and on another, white beans and shredded cabbage, which will almost have melted to give a fresh, intriguing, wonderful taste and texture.

Place all round – gathered in little bunches – the leeks, carrots and turnips, along with the slices of crisp sausage.

This invigorating dish will conquer all hearts at first sight and first bite and be a candidate for frequent re-election throughout the winter. Potée is neither expensive nor complicated to prepare and cooks mostly unattended, but you must take time to share and enjoy it, for this is for the serene and rich hours. Be generous in your offerings of vegetables and meats: 'the most is the best here', as the Gauls might have said, and left-overs will turn into succulent preparations for days to come.

FOR 8 PEOPLE

VEGETABLES

> 2 cups white beans
> Salt
> 1 large green cabbage (about 2 lb/900 g) shredded
> 1 oz/25 g unsalted butter
> 2 tbsp vegetable oil
> 6 carrots, peeled and cut into 2-in/50-mm pieces
> 2 onions, peeled and quartered
> 1–2 celeriac (about 2 lb/900 g), peeled and cut into 2-in/50-mm pieces, or 5 small white turnips, peeled and quartered
> 10 cloves garlic, peeled
> 4 leeks (white part only), cleaned and tied into a bundle (reserve greens for the cooking liquid)
> 3 bay leaves, crumbled
> 3 tsp dried thyme or a few sprigs of fresh thyme
> Freshly ground black pepper

SEASONINGS

1⅔ pt/900 ml water (approximately) for each 1 lb/450 g of meat
Stalk of celery, trimmed
2 medium onions (about 8 oz/225 g), peeled and stuck with 2 whole cloves
10 peppercorns
10 juniper berries
3 bay leaves
4 cloves garlic, peeled
Greens of 2 leeks

MEATS

1 lb/450 g (or more) cured ham
2 lb/900 g piece lean slab bacon or lean salt pork, with rind removed
3 lb/1.25 kg meaty pork spareribs, trimmed and left in 1 piece
2–3 lb/900 g–1.25 kg boneless shoulder of pork
1 meaty ham bone or blanched smoked ham hock (optional)
1 lb/450 g boiling sausage, such as Polish kielbasa or saucisson from Lyon
1 lb/450 g thin frying sausage, such as Italian sweet or hot, garlicky or peppery or smoky

ACCOMPANIMENTS

4 slices of whole-wheat bread
Mustards: Dijon, whole grain and tarragon
Sea salt
Small bowl of tiny sour gherkins (cornichons)
Bowl of vinaigrette with 3 tbsp finely minced chives or tarragon or fresh coriander or flat parsley

GARNISHES

¼ cup chopped chives and parsley sprigs

The day before the Feast, soak the beans in cold water for 1 hour. Drain, rinse and add cold water to cover. Bring to a boil, lower the heat and simmer for about 1 hour until cooked but not mushy. Drain, cool and reserve until ready to assemble the Potée.

Bring water to a boil in a large saucepan. Add salt (about 2 teaspoons for each 3 pt/1.8 l of water). Add the shredded cabbage and bring back to a boil. Lower the heat slightly and cook for 15 minutes. Drain and refresh under cold running water. When cool enough to handle, squeeze out as much water as possible with your hands. Reserve until ready to finish the Potée.

Melt the butter with the vegetable oil in a large frying pan over medium heat. Add the carrots, onions and celeriac. Cook, stirring frequently, for about 7 minutes, until lightly coloured. Add garlic and bundle of leeks. Continue cooking for about 3 minutes more. Season with bay leaves, thyme, salt and pepper. Remove to drain on paper towels and reserve until ready to assemble the dish.

Bring 13–14 pt/7–8 l of water to a boil and add all the seasonings. Boil for 5 minutes.

Trim the cured ham, bacon, spareribs and shoulder of pork of as much fat as possible. Place in the pot with the seasonings (and ham bone if you have it) and bring back to a boil. Lower the heat and simmer for 1 hour. Add the lightly browned vegetables, the cabbage and the bundle of leeks. Simmer for 15 minutes. Add the cooked beans and cook for 15 minutes. Stir with a long-handled spoon so you have meats and vegetables on top of the cabbage to prevent it from floating.

Prick the boiling sausage with a fork to prevent splitting and add it to the pot. Cook 20 minutes more. Remove from the heat, cool to room temperature and then refrigerate.

On the day of the Feast, 2 hours before the party, take the Potée out of the refrigerator. Forty minutes before you sit down to dinner, preheat the oven to 350°F/180°C/Mark 4. Bring the Potée to a boil on top of the cooker, then lower the heat, stirring a few times with a long-handled spoon.

When you feel the meat is warm, remove all the pieces from the saucepan and slice them, removing all the loose bones, rind and gristle. Place in 1 or 2 serving dishes. Spoon 1 or 2 ladlefuls of hot broth on top, cover with foil and place in the oven while you finish preparations.

Toast the whole-wheat bread until crisp and then slice in half. Sauté the frying sausage in a little oil until crisp and brown, and place in the oven to keep warm. With a wide, long-handled sieve, remove the beans and cabbage from the broth and put into a shallow serving dish. Place the various boiled vegetables all round. Remove and discard the string from the leeks and cut each into 2-in/50-mm pieces.

Spoon warm broth over everything. Sprinkle with salt and pepper and a little chopped chives. Take the sliced meats out of the oven and place a few parsley sprigs in the centre. Sprinkle with salt and freshly ground pepper. Spoon a little more broth over the platter. When your guests are seated, bring the serving dishes, warm plates, slices of toast and a bowl or pot of hot broth into the dining-room.

You may let your guests get up and help themselves from a side table, or you can serve each plate yourself. Ask a friend to pass the plates for a quicker service, as Potée is best warm. Each serving should have a piece of sparerib, a slice of boiled sausage, a slice of crisp sausage, a slice of raw cured ham, a piece of lean salt pork, a piece of shoulder, a generous helping of white beans and cabbage, and a few boiled vegetables. Moisten the vegetables with a little warm broth.

Pass the different mustards, salt, gherkins and vinaigrette round the table.

Return what is left of the Potée to the kitchen at once. Put it on the cooker or in the turned-off oven and return to your guests. Later, bring a steaming lavish platter of meats and vegetables to the dining-room for second helpings.

WINE

A dry white wine or a red wine with bouquet from Burgundy, Beaujolais, Médoc, or Graves.

WHAT TO SERVE BEFORE AND AFTER POTÉE

This is a hearty country dish, so you should have a light hors-d'oeuvres.

HORS-D'OEUVRES

1. Pissenlits aux Lardons
2. Poireaux Tièdes Vinaigrette
3. Crudités with a sauce
4. Caviar d'Aubergines with warm toast and crisp vegetables

DESSERTS

1. Granité au Vin
2. Cervelle de Canut with warm toast
3. Flan au Caramel and a plate of thin biscuits
4. Mousse au Chocolat Glacée
5. Panier de Frivolités

TABLE DECORATION

With such a glorious offering you don't need to decorate the table elaborately. You could, for instance, choose a solid brown tablecloth or brown and caramel tablecloth, and add red accessories. You could use red napkins and roll and tie each one with a piece of brown ribbon and a soft bow.

You might like to use baskets painted a rich brown or deep red for the bread, and you could cover a round plate or small tray with one of the red napkins and place the mustards, salt, gherkins and vinaigrette on it. You can use brown and red candles to continue the theme.

In the centre you may want a wooden bowl filled with a mixture of walnuts in their shells, kumquats and crab apples, and with a few twigs of green here and there.

Your wine bottles could have a little brown napkin wrapped round their necks, and don't forget to put jugs of water on the table.

STRATEGY FOR THE SUGGESTED MENU

- Guests invited for 7.30 p.m.
- Dinner served at 8.30 p.m.

- The day before the Feast: cook the Potée and prepare the Granité au Vin. Trim all the salad greens and prepare the dressing.

- On the day of the Feast:
  7.00 Reheat the Potée over a low heat, stirring once or twice very, very gently with a long-handled spoon. Take the salad greens out of the refrigerator. Prepare the salad plates and cut bacon. Preheat the oven to 350°F/180°C/Mark 4.
  7.30 Your first guests arrive.
  8.15 Sauté the bacon, toss the salad and arrange on individual plates. Prepare the pork, sausages and spareribs, cover with broth and foil, and keep warm in the oven. Sauté the frying sausage; place it with the sliced pork in the oven.
  8.30 Light the candles. Ask your guests to the table and serve the Pissenlits.
  8.45 Arrange serving dishes according to the recipe and bring everything to the dining-room. Remove small salad plates, bring in warm plates and serve Potée as described.
  9.20 Change plates and serve Granité au Vin with a plate of thin biscuits.

LEFT-OVERS

1. A country soup: float some crisp *croûtons* on top of the left-over broth for a delicious soup.
2. Add diced left-over meat and vegetables to the broth and serve piping hot with a sprinkling of chives.
3. Serve the cold sliced left-over pieces of pork with a very tart lemony mayonnaise, or a very lively vinaigrette.
4. Left-over pork can be used for Plat de Farcis.
5. Left-over pork can be used for Chou Farci.
6. Left-over pork can be used for the Poule Verte stuffing.
7. Gratin: delicious with diced left-over vegetables, seasoned with a little tomato sauce and covered with grated cheese.

Poulet Fricassée Provençale

Marinated chicken sautéd with onions and seasoned with a heady purée of chicken livers, garlic, fresh herbs and capers.

SUGGESTED MENU
Olives Sautées

Poulet Fricassée Provençale
Rice
Ratatouille

Mousse au Chocolat Glacée
Thin Biscuits

White Burgundy

The cornerstone of a good meal is each guest's feeling that he or she is in good hands. This is the case when you serve Poulet Fricassée Provençale. This light and vibrant dish is easy to prepare, easy to reheat, easy to serve. The chicken is marinated with herbs, sautéd in butter, deglazed with wine and at the last moment a heady mixture is stirred into the dish. Tiny courgettes, spring carrots and baby turnips or a Ratatouille will complement this Chicken Fricassée, and with everything prepared in advance you can be confident of a superb Feast.

Le Corbusier said, 'God is in the details', and so is the good cook. As always, take care of little things – the crispness of each piece of chicken before you add the wine, the firmness of the carrots and the courgettes – and you will soon notice that the big things will take care of themselves.

FOR 8 PEOPLE

FRICASSÉE

> *20 pieces of chicken: either 3 × 4-lb/1.8-kg chickens cut into serving*
> *pieces, discarding the wings and backs, or 20 chicken breasts*
> *Juice of 1 lemon*
> *4 tbsp dried thyme*
> *3 oz/75 g butter*
> *6 tbsp olive oil, plus oil for marinating the chicken*
> *2 tsp marjoram*
> *2 tsp sage*
> *Salt*
> *Freshly crushed pepper*
> *2 large onions, peeled and chopped*
> *8 fl oz/225 ml dry white wine*
> *8 fl oz/225 ml dry white vermouth*
> *1–2 tsp peppercorns (a mixture of green, red and black, if available)*
> *12 small shallots with stems on*
> *12 oz/350 g chicken livers*

1 tbsp flour
5 cloves garlic, peeled and crushed
¾ cup chopped parsley
3 tbsp chopped basil or *any fresh herb*
4 tbsp capers

ACCOMPANIMENTS

2 cups rice
Ratatouille or *a mixture of turnips, courgettes and carrots sautéd in*
  butter

GARNISH

4 thin slices of bread, toasted
Olive oil

The day before the Feast, dry the pieces of chicken with paper towels. Sprinkle them with lemon juice and then rub all the pieces with a great deal of thyme and olive oil. Cover and marinate for a few hours, turning once or twice.

Meanwhile, prepare the accompaniments. Cook the rice. Cool, cover and keep in the refrigerator. Prepare the Ratatouille or sauté the vegetables briefly in a frying pan, so they are truly *al dente* (they will have to be reheated). Cool, cover with cling film and place in the refrigerator.

Heat half the butter and oil in a large frying pan. Sprinkle each piece of chicken with a little marjoram, sage, salt and fresh crushed pepper. Cook over a medium-high heat for 5–10 minutes so each piece is golden on all sides. Do this in as many batches as needed so that each piece has enough room to brown on both sides. Transfer the chicken to a large casserole in which 1 oz/25 g of butter and 2 tablespoons of oil are heating and continue cooking, uncovered, for 10 minutes. Sauté the chopped onion in the frying pan and add to the casserole. When all the chicken pieces are in the casserole, discard any excess cooking fat left in the frying pan and pour the white wine and vermouth into the pan. Scrape the coagulated juices in the bottom with a fork and pour this on the chicken pieces into the casserole.

Add the peppercorns and cook over a medium heat, uncovered, for 20 minutes. Turn the chicken pieces with a wooden spoon to make sure every piece is brown and impregnated with the onion-wine sauce. Add the shallots and cook for 10 minutes more, uncovered. Check with a fork to make sure the chicken is cooked.

Heat ½ oz/15 g of butter and 1 tablespoon of oil in the frying pan. Sprinkle the chicken livers with a little flour and sauté for 1 minute or so, until they stiffen. Pour them and the crushed garlic into a food processor or a blender and process for 1 minute. Pour into the chicken casserole, turn off the heat at once and stir carefully. When cool, cover with cling film and leave in the refrigerator.

On the day of the Feast, 1 hour before the meal, place the parsley and basil (or other fresh herb) in a bowl with the capers. Remove the Fricassée from the refrigerator and reheat it over a low heat with the lid half covering the dish. This is a *sauce courte*, a short sauce, since most of the sauce has been absorbed by the chicken. Reheat the Ratatouille or sautéd vegetables briefly. Reheat the rice with a little butter, fluffing it lightly. Warm the plates. Toast the bread slices lightly on both sides and dot with a few drops of olive oil. Cut them in triangles and stack them on a small plate.

When you are ready to serve dinner, stir the chopped parsley, basil (or fresh herbs) and capers into the casserole, turn off the heat, cover, wrap in a pretty tea-towel and bring to the table with the warm plates, rice, Ratatouille or vegetables, and crisp toasted bread.

When you serve your guests, each plate should have 2 pieces of chicken with a little sauce poured over them, 1 or 2 shallots, 2 pieces of toast, 2 spoonfuls of rice and 2 spoonfuls of Ratatouille or sautéd vegetables.

WINE

Serve a chilled white Burgundy, a white Bordeaux or a Côtes du Rhône.

WHAT TO SERVE BEFORE AND AFTER POULET FRICASSÉE PROVENÇALE

HORS-D'OEUVRES TO BE SERVED WITH THE DRINKS

1. Olives Sautées
2. Terrine aux Herbes
3. Crudités à la Tapenade

DESSERTS

1. Mousse au Chocolat Glacée and a plate of thin biscuits
2. Grand Baba
3. Crémets aux Fruits
4. Poires, Pruneaux, Oranges au Vin Rouge et aux Épices
5. Oeufs à la Neige et aux Fruits

TABLE DECORATION

You may wish to cover your table with a richly coloured tablecloth – either a piece of thick quilted cotton or an Indian cotton bedspread large enough to reach the floor. You can spread a piece of ivory or white crochet work, macramé or heavy lace over the long cloth. Then you may place a china or earthenware tureen in the centre and set two round, chubby bunches of cut flowers in plain glass vases on either side. Scatter candles and tiny pots of butter all round, along with two wine decanters, water jugs and baskets of assorted bread.

This setting should suggest a feeling of cosy pleasure, of easy, sensual well-being. It should be sensible and cheerful and avoid at all cost the magazine rendering of a utopian 'good celebration'.

STRATEGY FOR THE SUGGESTED MENU

- Guests invited for 7.30 p.m.
- Dinner served at 8.30 p.m.

- One day before the Feast: prepare the Poulet Fricassée, Rice, Ratatouille, Mousse au Chocolat and sliced oranges. Refrigerate.

- On the day of the Feast:
  7.15 Take everything except the Mousse au Chocolat out of the refrigerator. Sauté the olives.
  7.30 Your first guests arrive. Serve Olives Sautées with the drinks.
  8.00 Reheat the Fricassée, Ratatouille and Rice. Warm the plates. Place the bread in the oven to dry.
  8.30 Stir the parsley and capers into the casserole. Turn off the heat. Wrap the casserole with a wide, pretty napkin. Light the candles. Ask your guests to the table. Bring the warm plates, Poulet Fricassée, toast, Ratatouille and Rice to the table.
  8.50 Take the Mousse au Chocolat out of the freezer. Unmould it on to a plate lined with a white napkin. Sprinkle it with chocolate shavings and bring it to the table with the sliced oranges and a plate of thin biscuits.

LEFT-OVERS

1. Paella, page 165.
2. Croquettes: add 2 eggs and pass everything through a good mill or food processor. Form little balls, roll them in flour lightly, dip them in a lightly beaten egg, and fry for 1–2 minutes. Drain the croquettes and serve them with lemon wedges.

3. Crêpes: chop the chicken left-overs and spoon in the centre of each crêpe. Roll them, pour a little butter on top, and reheat in the oven at 350°F/180°C/Mark 4. Serve with a plain tomato sauce.

4. Gratin: pour into a buttered gratin dish, cover with tomato halves and sprinkle with salt and pepper, breadcrumbs and chopped parsley. Dot with olive oil and bake until warm at 375°F/190°C/Mark 5 for 30 minutes.

Poulet en Gelée

Chicken cooked with vegetables and herbs, served cold in its natural aspic and decorated with parsley and lemon.

> **SUGGESTED MENU**
>
> *Crudités with Anchoyade and Tapenade Sauces*
>
> *Poulet en Gelée*
> *Lentilles en Salade*
>
> *Crémets aux Fruits*
> *Thin Biscuits*
>
> *Côte de Beaune*

This is a wonderful dish for summer. It must be patiently prepared a day in advance to allow the chicken to rest in its juice and for all the flavours to mingle. This is not an improvised preparation, nor is it complicated or laboured. The cook remains calm knowing nothing can go wrong.

No gelatin is added, so the taste and the texture are wonderful, not rubbery like the 'plastic' fantastic aspic offered in ready-to-eat concoctions. It is a bit harder to serve than the chemically superfirm gelatin, but the flavour makes up for it. All the time and effort devoted to this preparation are rewarded the minute you bite into this luscious and fragrant dish.

Try to use a rather shallow bowl; a deep dome may be more difficult to serve when you have many guests. The chicken should be presented on a very large round serving dish so there is room for a wreath of green all round. Both the tossed salad and the lentils or chick-peas should be in bright, pretty ceramic bowls. Have a stack of paper napkins along with wide cotton napkins.

FOR 8 PEOPLE

BROTH

> *3 lb/1.25 kg chicken wings, necks or backs (gizzards as well), trimmed of skin, fat and gristle*
> *1 large veal bone, cracked (optional)*

1 onion, peeled and studded with 2 cloves
Twig of thyme
3 bay leaves
Salt
4 fl oz/100 ml sherry

VEGETABLES AND CHICKEN

2 cups carrots sliced on the bias (about 1 lb/450 g)
Salt
1 tbsp oil
2 medium onions, chopped (1 cup)
½ cup diced lean salt pork or bacon
16 fl oz/450 ml dry white wine
2 chickens, trimmed and cut in half
Freshly ground pepper
2 tsp dried thyme
½ cup coarsely chopped celery or 2 tbsp coarsely chopped green
  pepper
Juice of 3 large lemons
1 lemon rind grated
5 cloves garlic, peeled and sliced
2 veal bones (optional)
3 bay leaves
1 cup chopped parsley

GARNISH

Bunch of parsley or watercress, with stems removed
2 lemons, thinly sliced
1 lime, thinly sliced (optional)
4 tbsp minced parsley or chives or basil

ACCOMPANIMENTS

Lentilles ou Pois Chiches en Salade
Green salad

Prepare the Poulet en Gelée the day before the Feast. Place the sliced carrots in a medium saucepan with a pinch of salt. Cover with water. Bring to a boil, lower the heat and simmer for about 10 minutes, until soft. Refresh under cold water. Drain.

Prepare the broth. In a large saucepan place the chicken parts, veal bone, onion, thyme, bay leaves and salt. Add cold water to cover. Slowly bring to a boil. Skim off scum as it rises. Simmer for 1 hour. Pour the contents through a sieve and retain broth. Bring the sieved broth to a boil. Pass through a fine sieve lined with a clean linen tea-towel or piece of cheesecloth. Add the sherry. Check and correct the seasoning.

Meanwhile, heat 1 tablespoon of oil in a frying pan and cook the chopped onions and lean salt pork for a few minutes, until the onions are soft and translucent. With a slotted spoon, add the onions and pork to the chicken broth and add the white wine. Cook a few minutes more, then turn off the heat.

Place the chicken halves flat in a large roasting pan. Sprinkle with salt, pepper and thyme. Add the chopped celery and then the prepared chicken broth, lemon juice, lemon rind, garlic and veal bones, if used. The meat should be barely covered. You may need 2 pans. Cover with foil, bring to a boil, lower heat, simmer for 1½ hours.

Remove the pieces of chicken and set aside. Reduce the liquid over high heat for 15 minutes in an uncovered saucepan. You should have about 2¼ pt/1.4 l of liquid. Correct the seasoning.

Meanwhile, discard the veal bones. Bone and remove the skin from the chicken with a pointed knife and cut the meat into large pieces, 1½–2 in/35–50 mm. Place a few of the cooked carrot slices round them, alternating with the chopped parsley. Place the chicken pieces and the rest of the cooked vegetables in the bowl, and then pour all the broth on top. The meat will be barely covered. Cool to room temperature, cover with cling film and refrigerate overnight. It will become firm but tender.

On the day of the Feast, a few minutes before serving, dip the bowl into warm water for a second (or dip a tea-towel into warm water, squeeze and then place on top of the bowl for a minute). Run a long knife round the rim of the bowl. Place a serving dish on top of the bowl and, holding it and the bowl firmly, turn them upside down in a decisive movement.

Tuck twigs of parsley or watercress all round the jellied chicken and arrange very thin slices of lemon and lime on the lower part of the jellied dome. Stick 3 short sprigs of parsley on the top of the preparation and sprinkle finely minced parsley, chives or basil all over the dome surface.

Prepare a salad bowl. Pour dressing into the bottom of the bowl, cross the salad spoon and fork over it and place the salad on top. Pour the dressing over lukewarm lentils (or chick-peas), and pour them into a pretty side dish.

Bring the Poulet en Gelée to the table with the lentils and the tossed green salad. Make sure all your guests see the pretty chicken dome as you bring it, and then pass it round with a wide flat spatula and a large serving spoon. You may prefer to serve each guest yourself, placing 2 tablespoons of Poulet en Gelée and 1 tablespoon of lentils on each plate. Leave the tossed salad on the table to be passed round later.

WINE

A light red Burgundy wine, Côte de Beaune or Mercurey, served cool.

WHAT TO SERVE BEFORE AND AFTER POULET EN GELÉE

HORS-D'OEUVRES TO BE SERVED WITH THE DRINKS

1. Crudités with Anchoyade and Tapenade sauces
2. Warm salted almonds, hazelnuts or walnuts
3. Pissaladière
4. Olives Sautées and/or Olives Farcies
5. Tiny sliced tomatoes served on a platter with hard-boiled eggs, sliced lengthways, with a thick paste of basil, garlic, olive oil, salt and pepper. Dot each of them with a black olive.

DESSERTS

1. Crémets aux Fruits and thin biscuits
2. Granité au Vin
3. Panier de Frivolités and a large bowl of Oeufs à la Neige

TABLE DECORATION

This is a summer Feast and your table should be light and crisp. You may choose an ivory or peach tablecloth, a wide basket painted peach or off-white filled with a soft bundle of rambling roses and branches of ferns, wistaria and honeysuckle. You may want to use terracotta accessories – butter pots, salt and pepper shakers – and offer two kinds of bread in napkin-lined baskets. Wrap a fresh napkin round the wine bottle necks, and don't forget the jug of cold water.

STRATEGY FOR THE SUGGESTED MENU

- Guests invited for 7.30 p.m.
- Meal served at 8.30 p.m.

- One day before the feast: prepare the Crudités, sauces, Poulet en Gelée, Lentilles ou Pois Chiches and Crémets

- On the day of the Feast:
  7.30 Your first guests arrive. Bring Crudités basket and two bowls of sauces with the drinks into the sitting-room. Reheat the lentils on a very low heat.

8.25 Light the candles. Ask your guests to the table. Season and toss the salad. Unmould the Poulet en Gelée.
8.30 Bring the Poulet en Gelée and the salad to the table.
8.50 Bring the Crémets and fruits to the table with the plate of thin biscuits.

LEFT-OVERS

1. Omelette: add a few eggs, salt and pepper to the chopped chicken left-overs and make a flat omelette. Dot the surface with a little olive oil or butter and serve it with a light tomato sauce.
2. Chicken fritters: prepare a light batter. Dip 1 tablespoon of chopped left-over chicken in it and deep-fry until golden. Serve the fritters with lemon wedges.
3. Croquettes: add 2 eggs and a little chopped parsley to the chopped chicken left-overs. Check the seasoning. Make into small balls and roll them in a beaten egg and then in breadcrumbs. Fry the croquettes in a little oil or butter and serve surrounded with sprigs of parsley.

Poule Verte

A chicken stuffed with spinach, ham, eggs, herbs, spices and garlic, and served with eight 'baby chick' bundles, a variety of vegetables and a pungent sauce.

SUGGESTED MENU
Gougère

Poule Verte and Stuffed Cabbage Bundles with Vegetables and their Sauces

Mousse au Chocolat Glacée

A Light Red Wine

When Carême stated that 'gastronomy marches like a queen at the head of civilization', he probably had Poule Verte leading the way.

Spread across a platter like a glorious monarch, the 'green' chicken surrounded by her plump 'baby chicks' is indeed a dazzling sight with its moist ivory meat, assortment of firm vegetables, thick slices of stuffing and bowls of pungent sauce and fragrant cooking broth. Toulouse-Lautrec, a fine artist and a superb gourmet, prepared the stuffed hen and her little green bundles in his native Perigord, and celebrated and enjoyed them as often as he could. To him Poule Verte evoked family gatherings and those large Feasts around important occasions when only such an opulent traditional dish will do. It is one of those great reassuring dishes we long to have a few times a year to keep our faith in good things.

Poule Verte is not prepared in a jiffy, but it can be put together calmly in advance and with mostly unattended, foolproof cooking.

The stuffed chicken needs to be cut up at the last minute: the other pieces of chicken, the baby chicks and the vegetables are taken directly from the saucepan to the serving platter. The sauces are ready to be passed round.

FOR 8 PEOPLE

BROTH

> *1 veal skin*
> *8 pt/4.5 l water*
> *1 chicken gizzard and neck*
> *A few chicken bones*
> *Bouquet garni*
> *2 onions, peeled and studded with cloves*
> *Salt*
> *10 peppercorns (approximately)*

VEGETABLES

> *8 carrots, peeled and cut in half lengthways*
> *8 turnips, peeled and halved or quartered*
> *8 leeks (white part only), trimmed, split lengthways, cut into*
> *   4-in/100-mm pieces, and tied into a bundle with string*
> *4 onions, peeled and halved or quartered*
> *5 bulbs fennel, cut in half lengthways*
> *8 stalks celery, cut into sticks*
> *1 large cabbage: to yield at least 10 large cabbage leaves for the 'baby*
> *   chicks' bundles*

SAUCES

> *Bowl of vinaigrette with minced fresh herbs*
> *Bowl of vinaigrette with 2 tbsp minced shallots, 2 hard-boiled eggs,*
> *   chopped, and 1 tbsp Dijon mustard*

STUFFING

> (Enough for 1 chicken and 8 cabbage-wrapped bundles)
> *2 tbsp vegetable oil*
> *2 medium onions, peeled and chopped*
> *½ cup chopped chicken livers*
> *2 lb/900 g fresh spinach, trimmed, cooked and drained; or*
> *   10 oz/275 g package frozen spinach, thawed, drained and squeezed*
> *   dry*

3 lb/1.25 kg cured ham and/or lean salt pork, coarsely chopped
4 cloves garlic, peeled and sliced
4 cups chopped flat parsley
4 shallots, peeled and chopped
3 tsp dried thyme
Pinch of freshly grated nutmeg
2 slices bread, moistened and squeezed
4 eggs, lightly beaten
Salt
Freshly ground pepper

CHICKEN

1 large chicken, ready for stuffing (about 4½ lb/2 kg)
½ oz/15 g butter
1 tbsp oil or more if needed
6 chicken drumsticks
6 chicken thighs

GARNISH

Bowl of minced parsley or *chives*

You can prepare the broth, vegetables, stuffing, chicken and sauces one day in advance. Then you have only to reheat the chicken and cook the vegetables 1½ hours before the dinner.

Prepare the broth. Place the veal in a large saucepan. Add the water, chicken gizzard and neck, bones, bouquet garni, onions, salt and peppercorns. Bring to a boil and simmer for 1 hour, uncovered.

Wash and trim the raw vegetables, cover with cling film and refrigerate.

Prepare the sauces, cover and refrigerate.

Prepare the stuffing, which should be very tasty and heavily spiced. Heat the oil in a frying pan and sauté the onions for a few minutes. Add the chicken livers for 1 minute, stir with a wooden spoon and then remove from the heat. Place in a large bowl and add the spinach, sautéd onions and chicken livers, chopped ham, garlic, parsley, shallots, thyme, nutmeg, soaked bread squeezed dry, eggs, salt and pepper. Chop the mixture coarsely with a knife or scissors, or pulse a few times in a food processor. The mixture should not be too fine. Stir it carefully and stuff it into the chicken with a spoon, making sure it is not tightly packed. Set aside the rest of the stuffing. Sew up the openings of the stuffed chicken and truss it so that it will keep its shape as it cooks.

Heat the butter and 1 tablespoon of vegetable oil in a large frying pan and brown the stuffed chicken for a few minutes. Remove from the heat and set aside. Add a little oil to the pan and sauté the drumsticks and thighs until they are nicely browned all over. You may need to do this in 2 batches.

Add the stuffed chicken to the broth and bring gently to a boil. Simmer for 30 minutes, then add the chicken pieces to the broth. Simmer 30 minutes more. Let the chicken cool in the broth. Transfer both to a large bowl, cover with cling film and refrigerate.

Meanwhile, blanch the cabbage for 15 minutes in a saucepan of boiling water or steam it. Remove the cabbage from the water and separate the leaves, reserving about 10 large ones or 20 small ones. Discard the rest of the cabbage or use it puréed as an accompaniment.

Place a piece of cheesecloth on a work surface. Spread 1 large cabbage leaf or 2 small ones overlapping slightly at the stem end. Sprinkle with salt and pepper, and place 1 tablespoon stuffing in the centre. Tuck in the leaf to make a little bundle and fold the cheesecloth loosely round it. Proceed until you have 8 bundles. Place the bundles, folded side down, on the perforated tray of the steamer. Steam for 30 minutes. If you do not have a steamer, use a wide saucepan and colander. Let the bundles cool to room temperature, cover with cling film and refrigerate.

On the evening of the Feast, 1½ hours before your dinner, take everything out of the refrigerator, including the trimmed raw vegetables and the sauces.

Remove all the fat from the broth and correct the seasoning. Place the broth only in a saucepan and bring it to a boil. Check every piece of poultry to make sure it has no gristle or fat. Remove the skin from the stuffed chicken and from the thighs and drumsticks. Place the stuffed chicken and chicken pieces in the boiling broth, cover and simmer for 30 minutes.

Bring the water in the bottom of the steamer to a boil. Place the vegetables on a tray and cook for 15 minutes. Add the 8 green bundles to the second tray and cook 20 minutes more. If you do not have a multi-tiered steamer, cook the vegetables in a saucepan of salted water and the bundles in another saucepan of fresh water.

Warm 2 large serving platters. When you are ready to serve, carve the stuffed chicken, remove its stuffing, which should be in one compact piece, and slice it. Place the overlapping slices of the stuffing in the centre of the platter and place the pieces of carved chicken round it. Add the thighs and drumsticks to the platter. Spoon a few tablespoons of hot broth over everything and sprinkle with salt, pepper and chives. Cover tightly with foil to keep warm.

Place the little cabbage bundles on another serving dish, remove the pieces of cheesecloth and discard them. Surround with the steamed vegetables, spoon a little hot broth over everything and season with salt and pepper. Cover with a piece of foil.

When everybody is seated at the table, remove the foil from the serving dishes and bring them to the dining-room with the Poule Verte, warm plates, 2 bowls of sauce, chicken broth and bowl of minced fresh parsley or chives.

Serve a piece of chicken, a slice of stuffing, a green cabbage bundle and a few vegetables on each plate. Spoon a little hot broth and a pinch of minced herbs on top before handing a plate to each guest. Pass the bowls of sauce and warm broth round the table.

Note: If you are a good carver, you may prefer to show the Poule Verte surrounded by the little green chicks and the lovely vegetable assortment. It is a beautiful and appetizing sight.

I tend to think that once you have more than 6 people at a table the process of carving, slicing and serving takes so long that by the time all guests are served the meal is lukewarm, at best, or cold, which is a great pity for such a delicious dish. However, if you have a good carver you can trust to help, you may serve the rest of the dish on each plate while he or she carves so that serving does not take too long and the theatrical aspect of the process remains.

WINE

A light red, a dry white wine or a full-bodied red wine.

WHAT TO SERVE BEFORE AND AFTER POULE VERTE

HORS-D'OEUVRES TO BE SERVED WITH THE DRINKS

1. Gougère
2. Pissaladière
3. Pissenlits aux Lardons

DESSERTS

1. Mousse au Chocolat Glacée
2. Grand Baba
3. Poires, Pruneaux, Oranges au Vin Rouge et aux Épices
4. Tarte Tatin aux Poires et aux Pommes

TABLE DECORATION

This is a fairly messy dish, although you will keep the serving dishes themselves on a side table.

You may wish to use two short vases instead of a single centre-piece and fill them with a variety of tulips or peonies a few hours before your party. By the time you light the candles, the stems will have taken unpredictable curves.

Better not use a delicate, light-coloured tablecloth. A thick fabric, woven like a country rug, with many shades of brown, rust and beige, or a piece of patchwork quilted fabric (not a valuable antique – you are interested only in a pretty print rendering) could be lovely, and you might like a few faded or dark green accessories for the crockery, salt and pepper shakers, butter pots and napkins.

Even if you have the plainest setting, set a pile of raw eggs in a pretty basket in the centre of the table and relax: your royal platter with the mother hen and her green baby chicks is so overwhelming that it will steal the show.

STRATEGY FOR THE SUGGESTED MENU

- Guests invited for 7.30 p.m.
- Meal served at 8.30 p.m.

- One day before the Feast: prepare the Mousse au Chocolat and freeze it. Cook the stuffed chicken, cabbage bundles, drumsticks and thighs as indicated. Wash and trim the vegetables and garnish. Prepare the sauces. Prepare the orange salad for the Mousse.

- On the day of the Feast:
  5.00 Take everything except the Mousse out of the refrigerator.
  7.00 Make the Gougère and bake it as indicated.
  7.30 Bring chicken broth and water to a boil. Your first guests arrive.
  8.00 Serve Gougère with the drinks. Cook the vegetables and stuffed cabbage bundles in water and reheat the stuffed chicken and cut-up thighs and drumsticks in the chicken broth.
  8.30 Light the candles. Prepare platters as indicated and serve when all your guests are seated at the dining-room table. Return all left-overs to the steamer or saucepan to keep warm until second helpings are needed – about 15 minutes.
  9.00 Change plates and serve the Mousse au Chocolat with the orange sauce and a plate of thin biscuits.

LEFT-OVERS

1. Croquettes: mix the chopped left-over chicken with 2 eggs and a little fresh parsley. Check the seasoning. Make into small balls, and roll in beaten egg and then in breadcrumbs. Fry in a little oil or butter.

2. Omelette: add chopped left-over chicken and stuffing to beaten eggs. Season with salt and pepper.

3. Chicken soup made from the broth, some chopped left-over chicken and a little rice.

4. Gratin: can be made with left-over stuffing thinned with a little broth, sprinkled with breadcrumbs, dotted with butter and baked for 30 minutes at 375°F/190°C/Mark 5. You may also add chopped left-over meat and chopped left-over vegetables to the mixture.

5. You can freeze any left-over chicken stock and use it later as a base for a sauce or a soup, such as Gratinée Lyonnaise.

DESSERTS

Cervelle de Canut

This herbed fresh cheese is whipped with cream and dry white wine.

A '*canut*' is a worker in the silk factories of Lyon. This dish was called a 'worker's brain' because it is like a true *canut*: high-spirited, demanding, passionate and colourful.

One of the most invigorating and fresh ways of ending a heavy meal, Cervelle de Canut is made with a variety of herbs and must be beaten vigorously – 'just as if it were your wife', as the appalling saying goes. Mores have changed in Lyon as elsewhere, but this delicious dish prevails.

FOR 8 PEOPLE

INGREDIENTS

>*1 lb/450 g cottage cheese*
>*4 tbsp soured cream*
>*3 tbsp double cream*
>*1 cup finely minced chives, tarragon, dill or parsley*
>*2 cloves garlic, peeled and finely minced*
>*2 tbsp dry white wine*
>*1 tbsp red wine vinegar*
>*2 tbsp olive or vegetable oil*
>*Salt to taste*
>*Freshly ground pepper to taste*

ACCOMPANIMENT

>*Bread, toasted and cut into triangles*

Whip all the ingredients by hand for a few minutes. It should be smooth but not frothy. Correct the seasoning. Cover with cling film and refrigerate.

Serve with a large spoon and a linen-lined basket of warm toast points.

Note: You can also serve it with a basket of Crudités as an hors-d'oeuvres.

Compote de Poires

These pears, simmered in butter and flavoured with grated lemon rind and fresh ginger, are served with home-made crème fraîche.

A light, fresh family dessert to make in advance, this is wonderful after a heavy *plat de résistance*. You can serve the pears with thin biscuits and pass a bowl of home-made crème fraîche. French crème fraîche is a cream that has been allowed to mature. Its distinctive nutty flavour is hard to reproduce, but you can make a very good home-made version. Bitter chocolate sorbet store-bought is fine and is splendid with this.

FOR 8 PEOPLE

CRÈME FRAÎCHE

> *8 fl oz/225 ml double* or *whipping cream*
> *1 tbsp buttermilk*

PEARS

> *8 firm, ripe, preferably Anjou pears, cored, peeled and quartered*
> *4 oz/100 g unsalted butter*
> *4 oz/100 g fresh ginger (approximately) peeled and cut up into tiny thin sticks*
> *Rind of 1 lemon, thinly grated*
> *½ cup sugar*
> *1 tbsp cold water*

Mix the cream with the buttermilk in a saucepan. Heat the mixture gently to lukewarm, then pour it into a bowl. Cover and keep it in a warm place (60–80°F/16–27°C) for a day. Stir to make sure the mixture has thickened, then place it in the refrigerator until ready to serve. It will keep for a week.

Prepare the pears. Preheat the oven to 375°F/190°C/Mark 5. Place the quartered pears in a pretty ovenproof dish. Dot with butter, sprinkle on the ginger sticks and grated lemon rind, dot with butter again.

Pour the sugar into a thick-bottomed saucepan, add 1 tablespoon of cold water and bring to a boil over high heat without stirring. As soon as it turns deep brown, pour this caramel over the pears.

Bake the pears for 10 minutes, then lower the temperature to 350°F/180°C/Mark 4 and cook for 10 minutes more. Remove from the oven when the pears are soft, but not mushy.

Serve the pears lukewarm in their ovenproof dish or cold in a pretty glass bowl. Pass the crème fraîche and, if you like, a dish of bitter chocolate sorbet.

Crémets aux Fruits

A delicate mixture of whipped cream, whipped egg whites, lemon and sugar, drained overnight and served with puréed and fresh berries.

They are no longer served in Normandy's country inns or along the Loire valley's little restaurants, but Crémets remain the proper dessert in well-run homes where the traditions of fine food have been carefully maintained.

Crémets appear on the table for big occasions after a hearty *plat de résistance*, when their light and delicate texture, enhanced by the sharpness of a fruit purée and the crispness of fresh fruit, makes for the most delicious of combinations.

You can mould the Crémets in little heart-shaped moulds with draining holes or in a colander lined with cheesecloth so that the liquid will easily drain away.

They are served with raspberry or strawberry purée, fresh berries and fresh cream for 'complete pleasure', as the farmers put it.

A rich cousin of Crémets is Coeur à la Crème, which is generally made with cream cheese, cottage cheese and cream.

FOR 8 PEOPLE

CRÉMETS

> *1⅔ pt/900 ml double* or *whipping cream*
> *1 tbsp soured cream*
> *5 egg whites*
> *3 tsp finely grated lemon rind*
> *2 tsp sugar*

PURÉE

> *1⅔ pt/900 ml fresh berries, trimmed and cleaned*
> *1 cup sugar (approximately)*
> *Juice of 2 large lemons (approximately)*
> or
> *2 packages of frozen berries (10 oz/275 g)*
> *Juice of 2 large lemons*
> *Sugar to taste*

ACCOMPANIMENTS

> *3 tbsp single cream*
> *Bowl of fresh raspberries* or *strawberries, cleaned and drained*

One day and a night before the Feast prepare the Crémets and fruit purée.

Whip the cream until it makes soft peaks. Fold in the soured cream. In a separate bowl, whip the egg whites until firm, then fold them gently into the whipped cream until stiff.

Mix in the grated lemon rind and sugar. Gently pour into the pierced little moulds or a colander lined with cheesecloth and fold the piece of cloth over the top. Set the moulds or colander into a bowl and allow to drain for a few hours in a cool place. Refrigerate overnight.

Make the purée. If you are using fresh fruit, whip the ingredients in a blender until smooth. Add more sugar or more lemon to taste. If you are using frozen fruit, first thaw the berries, preserving any juice that melts off. Put the berries in a blender with a little of the juice, add lemon juice and whip until blended. Add sugar to taste. (Frozen fruits often have sugar added already, so read the information on the packet.)

Just before serving, unfold the cheesecloth and invert the contents on to a wide serving plate or platter. Pour some single cream on top and spoon a little fruit purée round. Make it as neat as possible.

Serve the rest of the purée in a bowl or jug and the fresh berries in a flat basket lined with a paper doily or a few fresh green leaves.

Crêpes Normandes

Thin crêpes stuffed with diced apples, simmered in brown sugar, sprinkled with Calvados, spread with a pungent redcurrant sauce and reheated at the last moment.

The name evokes austere ladies in lace head-dresses officiating over their open-air griddles in Brittany market-places and spreading salted butter on their large golden crêpes in front of gasping children. But the name also brings to mind bad memories of fancy burning affairs prepared out of copper dishes in pretentious restaurants.

Even though crêpes are the simplest and cheapest of desserts, for all children and most adults they will always spell 'the best'.

Crêpes Normandes offers a spectacular finale for any family Feast, and it is an easy dessert to prepare and to serve. Cooked in advance and reheated 30 minutes before serving, Crêpes Normandes will go straight from the oven to the table in its baking dish.

Once again I have given you too big a recipe for eight people, and you may have five or six crêpes left at the end of the meal. But the sight of so many plump crêpes under their red foamy sauce is truly exciting and festive. And any left-over crêpe will reheat beautifully the next day as long as you dot it with butter and cover it with foil. In this recipe I use beer and water instead of the usual cream and milk for a thinner crêpe batter, and I choose the tangiest and sharpest apples I can find on the market, adding more lemon if I find them too sweet.

FOR 8 PEOPLE

CRÊPE BATTER

> *2 cups flour*
> *2 eggs, lightly beaten*
> *Pinch of salt*
> *8 fl oz/225 ml beer*
> *8 fl oz/225 ml water, or more if needed*
> *2 tbsp vegetable oil or 1 oz/25 g butter, melted*
> *1 tbsp orange-blossom water (optional)*
> *1 oz/25 g butter or vegetable oil or a small piece of pork fat*

FILLING

> *3 lb/1.25 kg (approximately) apples, such as Granny Smith*
> *1 oz/25 g butter*
> *10 tbsp brown sugar*
> *1–2 tbsp lemon juice*
> *1 lemon rind, grated*

TOPPING

> *8 tbsp redcurrant jelly*
> *1 tbsp water*
> *2 tbsp Calvados (optional)*

Make the batter. Put the flour in a bowl. Make a well in the centre and place in it the lightly beaten eggs and salt. With a whisk or a fork stir the flour gradually into the eggs. Beat in the beer, water and oil until the batter is smooth; also add orange-blossom water if you wish. Let stand for 1 hour or so.

Make the filling. Peel, core and dice the apples. Place them in a pan with the butter, brown sugar, lemon juice and lemon rind. Cover and cook slowly for about 30 minutes (depending on the apples), until soft. They should not turn into purée. Set aside.

When you are ready to prepare the crêpes check the consistency of the batter and add more water if it is too thick: it should feel like a thick cream or a light custard. Heat the 2 crêpe pans. Rub them either with butter, oil or pork fat. (You can put the fat on a fork or use a piece of cheesecloth dipped in oil and put on the end of a fork. The main thing is to feel comfortable while you oil the pans and be ready to act quickly. Very little fat is needed in the pans after the third crêpe.)

When the first pan is warm, add 2 or 3 tablespoons of batter, turning the pan so the surface is evenly coated. Use as little batter as possible so the crêpes are really thin. Cook over a high heat. Oil and fill the second pan. After 1 minute or less turn the first crêpe on the other side with a spatula. It should detach easily if it is cooked. Wait 1 minute longer and then slide the crêpe on to a plate. Turn the second crêpe. Stack the cooked crêpes together and place a large plate over them so they keep moist while you continue to make the other crêpes.

Place a large tablespoon of cooked apples in the centre of each crêpe. Roll the crêpe so it looks like a 2-in/50-mm wide cigar. Butter 2 baking dishes and place the rolled crêpes in them side by side and slightly overlapping. Dot the surface with butter. Cover with a sheet of foil. Set aside in the refrigerator or a cool place.

Thirty minutes before you sit down to dinner, preheat the oven to 350°F/180°C/Mark 4. Pour the redcurrant jelly and the water into a pan, and cook over a slow heat, stirring until it turns into a syrup. Cover and keep warm.

When you sit down to dinner, place the 2 covered gratin dishes with the crêpes in the oven to reheat. As you go to the kitchen to change plates for the dessert course, remove the foil from the crêpe dishes, pour half of the warm jelly over the crêpes and put them back in the oven for a few minutes to lightly glaze the surface. Bring the liquid refreshments to the table (see Wine below). Remove the baking dishes from the oven, sprinkle on a little Calvados, then pour the rest of the warm redcurrant syrup on the surface. Wrap each dish with a large tea-towel or napkin and bring them to the table. Use a spatula to slide each crêpe on to a plate and use a spoon for any juice left in the bottom of the baking dish.

WINE

Serve cider or a sweet white wine, perhaps a heady Muscat wine or a fortified wine to which alcohol was added during fermentation to seal the sweetness of the grape. Chilled sweet champagne would also be lovely.

Flan au Caramel

An unmoulded caramel custard.

An old favourite that is easy to prepare in advance, easy to serve and loved by all, whether served in individual pots or as a spectacular unmoulded amber dome. For a flamboyant finale you may want to serve it with an assortment, or a *Farandole* (the mad dance done hand in hand down the hills of Provence), of desserts, together with Mousse au Chocolat Glacée and a basket of Frivolités, since all can be prepared in advance.

Flan au Caramel is always best served at room temperature, and if you serve it in individual pots it is even better lukewarm.

FOR 8 PEOPLE

CARAMEL

> *½ cup sugar*
> *2 tbsp water*
> *Dot of butter*

CUSTARD

> *2 cups sugar*
> *2 pt/1.1 l milk*
> *1 vanilla pod*
> *6 eggs*
> *6 egg yolks*
> *1 tbsp candied orange peel shavings or very finely grated fresh*
>   *orange rind*

The Flan must be prepared a few hours before you serve it. Prepare the caramel. Bring the sugar and water to a boil in the frying pan. Lower the heat and let the caramel slowly develop a deep amber colour; do not stir. Add the butter and quickly pour the amber-coloured syrup into the moulds, turning in all directions so the caramel coats the bottom and sides before it hardens.

Preheat the oven to 350°F/180°C/Mark 4. Make the custard by combining the sugar, milk and vanilla in a thick-bottomed saucepan rinsed with cold water. Bring to a boil. Meanwhile, beat the eggs and egg yolks together until pale. Add the warm milk slowly, stirring constantly, then pour the custard mixture into the caramelized moulds.

Place the moulds in a large baking pan and pour in hot water to come half-way up the sides of the moulds. Bake for 40 minutes for a large mould or 20 minutes for individual moulds. Test by plunging a knife into the custard – if it comes out clean, the custard is finished.

Cool the custards to room temperature. To serve, run a knife round the edges of the moulds and unmould in a decisive movement just before serving. Sprinkle the tops with candied orange peel or grated orange rind. Reheat the moulds to soften any left-over caramel in the bottoms and pour it over the orange peel.

If you have china moulds and do not want to unmould the custard, you can make a little extra caramel, grate some orange rind on top of each pot, reheat the caramel and pour it on top.

It is better to serve this at room temperature or even lukewarm rather than cold, so leave it in the oven with the heat off if prepared a few hours in advance.

WINE

A mellow white dessert wine, Sauternes, Barsac or a demi-sec champagne.

Grand Baba

A moist plump cake filled with fruit, flavoured with syrup and brandy, and decorated with apricot glaze and candied fruit.

The small cylindrical Rum Baba, like a golden toy, with a touch of whipped cream and heavy dose of dark rum, is the traditional bistro dessert. But for a family extravaganza, for a big family Feast, the Baba grows. Made in a large ring mould, its name changes to 'Savarin', in memory of the grand gourmet Brillat-Savarin. For the true Baba lovers, and for children who don't care to master such differences, there are only two desserts worth mentioning: Petit Baba and Grand Baba; Savarin is too highbrow.

Where do babas come from? Apparently from a gourmet king. The story is that a Polish king, Stanislaw Leszczyński, on tasting a delicious brioche-like little cake impregnated with Malaga wine, named it Ali Baba after his favourite character in the *Thousand and One Nights* because he considered it worthy of the cavern of treasures in this famous book. The name has become plain Baba to us.

For a memorable dessert, make two Grand Baba rings. Fill the centre of one with diced apples sautéd in butter, brown sugar and lemon, and impregnate the cake with a kirsch-flavoured syrup. Fill the centre of the other with fresh sliced oranges and Grand Marnier. Pass a bowl of whipped cream round.

Some cooks add raisins that have been soaked in Malaga or port for an hour, or diced candied fruit, to the dough before baking the Babas. I find the fruit garnish, glaze and syrup enough to dress up these delicious cakes.

Make the cakes a day or so in advance and freeze them. Prepare the syrup and jam glaze in advance too. Cook the apples and slice and flavour the oranges. Cover both dishes and leave in the refrigerator until a few minutes before serving the cake. Three hours before the dinner, reheat the cakes, syrup and glaze for a few minutes.

Grand Baba should slowly soak up the syrup and be very moist but not soggy. Pour out excess syrup. It can be glazed with an apricot glaze and decorated with (glacé) fruits or if you have tiny strawberries you may prefer, just before serving, to make tiny incisions on top of the Baba and insert the strawberries before pouring on the glaze.

This is one of the most relaxing yet spectacular and popular of family desserts.

FOR 8 PEOPLE

PASTRY

> *4 oz/100 g butter*
> *⅔ oz/16 g fresh yeast*
> *4 tbsp sugar*
> *1 tsp salt*
> *4 eggs, lightly beaten*
> *4 cups flour*
> *1 oz/25 g butter, softened (for the moulds)*
> *Fine breadcrumbs*

FILLINGS

FOR BABA 1:

> *1 oz/25 g butter*
> *3 large apples (Granny Smith, MacIntosh), peeled, cored and cut into 1-in/25-mm dice*
> *2 tsp brown sugar*
> *Lemon juice (optional)*

FOR BABA 2:

> *5 oranges*
> *Juice of 1 lemon*
> *3 tbsp Grand Marnier*
> *Sugar*

CHANTILLY CREAM

> *8 fl oz/225 ml double* or *whipping cream*
> *2 tbsp sugar*
> *2 tsp vanilla extract (optional)*

GLAZE

> *½ cup apricot preserves*
> *3 tbsp sugar*
> *2 tbsp rum*
> *Lemon juice*

SYRUPS

FOR BABA 1:

> *16 fl oz/450 ml water*
> *1 cup sugar*
> *Juice of 1 lemon*
> *5 fl oz/150 ml dark Jamaican rum* or *kirsch*

FOR BABA 2:

> *1 cup sugar*
> *16 fl oz/450 ml orange juice*
> *3 tbsp Grand Marnier*

Make the pastry. Melt the butter over a low heat. Let it cool. In a bowl crumble the fresh yeast and add sugar, salt and eggs. Beat until well blended. Pour the flour in a large bowl. Add the cooled butter and stir carefully. Add the yeast and egg mixture, and knead with your fingers, lifting the dough and pulling it for a few minutes. After 5 or 6 minutes it turns smooth and elastic. Pull it between your hands to make sure it is no longer too sticky and it can stretch.

Scrape the dough into a large ball and place it in the bottom of the bowl. Cut a cross on top of the dough and sprinkle it with 1 tablespoon of flour. Cover the bowl with 2 folded wet towels and keep it in a warm place, even in a *very* low oven or one that has been heated slightly and turned off.

After 2 hours punch the dough with your fingers and fold the outside back into the centre.

Butter the 2 ring moulds. Sprinkle 1 tablespoon of fine breadcrumbs or a little flour in each, shaking and twisting the moulds to coat the sides and bottom lightly. Pour the dough into the 2 moulds. They will be about one-third full.

Let them rise in the lukewarm oven, uncovered, for 1 or 2 hours. Punch with a finger to deflate the dough again. Remove from the oven.

Preheat the oven to 375°F/190°C/Mark 5 and bake both rings for about 20 minutes. The sides will shrink a little and the top will be golden.

Turn each cake upside down on a rack. After 5 minutes, remove the moulds and cool to room temperature. You can freeze them as soon as they are cool.

To make the filling for Baba 1, heat the butter and cook the prepared apples until soft but not brown. Cool to room temperature. Sprinkle with the brown sugar and a little lemon juice, if desired. Cover and refrigerate.

To make the filling for Baba 2, peel and thinly slice the 5 oranges. Put the slices in a bowl with the lemon juice, Grand Marnier and a little sugar. Cover and refrigerate.

To make the Chantilly Cream, pour the chilled cream into a large chilled bowl and beat it, lifting the cream and turning the beater round as you go. It is ready when a bit of cream retains its shape when you lift it. Fold in the sugar and vanilla. Cover and refrigerate.

To prepare the glaze, press the apricot preserve through a sieve into a small saucepan over a medium heat. Stir for 3 minutes or so; it will become syrupy and sticky. Stir in sugar, rum and lemon juice and cook for a few moments more. Keep in a jar or in the pan to use later.

Prepare the syrups.

For Baba 1, mix the water, sugar and lemon juice together in a small saucepan over a low heat until the sugar is completely dissolved and you have a syrup consistency. Remove from the heat.

For Baba 2, mix the sugar and orange juice together in a small saucepan over a low heat until the sugar is completely dissolved and you have a syrup consistency. Remove from the heat.

When the syrups are at room temperature, add rum or kirsch to one and Grand Marnier to the other.

When you are ready to assemble the cakes, place the 2 frozen cakes on the middle rack in the oven at 300°F/150°C/Mark 2 for about 30 minutes, until the insides are lukewarm. Prick the top and side of each cake with a fork delicately. Place the cakes on 2 wide plates, upside down, the brown flat side against the plate, the porous bottom side up.

Reheat the syrups and spoon half of each syrup slowly over its respective cake. Let it soak for about 30 minutes, then add the rest. The dough is very spongy so all the syrup should soak in after an hour. Pour off any excess syrup after 30 minutes more. The Babas should be moist, not soggy.

Sprinkle a little extra kirsch, rum or Grand Marnier on top of each cake. Reheat the glaze for a minute or so and apply lightly on the tops of the 2 rings. It will cool into a shiny glaze. You may want to apply pieces of angelica cut into little diamond shapes and glacé cherries cut in half. Pour a bit of glaze over them too.

Spoon the cooked apples into the centre of one of the Babas and the sliced oranges into the centre of the other. Pour the Chantilly Cream into a pretty serving bowl and bring it, the 2 Grand Babas and the dessert plates to the dining-room.

Pass the Babas and the bowl of Chantilly Cream round the table. Each guest will have a piece of both Babas with their respective garnish and some Chantilly Cream.

WINE

Serve with a sweet white wine. Also serve iced water.

Granité au Vin

A red or white, sweet or dry wine sorbet served with chopped mint leaves.

This must be done with a good wine: a sweet Sauternes, a good port or a heady Bordeaux. Taste the wine to make sure of its quality. Prepare the Granité a day in advance and then spoon into pretty glasses and decorate with a few mint leaves, if you have them, or a small cut flower or a tiny swirl of lemon peel.

This is clearly not nursery food, so keep it for the finale of a rich meal and serve a plain ice cream to children and timid souls.

You may like to serve the Granité in a large crystal bowl surrounded by poached peaches or pears. Their sweetness, texture and colour will be a pleasant counterpoint to the Granité. Scatter mint leaves on top.

FOR 8 PEOPLE

GRANITÉ

>*1½ cups sugar*
>*6 fl oz/175 ml water*
>*Grated rind of 3 oranges and 2 lemons*
>*Juice of 2 large oranges*
>*Juice of 2 lemons*
>*24 fl oz/675 ml Bordeaux or Sauternes or port wine*

GARNISH

> *Several mint leaves*
> *Several tiny cut flowers* or *8 little lemon twirls*
> *4 poached peaches* or *pears*

Place the sugar, water and grated lemon and orange rinds in a saucepan and bring to a boil. Turn off the heat after 5 minutes. Cool. Add the fruit juices and the wine. Stir thoroughly and then pour into a wide shallow dish. Cover with foil and put in the freezer. After 1 hour or so use a fork to scrape all the solid icy parts on the bottom and sides of the dish, and stir well. Repeat after another hour. The Granité should be flaky and a little mushy. Cover with foil and freeze overnight.

Just before serving the Granité, remove the foil and stir once more with a fork so the ice is crisp and even. Spoon the Granité into either parfait, champagne or tall Pilsner-type glasses and shape the tops into pretty domes. Plant a mint leaf, a small cut flower or a tiny swirl of lemon peel on top. Or place poached peaches or pears in the bottom of a shallow dish, put the Granité on top and scatter mint leaves over both. You might also like to pass a plate of thin biscuits.

WINE

The same you have used in the Granité, or champagne.

Madeleines Tièdes aux Fruits

Lukewarm madeleine cakes with an assortment of fruit preparations.

Even if they don't remind you of Proust, even if they don't evoke memories of grand visits with elderly relatives in nostalgic manors, Madeleines are inspired and inspiring. Composed in the spirit of yester-year, they speak of lazy afternoons under a linden tree, deep wicker chairs, Chinese tea in fine china cups, mint and verbena infusions, and they are a wonderful response to stress, anguish, anxiety or whatever it is you try to banish when you organize your Feast.

Madeleine cakes should always be served lukewarm, with their plump shell-like sides up, with a tray of assorted preserves, compotes, honeys or fruit preparations. They can be prepared in advance and reheated. If Madeleines are served with dessert, a sweet wine or champagne is perfect.

FOR 8 PEOPLE

MADELEINES

> *4 oz/100 g butter*
> *4 eggs, separated*
> *1 cup sugar*
> *Salt*
> *1¾ cups flour*
> *Rind of 2 small or 1 large lemon, grated*

GARNISH

> Choose 1 or more of the following:
> *Bowl of sliced oranges marinated in lemon juice and Campari then
>   sprinkled with sugar*
> *Bowl of cooked apples and pears sprinkled with a little lemon juice*
> *Mousse au Chocolat Glacée*
> *Bowl of raspberry and lemon purée*
> *3 bowls of different preserves gathered on a round tray*
> *Assortment of honeys*

Soften the butter. Beat the egg yolks and sugar until pale yellow. Add the butter, stirring until totally smooth and light yellow.

Whip the egg whites until firm, then add a little salt. Add the egg whites, spoonful by spoonful, to the yolk mixture, alternating with spoonfuls of flour and lifting with a spatula delicately. Add the lemon rind.

Preheat the oven to 300°F/150°C/Mark 2. Butter the Madeleine mould thoroughly and pour the batter into the mould. Each Madeleine should be three-quarters full.

Bake for 5 minutes, then raise the temperature to 350°F/180°C/Mark 4 and bake for 10 minutes more. Unmould.

A few minutes before serving, place the Madeleine cakes on a baking sheet. Cover them with a sheet of foil and reheat in a 350°F/180°C/Mark 4 oven for a few minutes.

Put the Madeleine cakes on a flat plate lined with a paper doily and serve with the garnish you have chosen.

WINE

A sweet wine or champagne.

Mélange de Fruits

A fresh fruit salad.

A lovely finale after a heavy meal, this can be prepared entirely in advance. Whether it is a simple mixture of fresh ripe fruits or a sophisticated dessert enhanced with a mixture of lemon, orange juice and brandy or a purée of fruits, Mélange de Fruits is delicious. Served with a chilly champagne it turns into a Mélange de Fruits Royal.

FOR 8 PEOPLE

FRUITS

> *Choose 12 to 15 ripe fruits to make about 9–12 cups of cut-up fruit.*

In autumn and winter

> *Melons, oranges, kumquats, tangerines, pineapples, apples,*
>   *bananas, nuts*

In spring or summer

> *Peaches, apricots, pears, plums, strawberries, raspberries,*
>   *blueberries, blackcurrants, redcurrants, grapes, figs,*
>   *mangoes (wonderful all year round)*

DRESSINGS

DRESSING 1:

> *Juice of 1 lemon*
> *Juice of 2 oranges*
> *4 tbsp of cognac, rum, kirsch or Grand Marnier*
> *⅔ cup sugar (approximately: according to taste and to the sweetness*
>   *of fruit selected)*
> *Several pieces of crystallized or fresh ginger, thinly shaved*
> *Mint leaves*
> *Bottle of chilled champagne (optional)*

DRESSING 2:

> *2 ripe mangoes, peeled*
> *2 very ripe peaches, peeled*
> *Juice of 1 orange*
> *Mint leaves*

If you are going to use Dressing 1, wash, peel and slice the fresh fruits and place them in a large bowl. Pour the lemon and orange juice on top and add the brandy, rum or liqueur to taste. Cover the bowl and refrigerate.

Just before serving, sprinkle a little sugar and ginger shavings on top. Bring the bowl to the table, toss gently, add mint leaves and serve. If you want to add champagne, bring the chilled bottle to the table, open and pour it on the fruit salad. Don't toss. Serve at once.

If you are going to use Dressing 2, blend the dressing ingredients in advance in a blender or food processor, then keep refrigerated. A few hours before the party, wash, peel and slice the fresh fruits. Place all of them except the berries in a large bowl and pour the dressing on top. Dot with the berries and fresh mint leaves. Cover with cling film and refrigerate until ready to serve.

Mélange de Fruits is served with either Panier de Frivolités or a plate of biscuits.

Mousse au Chocolat Glacée

A frozen chocolate mousse meringue with coffee and orange flavourings.

Everybody loves chocolate mousse, but there are two pitfalls to avoid. Some are so light and fluffy that they lack substance; you look forward to them but when they reach your mouth, there is nothing there. On the other hand, some chocolate mousses are rich and heady but so overwhelmingly buttery, chocolaty or sugary that your liver cries for mercy after the third spoonful.

This frozen version is wonderful and seems to avoid the pitfalls; it is velvety, tasty, yet quite light. It should be prepared one day in advance, then placed in the freezer and taken out a few minutes before serving.

FOR 8 PEOPLE

ORANGE SAUCE

> *Juice of 4 oranges*
> *2½ fl oz/65 ml honey*
> *5 large oranges, peeled and thinly sliced*

MOUSSE

> *3 tbsp water*
> *3 tbsp instant coffee powder*
> *14 oz/400 g semi-sweet chocolate, cut in pieces*

8 egg yolks
1 cup sugar
3 tsp grated orange rind
14 egg whites
Pinch of salt
10 tbsp icing sugar

GARNISH

Bowl of fine chocolate shavings
8 fl oz/225 ml fruit purée or 4 fl oz/100 ml whipped cream or
*   4 fl oz/100 ml soured cream combined with 4 fl oz/100 ml double*
*   cream and 4 tbsp sugar gently whipped together or 4 fl oz/100 ml of*
*   Orange Sauce poured over 4 sliced oranges*

To make the sauce, place the juice and honey in a saucepan, bring to a boil and pour over the peeled orange slices. Place in the refrigerator until ready to serve.

Make the mousse. Heat the water and instant coffee powder in a thick-bottomed saucepan. Add the chocolate pieces and cook over a low heat, stirring until smooth. Turn off the heat and set aside. In a bowl beat the egg yolks with the sugar until the mixture turns a pale yellow. Add to the coffee and chocolate mixture, stirring for a few minutes. Grate the orange rind into the pan. Taste to see if you should add more orange rind or some salt.

Beat the egg whites with a pinch of salt. When they turn white and frothy, add the sugar and keep beating until the egg whites are firm and solid.

With a spatula fold the egg whites into the lukewarm chocolate and eggs mixture, lifting gently as you draw the bottom to the top.

Pour into a lightly oiled charlotte mould and cover tightly with waxed paper or pour into an ice-cream mould and close it tight and place it in the freezer, where it should remain for at least 24 hours.

Just before you are ready to serve it, remove the Chocolate Mousse from the freezer and dip the bottom of the mould into a pan of hot water for a few seconds. Place a large serving plate over the mould and, holding tight to the sides of the charlotte mould and the edge of the plate, turn them over in a decisive movement. The Mousse should slide out of its mould easily.

Sprinkle the surface of the dome with chocolate shavings and pour some fruit purée or lightly whipped cream or a mixture of slightly beaten soured cream and double cream or some peeled oranges covered with light honey sauce all round the Chocolate Mousse.

If your meal is delayed, cover the unmoulded Mousse with a large bowl and return to the freezer until ready to serve.

Oeufs à la Neige et aux Fruits

Poached pears, covered with a light custard, topped with soft meringues and sprinkled with caramel and bitter chocolate shavings.

Some like to refer to Oeufs à la Neige as nursery food, but I always think of this dessert as *faux naif*, a falsely naive one. There is indeed nothing babyish or overly simple in this dessert and each guest goes from delight to delight, plunging his spoon into the beautiful snowy bowl, the crunchy chocolate and caramel top, the fluffy meringue balls, the silky custard and the mellow pear.

This can be prepared in advance. You may prefer to flavour the custard with a little orange blossom water and the pears with a little Calvados, but if you would rather omit them, the flavour of a vanilla pod in the custard is also quite lovely.

FOR 8 PEOPLE

MERINGUES

> *8 egg whites*
> *¾ cup sugar*

CUSTARD

> *21 fl oz/600 ml milk*
> *8 egg yolks*
> *1 cup sugar*
> *1 tbsp orange-blossom water or 1 vanilla pod or 1 tbsp vanilla extract*

PEARS

> *4 large pears, peeled and sliced, or 4 large canned pears, drained*
> *1 oz/25 g butter*
> *1 tbsp Calvados (optional)*

GARNISH

> *Piece of semi-sweet chocolate (to yield about 3 tbsp of shavings)*
> *½ cup sugar*
> *2 tbsp water*
> *Several drops of vinegar or lemon juice*
> *Dot of butter*

Make the meringues. Bring a wide frying pan or saucepan of salted water to the boil. Meanwhile, in a bowl beat the egg whites until stiff. Add the cup of sugar and continue to beat slowly for a few seconds.

Lower the heat and keep the water simmering. Slide the egg whites spoonful by spoonful into the hot water, which should not reach boiling point. After 5 minutes use a wide spoon to turn the meringues over. With a large slotted spoon remove them from the water to a wide tray placed so that it will drain. You will have to make the meringues in several batches.

Make the custard. Rinse a saucepan with cold water, leaving a few drops of water at the bottom to avoid scorching. Add the milk and bring to a boil. In a bowl beat the egg yolks and sugar until the mixture becomes pale yellow. Add a little hot milk and keep stirring with a wooden spoon. Add more milk and then pour the whole mixture back into the saucepan, stirring – the mixture should not boil at any time. Stir with a wooden spoon on a low heat until the custard thickens and coats the spoon. Place this pan in a pan of cold water and stir for a few minutes to cool the custard. Add the orange blossom water, vanilla pod or vanilla extract.

Prepare the pears. Cook them in the butter until soft or drain the canned pears and use them. Place the pears in the bottom of a wide bowl, sprinkle with a little Calvados, if wanted, and pour the cooled custard over them. Place the meringues delicately in the centre. Cover with cling film and leave in the refrigerator.

Shave the piece of softened chocolate. Place the shavings in a small bowl and cover with cling film. Keep refrigerated. Place the sugar and water in a saucepan and heat slowly, stirring with a wooden spoon. When the mixture starts boiling, add the vinegar. When the sugar caramelizes and turns brown, add the butter and turn off the heat. It will harden. Set aside for later.

About 5 minutes before serving the dessert, reheat the caramel on a medium heat. Take the bowl out of the refrigerator. Sprinkle the meringue balls with the chocolate shavings and dribble the hot caramel over them. Serve at once.

WINE

A sweet white wine, a Banyuls wine, any commercial *vin cuit* in which cognac and a little sugar have been added, or a home-made orange wine. A jug of cold water is also a good idea.

Panier de Frivolités de Tante Yvette

Crisp fritters.

These are *the* festive dessert *par excellence*. Traditionally served at carnival time and for Christmas, weddings, christenings, Sunday meals and all the family Feasts, they help celebrate the past as well as the ages to come. Frivolités is an exceptionally pretty dish, made for important occasions.

These may be called Merveilles (wonders) or Oreillettes (little ears) or Frivolités (little frivolous goodies), according to the region from which they come. They can be fried in olive oil, corn oil, peanut oil, lard or goose fat. The dough may be prepared with flour, eggs – or yolks only or whipped egg whites – with an addition of oil, butter or no fat at all, and flavoured with lemon rind, cognac, Grand Marnier or orange-blossom water.

My Aunt Yvette is living proof of what an organized mind can deliver when she prepares this traditional dessert, and there is nothing frivolous in the way she deals with Frivolités. She goes about kneading the dough, heating the oil and cutting strange geometric figures in record time. Then she demands total attention and total efficiency from her husband as he sprinkles sugar on both sides of each crisp, ethereal Frivolité, shakes off their excess sugar, and piles them into a wide flat basket as soon as they have cooled, keeping up with her most extraordinary pace and even taking time – it isn't for fun but out of duty – to nibble an occasional broken or twisted Frivolité and ponder briefly its texture and taste to make sure quality and traditions have once more been kept.

This is not an improvised dish. You must prepare the dough 2 hours or so in advance, own a good frying pan and count on about 1 hour to fry. A child, a friend, a husband, a wife – two, even three people – are welcome to dry the Frivolités on paper towels and sprinkle them with sugar while you attend to the frying.

In France most country cooks have a special smooth, unmarked bottle instead of a wooden rolling pin for spreading the dough. They think the glass, its weight and coolness, makes for paper-thin Frivolités, but a regular rolling pin is, of course, perfectly efficient. Frivolités are traditionally served in a big basket (generally a wide and flat linen basket) lined with big white napkins. Wide white ribbons are often gathered in bows on the basket handles for a truly festive touch. Make sure you prepare a huge stack of Frivolités. They are so light, so crunchy, so delicious that they are nibbled very quickly. For a grand finale, serve Frivolités with Oeufs à la Neige, Poires, Pruneaux, Oranges au Vin Rouge et aux Épices or Mousse au Chocolat Glacée. But Frivolités by themselves are most delectable. The difficulty lies in knowing how to stop nibbling them.

FOR 8 PEOPLE

INGREDIENTS

> *1 tsp dried yeast*
> *2 tbsp lukewarm water*
> *4 cups plain white flour*
> *2 eggs*
> *1 tbsp orange-blossom water*
> *1 tsp finely grated lemon rind*
> *Cooking oil*
> *Crystallized sugar*

You can prepare the dough on the morning of the Feast and leave it in a cool place, covered with a piece of cloth, or you can prepare it a day in advance if that is easier.

Stir the yeast in the lukewarm water and wait a few minutes, according to the directions on the packet. Put the flour in a bowl. Make a well in the centre and stir in the dissolved yeast and the eggs. Mix vigorously until smooth. Knead for a few minutes – the dough should be quite elastic. Cover with a wet towel and let it rest for about 3 hours. Then add the orange-blossom water and lemon rind, kneading for a minute and adding a little flour or a little cold water so you have a supple dough. Let it rest, covered, for 1 hour more.

Sprinkle a little flour on the work surface and spread the dough paper-thin, or as thin as you possibly can, stretching as you roll the pin.

Cut the dough into uneven pieces, whichever comes easiest: triangles 3 x 3 x 3in/75 x 75 x 75mm, strips 3 x 2 in/75 x 50 mm, squares 3 x 3 in/75 x 75 mm. Then with a sharp knife make a 1-in/25-mm slit in the centre of each Frivolité for 'breathing' as it fries.

Heat the oil until it is very hot but do not let it reach the smoking point. Add a few Frivolités. After frying a batch, let the temperature return to the same level before frying the next batch. Do not crowd the pan. Keep skimming off the bits of dough or crumbs that appear on top of the fat. Have a large supply of paper towels to drain the crisp Frivolités. Since the dough has no butter, oil or sugar, it will not absorb fat, unlike rich doughs.

Cook several small batches, remembering that they should not be too close together while they cook. Be careful at all times not to overheat the oil. The Frivolités must be 'surprised' by the hot oil and turn crisp and golden in the process, but they do so very quickly, so remain very attentive. Turn them once, cook 1–2 seconds more, then place them on a tray lined with paper towels. Sprinkle on both sides with crystallized sugar. Shake off the excess sugar and place the Frivolités in a clean linen-lined basket.

When all are done, cover with a clean towel and keep in a dark place or tightly closed container until ready to serve. These are best eaten the day they are made, but will keep for 4 or 5 days in a container.

Note: Sometimes a small decanter of good brandy, Calvados, cognac or grappa, is passed round the table so each guest may sprinkle a drop as he bites into the crisp Frivolité. Timing and a good hand are essential here so the Frivolité will have no time to turn soggy.

WINE

Serve with a good sparkling wine, a champagne, or a sweet and mellow dessert wine.

Poires, Pruneaux, Oranges au Vin Rouge et aux Épices

Pears, prunes and oranges cooked in red wine with fresh oranges and spices.

This is a racy, pungent, spirited dessert, perfect to conclude a rich meal. Prepared a day in advance, the fruit will cool in its own juices and be served in its pretty glass, porcelain, or earthenware bowl with a plate of thin biscuits or a basket of Frivolités.

FOR 8 PEOPLE

INGREDIENTS

> *1 cup raisins, preferably large black Spanish or California type, washed*
> *20 large pitted prunes (approximately)*
> *9–10 small thick-skinned pears, peeled but not cored, with stem on*
> *1⅔ pt/900 ml full-bodied red wine*
> *2 cups sugar*
> *1 tsp black peppercorns*
> *Pinch of grated nutmeg*
> *Pinch of cinnamon*

1 tsp coriander
2 cloves
4 bay leaves
Juice of 2 lemons
Juice of 1 orange
3 large pieces orange and lemon rind
3 oranges, peeled and thinly sliced
5 tbsp redcurrant jelly
Rind of 2 oranges, finely grated
1 tbsp grated fresh or ground ginger

Place the raisins and prunes in lukewarm water for 1–2 hours. Place the peeled pears, stem up, in a saucepan. Pour in the red wine and add the sugar, spices, lemon and orange juices, and pieces of orange and lemon rind. Cook on a low heat for 10 minutes. Drain the prunes and raisins, add to the saucepan and simmer for 15 minutes more. Add the sliced oranges and redcurrant jelly and turn off the heat. Let the fruits cool in their poaching liquid.

Place the prunes and raisins in the bottom of a pretty glass bowl. Place the pears, stem up, on top. Add the orange slices round the edges and set aside at room temperature.

Bring the poaching liquid to a boil, and reduce for a few minutes on a high heat. Add the finely grated orange rinds and the grated ginger. The juices should become a little syrupy. Check the taste and add more ginger if needed.

Remove the large pieces of orange and lemon rind and pour the syrup with the bay leaves over the cooked fruit. Cover and refrigerate.

Remove the bowl of fruit from the refrigerator just before serving. You may pass warm Madeleines, a basket of Frivolités or a plate of biscuits with the bowl of cooked fruit.

WINE

A sweet white dessert wine or, of course, champagne.

Tarte au Citron et aux Amandes

A tart and delicate lemon and almond pie.

This gourmet dessert is so delicate yet so tart that it is a perfect way to end a 'serious' festive meal. You must not be shy about the large quantity of lemon juice; it will make all the difference.

The mixture of lemons and almonds is traditional in Provence and along the Riviera. The two ingredients have grown there for centuries and are used in a variety of refreshing and pungent regional desserts.

I like to serve this tart with a brilliant raspberry purée; both are as pleasing to the eye as they are to the palate.

FOR ABOUT 10 PEOPLE

PASTRY

> 2 cups plain flour, sifted
> ¼ cup ground almonds
> ½ cup sugar
> ¼ tsp salt
> 1–2 tsp finely grated lemon rind
> 4 oz/100 g unsalted butter, cut into small cubes
> 1 egg yolk
> 3–4 tbsp ice cold water

FILLING

> 4 eggs
> ½ cup sugar
> 2 tbsp finely grated lemon rind (about 2 lemons) – retain the juice
> 8 oz/225 g unsalted butter, melted and cooled
> 1 cup coarsely ground unpeeled toasted almonds

GARNISH

> 16–24 fl oz/450–675 ml raspberry purée, page 219
> 2 tbsp icing sugar

Prepare the pastry. Combine the flour, almonds, sugar, salt and lemon rind in a large bowl. Lightly rub the butter into the flour, using your fingertips, until the mixture resembles coarse crumbs. Mix the egg yolk with 3 tablespoons of the ice water and stir into the crumbled mixture. The dough should form a soft ball. Add the remaining tablespoon of water if all the ingredients are not well combined. Wrap the dough in cling film and refrigerate for at least 2 hours or overnight.

Preheat the oven to 425°F/220°C/Mark 7. Roll the dough out to form a circle large enough for the tart ring. Butter the tart ring and line with the dough and refrigerate for 30 minutes. (*Note*: It is essential to butter the tart ring.) Prick the dough with a fork. Line the dough with greaseproof paper and beans and bake for 5 minutes. Set aside to cool.

Preheat the oven to 350°F/180°C/Mark 4. Prepare the filling. Beat the eggs, sugar and lemon rind together until pale and very fluffy. Slowly beat in the lemon juice and then the melted butter. Gently fold in the almonds with a spatula and transfer the filling to the prepared tart ring. Set the tart ring on a baking sheet and bake for 30 minutes, or until the filling is firm. Set aside to cool.

Prepare the raspberry purée according to the directions in the recipe.

When you are ready to serve, sprinkle the cooled tart with the icing sugar and cut into wedges. Spread a little raspberry purée on the bottom of each plate. Place a slice of tart on top and pour a little purée all round before handing it to each guest.

You may prefer to cut the Tarte au Citron into wedges and pass the plate round the table with a bowl of raspberry purée.

WINE

A sweet white wine or champagne.

Tarte Tatin aux Poires et aux Pommes

Warm caramelized apple and pear upside-down tart served with a bowl of whipped cream and ginger.

This is a sumptuous dessert with a long history. It was apparently invented by three old maids who ran the Hotel Tatin et Terminus's little restaurant in Lamotte-Beuvron, a tiny village not far from Paris. They were ambitious and resourceful, and since they did not have a proper oven, they had to improvise and cook their tart upside down on top of the cooker.

There Tarte Tatin, a true creation, became so famous that Maxim's restaurant quickly decided to obtain the recipe. A cook-spy disguised as a gardener was sent to the premises. He came back with the secret and it has been on Maxim's menu ever since.

The recipe that follows is a variation on the famous Tarte Tatin, but I use pears with apples for a more delicate texture. Because these fruits truly enhance each other, I also add quince on some occasions.

The problem is that one tart is not quite enough for eight people, so I suggest baking two. If there are any left-overs, who will complain?

Since the fruit is caramelized in a frying pan, no special mould is needed to bake this tart. Any ovenproof glass, copper, earthenware or aluminium mould will do, although there is a special copper mould for Tarte Tatin. If you own one, you can use it (whenever you are not preparing Tarte Tatin) in the centre of your dining-table filled with anemones or fruits.

You can prepare both the tarts and the whipped cream in advance and gently reheat the tart for a few minutes before serving it.

FOR 8 PEOPLE

PASTRY

> *2 cups plain flour, sifted*
> *2 tbsp sugar*
> *1 tsp salt*
> *4 oz/100 g chilled butter*
> *3 tbsp vegetable oil*
> *6 tbsp cold water*

FILLING

> *2½ lb/1.1 kg pears*
> *2½ lb/1.1 kg apples: Granny Smith*
> *6 oz/175 g butter*
> *3 cups sugar*
> *Juice of 3 lemons*
> *Rind of 1 lemon finely grated*

GARNISH

> *24 fl oz/675 ml chilled double* or *whipping cream*
> *6 tbsp icing sugar*
> *3 tbsp finely chopped crystallized ginger*

The dough must rest about 1 hour, so prepare it first. Place the flour, sugar, salt and butter in a large bowl. Rub flour and butter together between the palms of your dry hands until it feels crumbly, like coarse sand. Add the oil and cold water rapidly and press into a ball. The dough must not be sticky. Place on a floured work surface. Pressing the pastry with the heel of your hand, push it bit by bit away from you in a quick motion. When the flour and oil are well blended, gather into a ball and knead it for 1 second. Sprinkle with flour, wrap in cling film and place in freezer for about 40 minutes to firm while the fruit is cooking.

Peel, core and quarter the pears and apples. Heat the butter in the frying pan and add the fruit. (You may have to cook them in 2 or 3 batches.) Sprinkle with sugar, lemon juice and grated lemon rind. Cook on a high heat, uncovered, for 15 minutes. Butter the tart pans. Remove the fruit with a slotted spoon and place in the tart pans. Bring the left-over juice in the pan to a boil and cook until the liquid is brown and syrupy – about 5 minutes. Pour it on the cooked fruit. If the apples are watery, this process will be slower.

Meanwhile, whip the cream with the sugar and stir the ginger into it very delicately. Cover and place in the refrigerator.

Preheat the oven to 375°F/190°C/Mark 5. Take the pastry out of the refrigerator. Roll the dough quickly. Place it on a floured work surface and beat it with a rolling pin if it is too hard to handle. Knead it for a few minutes, then cut it into 2 balls.

Place the rolling pin in the centre of the first ball and roll back and forth firmly. Lift the dough, turn it once and continue rolling. Sprinkle a little flour as you go. When you have a circle about 14 in/350 mm in diameter and ⅛ in/3 mm thick, reverse the dough on the rolling pin and unroll it over the cooked apples and pears in the tart pan. Take the edge of the dough and slide it inside the dish, between the fruit and the side of the dish. With the tip of a knife cut a few holes in the dough so the steam can escape. Proceed with the second tart.

Place the 2 tart pans in the lower third of your oven and bake for about 30 minutes, until the pastry turns brown.

If you are ready for dinner, unmould on to a serving dish. If not, take out of the oven, cover with a piece of oiled foil and set aside.

Thirty minutes before serving dessert, preheat the oven to 350°F/180°C/Mark 4. Take the prepared Tarte Tatin out of the refrigerator. Place the tarts on the middle shelf of the oven for a few minutes. Remove from the oven; they should be lukewarm. Place a wide plate on top of a tart and in a decisive movement, holding the edges of the mould and the plate firmly, turn each tart upside down. The tops should be caramelized and brown, and the fruit should have a moist but consistent texture. It should not be runny. Take the ginger-flavoured whipped cream from the refrigerator and bring it to the table with the 2 warm tarts. Use a spatula and a deep spoon to serve.

WINE

A sweet white wine or champagne.

ACCOMPANIMENTS

Broccoli Purée

2 lb/900 g broccoli
4 tbsp single cream
Salt
Freshly ground pepper

Boil the broccoli for 10 minutes. Drain. Purée in a food processor. Stir in the cream, salt and pepper (to taste). Blend until smooth.

Cabbage Purée

2 heads of cabbage, core removed, quartered
1 oz/25 g butter
Salt
Freshly ground pepper

Blanch the cabbage until tender, about 20 minutes. Drain. Purée the cabbage in a food processor, then add the butter, salt and pepper to taste. Blend until butter is well mixed in.

Celeriac Purée

2 large celeriac, peeled and quartered
3 large potatoes, peeled
3 tbsp double cream or 1 oz/25 g butter
Salt
Freshly ground pepper
Milk (optional)

Prepare the celeriac and the potatoes and boil them for about 30 minutes in a pan of salted water until tender. Drain. Pass through a blender or food processor. Stir in the cream or the butter. Add salt and pepper to taste. Reheat on a low heat, stirring, and add a little milk if mixture is too dry.

Fennel Purée

5 bulbs fennel
2 potatoes, peeled
3 tbsp double cream or 1 oz/25 g butter
Salt
Freshly ground pepper
1 tbsp feathery fennel leaves, cut with scissors

Wash then trim the bulbs of any tough fibrous parts. Quarter them. Boil bulbs and potatoes in salted water for 20 minutes. Drain. Pass through blender or food processor. Stir in the cream or butter, salt and pepper. Sprinkle fennel leaves over the dish just before serving.

Green Salads

Whether served as a first course or as a refreshing accompaniment, tossed green salads are always welcome at festive meals.

Prepared in advance – washed, trimmed and kept in the refrigerator – they are seasoned and tossed at the last minute. Remember that you should be 'generous with oil, a miser with vinegar, and a wise man with salt' when you prepare a green salad, but you may definitely be bolder when you add shallots, mustard or herbs.

LETTUCES AND LEAVES

You need about 4 cups of trimmed salad for eight people. The variety available is immense: soft round-heart lettuce, long-leafed cos and the smaller Little Gem, crisp Webbs Wonder and Iceberg, as well as Chinese leaves, lamb's lettuce, rocket, young chard, endive and Batavian endive, watercress, spinach, sorrel, chicory and dandelion greens. To add a little colour, use red oak leaf lettuce, red chicory or radicchio.

Salad greens should be trimmed of rough stems, and tougher outer or discoloured leaves should be discarded. Separate the leaves and rinse carefully several times under very cold water. Tear them by hand into bite-size pieces, wrap in a thick tea-towel or paper towel or turn in a salad spinner to dry. Keep salad greens in the lower part of the refrigerator until ready to use.

You can mix several types of greens in one tossed salad. Endive, rocket, young dandelion, watercress, tender spinach and young chard are wonderful with a dressing of bacon and warm vinegar (page 42) or a vinaigrette dressing with mustard. They can be served with garlicky bread crusts – cut lengthways from a French loaf, preferably in 2-in/50 mm-long pieces – or thin rounds of bread, oven-dried or stale and then rubbed with garlic.

Batavian endive cut in small bite-size pieces can be seasoned with a vinegar and oil dressing, a few fork-mashed anchovy fillets and a little garlic for an invigorating salad.

Endive and round-heart lettuce or watercress and chicory will be delicious with a dressing of olive oil, fresh lemon juice and Dijon mustard sprinkled with fresh herbs.

Watercress, rocket and chicory also will make a refreshing accompaniment to a hearty dish when it is seasoned with vinaigrette flavoured with some mustard.

Chicory and Batavian endive, seasoned with a very mustardy vinaigrette and garnished with halved walnuts or quartered hard-boiled eggs, makes a lively accompaniment or a good first-course salad.

Round-heart and cos lettuce can be seasoned with vinaigrette and fresh chervil and parsley or a small amount of tarragon.

Lamb's lettuce grows wild and both it and rocket are worth growing yourself if you cannot find them at the greengrocers. Lamb's lettuce is a delicate autumn green that must be washed several times and trimmed carefully. It should have a light dressing and must be tossed very gently.

Green salads are best served in a very large glass bowl or in a long shallow dish so you can toss without bruising the greens or spilling the dressing. Whenever you serve chicory place the leaves round the dish or bowl like the spokes of a wheel then add the watercress or other greens in the centre. Sprinkle with herbs, such as mint and basil, crumble hard-boiled egg yolks on top, cover with cling film and keep refrigerated until used. Or you may wish to cut each chicory leaf crossways before adding it to other greens.

An hour or so before you serve dinner take the salad greens and dressings out of the refrigerator. Pour dressing in the bottom of the salad bowl, cross the serving fork and spoon on top and arrange the salad above so it does not come in contact with the dressing. Sprinkle herbs, walnuts or *croûtons* on top. Toss the salad just before you are ready to bring it to the dining-table. There is no such thing as usable left-over tossed salad, so discard whatever remains after the meal.

VINAIGRETTE DRESSING

This is the freshest and easiest of dressings, and it may also be the best with most of the dishes in this book. For 8 people you need about 10 tablespoons of dressing.

INGREDIENTS

> *4 tbsp red wine vinegar or fresh lemon juice*
> *8 fl oz/225 ml first-pressed, extra virgin olive oil*
> *1 tbsp salt*
> *½–1 tsp freshly ground pepper*

Stir well to blend and keep in a closed jar.

You may like to toss one or more of the following ingredients into vinaigrette dressing at the last moment:

> *2 tbsp chopped fresh herbs: flat parsley, dill, coriander, basil, mint,*
> *savory, chives, chervil or tarragon (in small quantities)*
> *2–3 tbsp Dijon mustard*
> *2 cloves garlic, peeled and crushed*
> *3 tbsp Roquefort, mashed with a little cream and a drop of cognac,*
> *pepper and sherry vinegar (use with Batavian endive or any tough*
> *leaf greens)*
> *3 tbsp finely minced shallots*
> *Anchovy fillets mashed with a fork*
> *Croûtons (bread rounds or pieces of crust, fried or oven-dried),*
> *sprinkled with olive oil and Parmesan or rubbed with a garlic clove*
> *Walnut halves or coarsely chopped walnuts*
> *Crumbled hard-boiled egg yolks*
> *Hard-boiled egg whites and egg yolks, finely diced*

Rice

> *1½ cups raw long grain rice*
> *3 bay leaves*
> *2 twigs fresh thyme or 2 tsp dried thyme*
> *1 oz/25 g butter*
> *2 tsp salt*
> *Freshly ground pepper*

Pour the rice in a large pan of boiling salted water, stirring with a fork. Add the herbs and boil uncovered for 15–20 minutes. Rinse under lukewarm water. Discard herbs. Stir in butter, fluffing the rice lightly with a fork. Season with salt and pepper and serve.

To reheat, dot top with butter, cover loosely with foil, and place in a lukewarm oven.

Note: About ¼ cup of raw rice per person is enough.

Index

A

Accompaniments 247–50
Broccoli Purée 247
Cabbage Purée 247
Celeriac Purée 247
Fennel Purée 248
Rice 250
Salads, Green 248–9
Vinaigrette Dressing for 250
see also Name of Entrée
Agneau au Pistou (Marinated Roast
Lamb with Garlic and Basil Sauce)
53–7
Accompaniments 53, 54
Hors d'Oeuvres and Desserts with 54
Left-Overs 57
Table Decorations 54
Wine with 56
Aioli Monstre (Fish, Meat, Vegetables
with Garlic Mayonnaise) 58–66
Hors d'Oeuvres and Desserts with 64
Left-Overs 65
Table Decorations 64
Wine with 64
Anchovy:
Anchoyade Sauce for Crudités 28
Bagna Cauda Sauce for Crudités 28
Sassoun Sauce for Crudités 27
Anchoyade (Anchovy) Sauce for Crudités
28
Apple:
Crêpes (Crêpes Normande) 220–2
and Pear Tart (Tarte Tatin) 241–3
Aspic:
Chicken in (Poulet en Gelée) 203–7
Ham (Jambon Persillé) 32–4
Aubergine:
Baked (Gratin d'Aubergines) 30–1
and Lamb (Moussaka Provençale)
160–5
Purée (Caviar d'Aubergines) 23–4

B

Baba, Rum or Brandy Flavoured (Grand
Baba) 224–8
Bagna Cauda (Garlic and Anchovy)
Sauces for Crudités 26
Basil:
Pistou Sauce for Crudités 27
Vegetable Soup with Garlic and Herbs
(Soupe au Pistou) 46–8
Beans, *see* Cassoulet; Potée
Beef:
and Chicken Fondue (Bourguignonne)
130–5
Marinated, Cold (Boeuf Froid en
Tranches) 77–80
Marinated, and Vegetable Stew
(Boeuf a l'Orange Niçoise) 72–6
Pot Roast, Cold (Daube de Boeuf en
Gelée) 124–9
Potato and Cheese Gratin (Hachis
Parmentier) 147–51
and Vegetable Boiled Dinner (Pot-au-
Feu) 184–93
Blanquette de Veau (Veal Stew)
66–71
Accompaniments 67
Hors d'Oeuvres and Desserts with 70
Left-Overs 71
Table Decorations 70–1
Wine with 70
Boeuf Froid en Tranches (Cold
Marinated Beef) 77–80
Hors d'Oeuvres and Desserts with 79
Left-Overs 80
Table Decorations 79
Wine with 79
Boeuf à L'Orange Niçoise (Marinated
Beef and Vegetable Stew) 72–6
Acompaniments 73
Hors d'Oeuvres and Desserts with 75
Left-Overs 76

Table Decorations 75–6
Wine with 75
Boiled Dinner (Pot-au-Feu) 184–93
Bouillabaisse Royale (Fish and Vegetable
   Stew) 81–7
   Hors d'Oeuvres and Desserts with
      85–6
   Left-Overs 87
   Table Decorations 86
   Wine with 85
Brandade (Dried Salt Cod and Potato
   Mousse) 87–91
   Accompaniments 88
   Hors d'Oeuvres and Desserts with
      89–90
   Left-Overs 90
   Table Decorations 90
   Wine with 89
Broccoli Purée 247

C

Cabbage:
   Purée 247
   Stuffed (Chou Farci) 104–9
   White Beans and Pork Dinner (Potée)
      198
Canard Farci (Stuffed Duck) 91–7
   Accompaniments 93
   Hors d'Oeuvres and Desserts with 95
   Left-Overs 97
   Table Decorations 95–6
   Wine with 95
Capers:
   Tapenade Sauce for Crudités 27–8
Caramel Custard (Flan au Caramel)
   223–4
Cassoulet (Bean, Meat and Vegetable
   Stew) 97–104
   Hors d'Oeuvres and Desserts with 102
   Left-Overs 103–4
   Table Decorations 102–3
   Wine with 102
Caviar d'Aubergines (Aubergine Purée)
   23–4
Celeriac Purée 247
Cervelle de Canut (Herbed Fresh
   Cheese) 217

Accompaniments 217
Cheese:
   Fondue Savoyarde 135–9
   Herbed Fresh (Cervelle de Canut) 217
   Pastry, Baked (Gougère) 28–30
Chick-Pea(s):
   Couscous 116–24
   Salad 35–6
Chicken:
   in Aspic (Poulet en Gelée) 203–7
   Fondue Bourguignonne 130–5
   Fricassée with Cheese (Gratin de
      Poulet au Fromage) 139–43
   Marinated Stew (Coq au Vin) 110–16
   Sauté (Fricassée Provençale) 199–
      203
   and Seafood Paella 165–9
   Stuffed (Poule Verte) 207–13
Chocolate Mousse Meringue, Frozen
   (Mousse au Chocolat Glaçée) 232–3
Chou Farci (Stuffed Cabbage) 104–9
   Accompaniments 105
   Hors d'Oeuvres and Desserts with 108
   Left-Overs 109
   Sauces for 106–7
   Table Decorations 108
   Wine with 108
Cod, Dried Salt, and Potato Mousse
   (Brandade) 87–91
Compote de Poires (Pears) 218
Coq au Vin (Marinated Chicken Stew)
   110–16
   Accompaniments 112
   Hors d'Oeuvres and Desserts with 114
   Left-Overs 116
   Table Decorations 114–15
   Wine with 114
Couscous (Meat and Vegetable Stew)
   116–24
   Hors d'Oeuvres and Desserts with 122
   Left-Overs 123–4
   Table Decorations 122
   Wine with 122
Cream, Moulded, with Fruit 219–20
Crémets aux Fruits (Moulded Cream
   with Fruit) 219–20
Crêpes Normandes (Apple-Stuffed
   Crêpes) 220–2

Wine with 222
Crudités en Panier (Raw Vegetables) 24–5
    Sauces for 25–8, 217
Curried Seafood Stew (Marmite Dieppoise) 156–60
Custard 234–5

D

Dandelions or Chicory and Bacon Salad (Pissenlits aux Lardons) 41–2
Daube de Boeuf en Gelée (Cold Beef Pot Roast) 124–9
    Accompaniments 126
    Hors d'Oeuvres and Desserts with 127–8
    Left-Overs 129
    Table Decorations 128
    Wine with 127
Desserts 217–43
    Apple and Pear Tart 241–3
    Apple-Stuffed Crêpes 220–2
    Baba, Rum or Brandy Flavoured 224–8
    Caramel Custard 223–4
    Chocolate Mousse Meringue, Frozen 232–3
    Fritters, Crisp 236–8
    Fruit Salad 231–2
    Herbed Fresh Cheese 217
    Lemon and Almond Pie 239–41
    Madeleine Cakes with Fruit 230
    Moulded Cream with Fruit 219–20
    Pears Compote 218
    Pears in Custard 234–5
    Pears, Prunes and Oranges in Red Wine 239
    Wine Sorbet 228–9
    see Table of Contents for Names of Desserts in French
Dips for Crudités 25–8, 217
    Anchoyade 28
    Bagna Cauda 26
    Pistou Sauce 27
    Sassoun 27
    Tapenade 27–8
Dressings, *see* Sauces and Dressings

Duck:
    Cassoulet 97–104
    Stuffed (Canard Farci) 91–7

E

Easter Table Decorations 56–7
Egg Custard 234–5
Endive and Bacon Salad (Pissenlits aux Lardons) 41–2
Equipment, Kitchen 19–20

F

Fennel:
    Purée 248
    Sassoun Sauce for Crudités 27
Festive Meals 1–6
    Preparations for 10–14
    Table Decoration 6–10
Fish: Dried Salt Cod and Potato Mousse (Brandade) 87–91
    Meat and Vegetables with Garlic Mayonnaise (Aioli Monstre) 58–66
    and Vegetable Soup (Bouillabaisse Royale) 81–7
Flan au Caramel (Caramel Custard) 223–4
    Wine with 224
Fondue Bourguignonne (Beef and Chicken Fondue) 130–5
    Hors d'Oeuvres and Desserts with 133
    Left-Overs 134–5
    Sauces for 131–2
    Table Decorations 133–4
    Wine with 133
Fondue Savoyard (Cheese Fondue) 135–9
    Accompaniments 136
    Hors d'Oeuvres and Desserts with 137–8
    Left-Overs 139
    Table Decorations 138
    Wine with 137
Fritters, Crisp (Panier de Frivolités) 236–8
Fruit:
    Moulded Cream with (Crémets aux

Fruits) 219–20
Salad (Mélange de Fruits) 231–2

G

Garlic:
  and Anchovy (Bagna Cauda) Sauce for
    Crudités 26
  Pistou Sauce for Crudités 27
Gougère (Baked Cheese Pastry) 28–30
  Wine with 29–30
Grand Baba (Rum or Brandy Flavoured
    Cake) 224–8
Granité au Vin (Wine Sorbet) 228–9
  Wine with 229
Gratin:
  d'Aubergines (Baked Aubergine) 30–1
    Left-Overs 31
  Dauphinois (Potato Gratin) 31–2
  Hachis Parmentier (Beef, Potato and
    Cheese) 147–51
  de Poulet au Fromage (Chicken
    Fricassée) 139–43
    Accompaniments 140
    Hors d'Oeuvres and Desserts with
      141–2
    Left-Overs 143
    Table Decorations 142
    Wine with 141
Gratinée Lyonnaise (Onion Soup) 143–6
  Hors d'Oeuvres and Desserts with
    145–6
  Left-Overs 146
  Table Decorations 146
  Wine with 145
Green Salads 248–9

H

Hachis Parmentier (Beef, Potato and
    Cheese Gratin) 147–51
  Hors d'Oeuvres and Desserts with 149
  Left-Overs 150–1
  Table Decorations 150
  Wine with 149
Ham:
  Aspic (Jambon Persillé) 32–4
  Marinated Fresh (Jambon en

Saupiquet) 155
Hors-D'Oeuvres 23–50. *See* Table of
    Contents for Names in French.
  Aubergine, Baked 30–1
  Aubergine Purée 23–4
  Cheese Pastry 28–30
  Country Paté 48–50
  Dandelion or Endive Salad 41–2
  Ham Aspic 32–4
  Leeks in Vinaigrette 43
  Lentil or Chick-Pea Salad 35–6
  Mussel Stew 36–8
  Olives Stuffed and Sautéd 38–9
  Onion Tart 39–41
  Potato Gratin 31–2
  Raw Vegetables 24–8
  Vegetable Stew 44–5
  Vegetable, Garlic and Herb Soup 46–8

J

Jambon Persillé (Ham Aspic) 32–4
  Accompaniments 33–4
  Wine with 34
Jambon en Saupiquet (Marinated Fresh
    Ham) 151–5
  Accompaniments 152
  Hors d'Oeuvres and Desserts with 54
  Left-Overs 155
  Table Decorations 154
  Wine with 154

K

Kitchen Equipment 19–20

L

Lamb:
  and Aubergine (Moussaka Provençale)
    160–5
  Breast, Stuffed (Pietsch) 170–4
  Cassoulet 97–104
  Marinated Roast (Agneau au Pistou)
    53–7
  and Vegetable Stew (Couscous) 116–24
Leeks in Vinaigrette (Poireaux Tièdes
    Vinaigrette) 43

Lemon and Almond Pie 239–41
Lentille ou Pois Chiches en Salade
    (Lentil or Chick-Pea Salad) 35–6
    Left-Overs 36

M

Madeleines Tièdes aux Fruits
    (Madeleine Cakes with Fruit)
    229–30
    Wine with 230
Man, as Cook 15–19
Marmite Dieppoise (Curried Seafood
    Stew) 156–60
    Hors d'Oeuvres and Desserts with
    158–9
    Left-Overs 160
    Table Decorations 159
    Wine with 158
Mayonnaise 131
Measurements 20
Meat:
    Bean and Vegetable Stew (Cassoulet)
    97–104
    Chicken and Shellfish Paella 165–9
    Fish and Vegetables with Garlic
    Mayonnaise (Aioli Monstre) 58–66
    and Vegetable Boiled Dinner (Pot-au-
    Feu) 184–93
    and Vegetable Stew (Couscous)
    116–24
Mélange de Fruits (Fruit Salad) 231–2
    Accompaniments 232
Meringue, Soft, in Custard 234–5
Mouclade (Mussel Stew) 36–8
    Wine with 38
Moulded Cream (Crémets aux Fruits)
    219–20
Moussaka Provençale (Lamb and
    Aubergine) 160–5
    Accompaniments 161
    Hors d'Oeuvres and Desserts with
    163–4
    Left-Overs 165
    Table Decorations 164
    Wine with 163
Mousse:
    au Chocolat Glacée (Frozen Chocolate

Mousse Meringue) 232–3
Dried Salt Cod and Potato (Brandade)
    87–91
Mussel Stew (Mouclade) 36–8

O

Oeufs à la Neige aux Fruits (Poached
    Pears in Custard with Soft
    Meringue) 234–5
Olives:
    Sautées, Olives Farcie (Olives Stuffed
    and Sautéd) 38–9
    Tapenade Sauce for Crudités 27–8
Onion:
    Soup (Gratinée Lyonnaise) 143–6
    Tart (Pissaladière) 39–41
Orange Sauce 232–3

P

Paella (Meat, Chicken, Shellfish and
    Vegetables with Saffron Rice) 165–9
    Hors d'Oeuvres and Desserts with 168
    Left-Overs 169
    Table Decorations 168
    Wine with 168
Panier de Frivolités de Tante Yvette
    (Crisp Fritters) 236–8
    Wine with 238
Pâté:
    Terrine aux Herbs 48–50
Pear(s):
    and Apple Tart (Tarte Tatin) 241–3
    Compote 218
    Poached, in Custard with Soft
    Meringue (Oeufs à la Neige) 234–5
    Prunes and Oranges in Red Wine
    (Poires, Pruneaux, Oranges au Vin
    Rouge) 239
Pies, Tarts:
    Apple and Pear Tart (Tarte Tatin)
    241–3
    Lemon and Almond Pie (Tarte au
    Citron) 239–41
    Onion Tart (Pissaladière) 39–41
Pietsch (Stuffed Veal or Lamb Breast)
    170–4

Accompaniments 171
Hors d'Oeuvres and Desserts with
    172–3
Left-Overs 174
Table Decorations 173
Wine with 172
Pissaladière (Onion Tart) 39–41
Wine with 41
Pissenlits aux Lardons (Dandelions or
    Endive and Bacon salad) 41–2
Pistou (Garlic and Basil):
Sauce for Crudités 27
Soupe au (Vegetable, Garlic and Herb
    Soup) 46–8
Plat de Farcis (Stuffed Vegetables) 174–8
Accompaniments 175
Hors d'Oeuvres and Desserts with 177
Left-Overs 178
Table Decorations 177
Wine with 176
Poireaux Tièdes Vinaigrette (Leeks in
    Vinaigrette) 43
Poires, Pruneaux, Oranges au Vin Rouge
    et aux Epices (Pears, Prunes and
    Oranges in Red Wine) 238–9
Wine with 239
Porc aux Herbes (Marinated Pork)
    179–83
Accompaniments 180
Hors d'Oeuvres and Desserts with 182
Left-Overs 183
Sauces and Dressings 180
Table Decorations 182
Pork:
Marinated (Jambon en Saupiquet) 155
Marinated (Porc aux Herbes) 179–83
White Beans and Cabbage Dinner
    (Potée) 198
Pot-au-Feu (Boiled Dinner) 184–93
Accompaniments 187
Hors d'Oeuvres and Desserts with 190
Left-Overs 191–3
Sauce for 186–7
Table Decorations 190–1
Wine with 190
Potato: Gratin Dauphinois 31–2
Potée (White Beans, Cabbage and Pork
    Stew) 193–8

Accompaniments 195
Hors d'Oeuvres and Desserts with 197
Left-Overs 198
Table Decorations 197–8
Wine with 197
Poule(t):
Fricassée Provençale
    (Sautéd Chicken) 199–203
    Accompaniments 200
    Hors d'Oeuvres and Desserts with
    201
    Left-Overs 202–3
    Table Decorations 202
    Wine with 201
au Fromage, Gratin de
    (Chicken Fricassée with Cheese)
    139–43
    Accompaniments 140
    Hors d'Oeuvres and Desserts with
    141–2
    Left-Overs 143
    Table Decoration 142
    Wine with 141
en Gelée (Chicken in Aspic) 203–7
    Accompaniments 204
    Hors d'Oeuvres and Desserts with
    206
    Left-Overs 207
    Table Decorations 206
    Wine with 206
Verte (Stuffed Chicken) 207–13
    Hors d'Oeuvres and Desserts with
    211
    Left-Overs 212–13
    Table Decorations 211–12
    Wine with 211
Preparation for a Feast 10–14
Purée:
Aubergines 23–4
Broccoli 247
Cabbage 247
Celeriac 247
Fennel 248

R

Ratatouille (Vegetable Stew) 44–5
Left-Overs 45

Rice 250
  Saffron 167
  see also Paella
Rouille sauce for Bouillabaisse 82, 83–4

S

Saffron Rice 167
Salads:
  Dandelion or Endive 41–2
  Green 248–9
  Lentil or Chick-Pea 35–6
  Vinaigrette Dressing for 249–50
  Watercress 78
Sauces and Dressings:
  Aioli 62
  for Crudités 25–8, 217
  Orange 232–3
  Pistou 27, 47
  Rouille 82, 83–4
  Tomato and Tarragon 77–8
  Vinaigrette 249–50
Saussoun (Anchovy and Fennel) Sauce
    for Crudités 27
'Savarin' 224
Seafood:
  Curried Stew (Marmite Dieppoise)
    156–60
  Paella 165–9
Sorbet:
  Wine (Granité au Vin) 228–9
Soup:
  Fish and Vegetable (Bouillabaisse
    Royale) 81–7
  Onion (Gratinée Lyonnaise) 143–6
  Vegetables, Garlic and Herb (au
    Pistou) 46–8
Spinach Stuffed Veal or Lamb Breast
    (Pietsch) 170–4
Stew:
  Blanquette de Veau 66–71
  Boeuf à l'Orange Niçoise 72–6
  Bouillabaisse Royale 81–7
  Cassoulet 97–104
  Coq au Vin 110–16
  Couscous 116–24
  Marmite Dieppoise 160
  Mouclade 36–8

Potée 198
Ratatouille 44–5
Swiss Chard Stuffed Veal or Lamb
    Breast (Pietsch) 170–4

T

Table Decoration 6–10
  Easter 56–7
Tapenade (Caper and Olive) Sauce for
    Crudités 27–8
Tarte au Citron et aux Amandes (Lemon
    and Almond Pie) 239–41
  Wine with 241
Tarte Tatin aux Poires et aux Pommes
    (Apple and Pear Tart) 241–3
  Wine with 243
Tarts, *see* Pies, Tarts
Terrine aux Herbes (Country Pâté)
    48–50
  Wine with 50
Thoionnade (Tuna sauce) for Crudités
    25–6
Tomato and Tarragon Sauce 77–8
'touiller' 145
Tuna Sauce (Thoionnade) for Crudités
    25–6

V

Veal:
  Breast, Stuffed (Pietsch) 170–4
  Stew (Blanquette de Veau) 66–71
Vegetable(s):
  Bean and Meat Stew (Cassoulet)
    97–104
  Broccoli Purée 247
  Cabbage Purée 247
  Celeriac Purée 247
  Crudités 24–8
  Fennel Purée 248
  Fish and Meat with Garlic
    Mayonnaise (Aioli Monstre)
    58–66
  and Fish Soup (Bouillabaisse Royale)
    81–7
  and Marinated Beef Stew (Boeuf a
    l'Orange Niçoise) 72–6

and Meat Boiled Dinner (Pot-au-Feu)
184–93
and Meat Stew (Couscous) 116–24
Stuffed (Plat de Farcis) 174–8
Soup (Soupe au Pistou) 46–8
Vinaigrette Dressing 249–50
Leeks in (Poireaux Tièdes) 43

W

Watercress Salad 78
White Beans Cabbage and Pork Stew
(Potée) 198
Wine Sorbet (Granité au Vin) 228–9
Wines, choosing 14–15
see also individual dishes

FOR THE BEST IN PAPERBACKS, LOOK FOR THE

In every corner of the world, on every subject under the sun, Penguin represents quality and variety – the very best in publishing today.

For complete information about books available from Penguin – including Puffins, Penguin Classics and Arkana – and how to order them, write to us at the appropriate address below. Please note that for copyright reasons the selection of books varies from country to country.

In the United Kingdom: Please write to *Dept E.P., Penguin Books Ltd, Harmondsworth, Middlesex, UB7 0DA.*

If you have any difficulty in obtaining a title, please send your order with the correct money, plus ten per cent for postage and packaging, to *PO Box No Ll, West Drayton, Middlesex*

In the United States: Please write to *Dept BA, Penguin, 299 Murray Hill Parkway, East Rutherford, New Jersey 07073*

In Canada: Please write to *Penguin Books Canada Ltd, 2801 John Street, Markham, Ontario L3R 1B4*

In Australia: Please write to the *Marketing Department, Penguin Books Australia Ltd, P.O. Box 257, Ringwood, Victoria 3134*

In New Zealand: Please write to the *Marketing Department, Penguin Books (NZ) Ltd, Private Bag, Takapuna, Auckland 9*

In India: Please write to *Penguin Overseas Ltd, 706 Eros Apartments, 56 Nehru Place, New Delhi, 110019*

In the Netherlands: Please write to *Penguin Books Netherlands B.V., Postbus 195, NL–1380AD Weesp*

In West Germany: Please write to *Penguin Books Ltd, Friedrichstrasse 10–12, D–6000 Frankfurt/Main 1*

In Spain: Please write to *Longman Penguin España, Calle San Nicolas 15, E–28013 Madrid*

In Italy: Please write to *Penguin Italia s.r.l., Via Como 4, I-20096 Pioltello (Milano)*

In France: Please write to *Penguin Books Ltd, 39 Rue de Montmorency, F-75003 Paris*

In Japan: Please write to *Longman Penguin Japan Co Ltd, Yamaguchi Building, 2–12–9 Kanda Jimbocho, Chiyoda-Ku, Tokyo 101*